The Physician's Comprehensive Guide to Negotiating

STEVEN BABITSKY, ESQ.

JAMES J. MANGRAVITI, Jr., ESQ.

S•E•A•K, Inc.
Excellence in Education since 1980

Falmouth, Massachusetts

The Physician's Comprehensive Guide to Negotiating

ISBN: 978-1-892904-31-7

CONTENTS

Acknowledgments

The authors wish to acknowledge the following persons whose assistance in the production of this book was invaluable: Bruce D. Armon, Esq.; Peter Greenbaum, Esq.; Dennis Hursh; Katherine L. Moore; Ryann Muir; Dee Netzel; Michael F. Schaff, Esq.; and Lisa D. Taylor, Esq.

Related Products by SEAK, Inc.

TEXTS

The A–Z Guide to Expert Witnessing
How to Become a Dangerous Expert Witness
National Guide to Expert Witness Fees and Billing Procedures
Cross-Examination: The Comprehensive Guide for Experts
Writing and Defending Your Expert Report
How to Excel During Depositions
The Comprehensive IME System
Writing and Defending Your IME Report

SEMINARS

Negotiating Skills for Physicians
Non-Clinical Careers for Physicians
National Expert Witness Conference
Advanced Cross-Examination Workshop
Advanced Deposition Skills Workshop
How to Be a Dangerous Expert Witness
Persuasion Skills Workshop for Experts
How to Start and Build a Successful Expert Witness Practice
Expert Report Writing Workshop
Testifying Skills Workshop
Law School for Experts
Expert Witness Practice Management Workshop
How to Be an Effective Medical Witness
How to Be a Successful Independent Medical Examiner

CD AUDIO PROGRAMS

Law School for Experts
Marketing Your Forensic Practice
Achieving Success As a Medical Witness
How to Be a Successful Independent Medical Examiner

DVD VIDEOS

The Expert Deposition: How to Be an Effective and Ethical Witness
Winning Over the Jury: Techniques for Experts That Work
Cross-Examination: How to Be an Effective and Ethical Expert Witness
The Most Difficult Questions for Experts: With Answers

DIRECTORIES (www.seakexperts.com)

SEAK, Inc. National Directory of Independent Medical Examiners
SEAK, Inc. National Directory of Experts

For more information, call SEAK at (508) 457-1111. Inquiries may also be addressed to SEAK, Inc. at P.O. Box 729, Falmouth, MA 02541. Fax (508) 540-8304; e-mail address: mail@seak.com; internet address: www.seak.com.

About the Authors

Steven Babitsky, Esq. (sbabitsky@aol.com), is the President and founder of SEAK, Inc. He serves as a negotiating consultant. He is the co-author of *The Successful Physician Negotiator: How to Get What You Deserve* and is the developer and trainer for SEAK's *Negotiating Skills for Physicians* seminar. Steve is also the co-editor of the text *The Biggest Legal Mistakes Physicians Make and How to Avoid Them.* He trains physicians and others on negotiation strategy and techniques and acts as a consultant to medical societies and journals in their negotiations with medical publishers, other organizations, and individuals. Steve has lectured nationally on negotiation strategies and techniques. He was a personal injury trial attorney for twenty years and is the former managing partner of the firm Kistin, Babitsky, Latimer & Beitman. He has trained thousands of physicians over the past 26 years.

James J. Mangraviti, Jr., Esq. (seakincjm@aol.com), has trained thousands of physicians and expert witnesses across the United States and Canada. He currently serves as Vice President and General Counsel of SEAK, Inc. Mr. Mangraviti received his BA degree in mathematics *summa cum laude* from Boston College and his JD degree *cum laude* from Boston College Law School. He is the co-author of *The Successful Physician Negotiator: How to Get What You Deserve,* the co-editor of *The Biggest Legal Mistakes Physicians Make and How to Avoid Them,* and serves as a trainer for SEAK's *Negotiating Skills for Physicians* seminar.

Preface

The authors have nearly 40 years of combined experience in negotiating with, against, and on behalf of physicians. We have reached several distinct and striking conclusions.

1. Most physicians have received little or no training in the art of negotiating.
2. As a result, many physicians are inexperienced or ineffective negotiators.
3. The physicians who have mastered the art of negotiating, understand negotiation techniques, and use effective negotiating strategies are far more financially successful and secure than their counterparts.

Another finding we made is that, for reasons we will discuss shortly, physicians frequently do not even attempt to negotiate for themselves. For example, let's say that you are asked by your church or civic organization to purchase $5,000 worth of food for a function. Would you go to your local supermarket and just load up a cart and pay for the food? Probably not. You would most likely feel an obligation to look for the best deal or at least negotiate a better price. Why would you do that? Your reasons may include the following.

1. You know your church or civic organization does not have money to waste.
2. You feel that you have a special fiduciary obligation to do the best you can for your organization.
3. You know you can get a better price if you try.
4. When you get a better price it will make you feel good about yourself and what you have accomplished for your organization.
5. You are neither embarrassed nor uncomfortable negotiating on behalf of a charity.
6. You will devote the time needed to get a good deal because it is for charitable purposes.

When physicians negotiate in their practices or in personal purchases, they are in fact negotiating for themselves and their families. Should these physicians be any less aggressive or diligent in their negotiating? The authors suggest that the answer is clearly and emphatically no.

As a preliminary matter, physicians need to accept the following five important premises about negotiating.

1. They, their practices, and their families have no extra money to waste.
2. They are under a special obligation to their families to do the best they can for them.
3. They very often can get better working conditions, salaries, prices, and deals when they negotiate.
4. There is nothing wrong with trying to negotiate better terms. It is neither rude nor pushy when done politely.
5. Employing negotiating skills correctly can be worth hundreds of thousands—perhaps millions—of dollars to the average physician.

Seeking the best price or deal should not embarrass physicians. It should, on the contrary, give them pride and satisfaction in knowing that they have done the best they could for themselves and their families. This is the kind of attitude that physicians need to be successful negotiators.

Many physicians do not negotiate effectively due to a lack of understanding of the process and/or because they are uncomfortable, embarrassed, and lack the skill set or mindset to do so. This point was driven home in a graphic fashion a few years ago when the authors witnessed a physician purchase an expensive piece of real estate. The negotiation between the doctor and the realtor was so short that it should be in the Guinness *Book of World Records*. Here is a verbatim transcript of the entire negotiation after the doctor was told of the (substantial) price:

Doctor: Can I negotiate?
Realtor: No.

This four-word "negotiation" concluded with the purchase of the piece of property at the full asking price.*

Physicians are notoriously poor negotiators despite being highly intelligent and highly educated. One important reason for this is a lack of training in this critical area. This text was written to bridge the gap between what physicians know about negotiating and what they need to know to be more financially successful and to get what they deserve. With the use of this text, the physician will understand the negotiation process, set realistic goals, and negotiate from a position of power and strength. Do you as a physician owe any less to yourself and your family?

This book has been designed to update and replace our previous work *The Successful Physician Negotiator: How to Get What You Deserve.* To take that work a step further, we have added numerous examples, included new strategies that take into account the sweeping technological changes of the past 8 years (the common use of cell phones, e-mail, PDAs, etc.), and tried to make the book even easier to use by adding executive summaries to most of our strategy chapters and headnotes to our numerous examples. We have also added several technical chapters dealing specifically with issues that physicians encounter in common negotiation situations (such as, employment agreements, leases, managed care contracts, and buying and selling a practice). As always, your feedback is welcome.

Steven Babitsky, Esq.
James J. Mangraviti, Jr., Esq.
SEAK, Inc.
www.seak.com

---

* The story does have a happy ending—the value of the property has (fortunately) greatly increased since the purchase.

Chapter 1 The Physician Negotiator

Executive Summary

- Most physicians negotiate for *millions* of dollars over their careers.
- Doing 5% or 10% better on negotiations translates into a huge amount of money and can also mean a much better lifestyle.
- Negotiating skills are critical in determining professional success.
- Physicians need to master fears of assertiveness and confrontation.
- The best way to get something is to ask for it.
- It is not unprofessional to negotiate.
- The best physician negotiators find the time to negotiate.
- Practice makes perfect. The more you negotiate, the more comfortable you will feel and the better your results will be.

How Much Are You Negotiating For?

As a physician, you can expect to negotiate for *millions* of dollars over the course of your career. Consider Box 1.1 below. In teaching physicians negotiation skills for the past 10 years, the authors have encountered many physicians who have reported negotiating for $10,000,000 to $20,000,000 or more over a 20-year period. This may represent an underreporting because many physicians have unknowingly left considerable amounts of money "on the table" by signing away rights to intellectual property, inventions, honoraria, and expert witness fees.

Box 1.1

Typical Physician Negotiations over 20 Years

Salary	$4,000,000
Salaries of Staff	$1,500,000
Purchase and Sale of Homes	$1,750,000
Purchase and Sale of Autos	$250,000
Professional Fees	$200,000
Office Leases	$500,000
Equipment Purchases	$200,000
Consumer Goods	$300,000
Other	$500,000
Total:	*$9,200,000*

As you can see in this very conservative example, a typical physician negotiates for tremendously large amounts of money over just 20 years of his career. Taking the example in Box 1.1, consider what would happen if the physician could save just 5% of this total. Five percent of $9,200,000 amounts to $460,000. If the physician could save 10%, the savings would be $920,000.

To appreciate how much you as a physician have at stake in learning to negotiate, consider approximately how much you will be negotiating for over the next 20 years. You can use Box 1.2 as a worksheet to arrive at a rough approximation.

Box 1.2

Negotiations over the Next 20 Years

Salary	$__________
Salaries of Staff	$__________
Purchase of Homes	$__________
Sale of Home	$__________
Automobile Purchases	$__________
Automobile Sales	$__________
Legal Fees	$__________
Accounting Fees	$__________
Equipment Purchases	$__________
Consumer Goods	$__________
Other	$__________
Other	$__________
Total:	*$*________________

The purpose of this book is to empower physicians to save an average of 5% to 10% (in some cases more) when negotiating. Multiply the total from Box 1.2 by 0.05 and 0.10 to determine how much you can save over the next 20 years through more skilled and effective negotiating. Saving 5%, 10%, or more requires superior negotiating skills. This book has been designed to help physicians develop such skills, techniques, and strategies.

More at Stake than Money

There are other important reasons why you should develop superior negotiating skills. First, superior negotiating skills will allow you to feel more comfortable during negotiations. Second, the assertiveness that is required of a savvy negotiator will help you in other aspects of your professional and personal life. Finally, once you have developed superior negotiating skills, you will be able to increase the level of satisfaction you have with the purchases and agreements you make. There is no reason you should feel "stage fright," awkward, or defensive about an upcoming negotiation. Properly trained physicians can learn to enjoy the give and take of negotiating.

Why Physicians May Not Be Skilled Negotiators

In general, some physicians have the reputation of being poor negotiators. There are many reasons for this. First and foremost is a lack of training in negotiation skills. Physicians are some of the most highly educated, intelligent, and trained professionals. Typically, not one minute of this training and education involves negotiation skills. Negotiation skills courses are offered by SEAK, Inc. (www.seak.com) and many other adult education organizations. A wise physician will further her skills and take such a course.

Another reason that some physicians are poor negotiators is that they are trained from internship on to follow the instructions of their teachers, mentors, and superiors. They are also trained to be responsive to patients' needs and to help them get better. The mindset that often develops after many years of this training is that confrontations with superiors, colleagues, and patients should be avoided almost at all costs. Physicians are told that if they do not fall into line, they risk getting labeled as difficult, thus jeopardizing their careers.

Example 1.1 Unassertive physician pays the price
Employer: The job pays $150,000 per year, okay?
Doctor: Ahh…, well, the going rate for my specialty in this part of the country is $180,000.
Employer: Look, we need team players here. We're all on the same team, right? You want to be a team player, don't you, just like Doctors Smith and Jones?

Doctor: Of course.
Employer: Okay then, the players on this team are paid $150,000, a very handsome salary, and they don't complain, they mind their own business, and they don't worry about what other people are doing.
Doctor: (embarrassed) Okay.

Lesson: To become successful negotiators, physicians must accept the fact that some confrontation or disagreement with the other party (i.e., the opponent in a negotiation) is sometimes necessary. The physician's unwillingness to be assertive in this case may have cost him $30,000 per year, or $150,000 over five years.

As attorneys, the authors accept the premise that confrontation and asking questions are *not* something inherently evil or to be ashamed of. If we did not, we would not meet our ethical obligation to represent zealously the interests of our clients. As a physician, you also need to accept the fact that there is nothing wrong with standing up for yourself, your family, your practice, or your professional beliefs and trying to obtain a fair deal. Doctors who learn to be assertive earn the respect of their peers and opponents and are generally more successful than doctors who are not assertive. Becoming a skilled negotiator is one of the single most important determining factors in the professional success of physicians. Often, it is not the "best doctor," but which doctor is the more skilled negotiator. Take as an example how a physician might have better handled the situation in Example 1.1.

Example 1.2 Negotiating yields huge rewards for new employee
Employer: The job pays $150,000 per year, okay?
Doctor: No, I'm sorry that's unacceptable. The going rate for my specialty in this part of the country is $180,000.
Employer: Look, we need team players here. We're all on the same team, right? You want to be a team player, don't you, just like Doctors Smith and Jones?
Doctor: I am a team player and very much look forward to being part of your team. However, I need to be paid what I'm worth, and what I'm worth is $180,000. You don't want an unhappy team member, do you?

Employer: Okay then, $180,000. We believe very strongly in paying our team members what they think they're worth.
Doctor: (enthusiastically) Okay. When do I start?

Lesson: The physician was able to get the salary she sought by being assertive and *asking* for it. Also note that the physician was not afraid to say no to the employer's low-ball offer of $150,000. The ability to say no is another extremely important skill that the savvy negotiator needs to master. (See pages 24–25 on saying no.) Note: The physician in Example 1.1 will second-guess herself for years, may be unhappy, and may leave the practice to achieve a fair and reasonable compensation package.

Also note the time invested and the reward. This negotiation took only 1 minute and made the physician $30,000 year. If she stays at the job 10 years, that's an extra $300,000 for 1 minute's work. This is what negotiating skills can do for a physician.

Another reason why many physicians are poor negotiators is their mindset, which many times includes the need to be liked. Some physicians do not like to negotiate because they don't want to be a "bad guy." Worse, they consciously or subconsciously give away everything in an effort to make sure that the person with whom they are negotiating likes them. A desire to be liked is natural. A *need* to be liked is understandable, but it can be extremely detrimental when negotiating. An opponent will quickly detect this weakness and use it against the physician. To be a successful physician negotiator, your primary focus should be on the deal under negotiation. If the goal is, instead, being liked by the opponent, the physician is heading for serious trouble.

Take as an example a person who negotiates professionally, say an attorney. Would you want an attorney who was representing you to be worried about whether the opponent would like him at the conclusion of the negotiation? The answer is clearly NO! You would want the attorney to use his negotiating skills, experience, and training to get you the best agreement or deal possible. Attorneys are successful during negotiating because they temporarily repress their human desire to be liked. Physicians need to do the same if they want to be successful negotiators. Consider the following example.

Example 1.3 Being Mr. Nice costs the physician
Salesman: (friendly and enthusiastically) Hi, Doctor. How's the family?
Doctor: Fine, thanks.
Salesman: What did you think of that game last night?
Doctor: That was something else, wasn't it?
Salesman: Yeah, it was. So are you ready to move on that Audi?
Doctor: Love to, but would it be possible to knock another two grand off the price?
Salesman: (taken aback and quiet) I thought we'd settled all that. I gave you a price of $42,000 and you didn't have a problem with it.
Doctor: (unsure) Yeah, but my wife thought it was a bit high.
Salesman: (sadly) If I don't close this sale at the price we had previously talked about, my sales manager is going to be furious. I already told him we had a deal, which is what I thought. My wife will kill me if I lose this job. She's expecting, you know.
Doctor: Okay, let's do it at $42,000.
Salesman: (friendly again) Doctor Jones, you're the best.

Lesson: Had Dr. Jones stood firm and not been concerned with his opponent's desires and with his own need to be liked, he would have been much more likely to purchase the car for the price he wanted.

Why Physicians Don't Negotiate

There are many reasons physicians use to justify their failure to negotiate. The five most common excuses are that:

- they do not have the time,
- they are embarrassed,
- they do not feel comfortable negotiating,
- they do not like conflict or disagreement, and
- they feel that asserting themselves during negotiations is not professional.

A successful physician negotiator moves beyond these excuses. Consider Box 1.3.

Box 1.3

Physician Excuses Not to Negotiate

1. I don't have enough time. A successful physician negotiator devotes the time needed to negotiating. There is simply too much at stake—possibly millions of dollars (see pages 1–2)—to not devote an appropriate amount of time to negotiating. If your schedule is tight, you need to make the time to negotiate. (See pages 75–91 on making time to negotiate.)

2. It's embarrassing. As a physician, you have trained intensively for years, paid for a very expensive education, and worked long hours under stressful conditions. You should not be embarrassed to ask for what you deserve.

3. I don't feel comfortable. This is a natural reaction. The way you develop a level of comfort is to learn about the negotiation process, to understand the tactics and defenses, and to actually negotiate a few times. It's just like riding a bike. The toughest part is doing it the first few times, then you are comfortable and never forget how to do it. In addition, many experienced physician negotiators report that once they learn how to negotiate, they actually enjoy the process. They like the give and take, they use their natural ability to read people, and they satisfy their needs and desires.

4. I don't like conflict or disagreement. This is a feeling shared by many physicians. Unfortunately, to be a successful physician negotiator, you must suppress this feeling during negotiations. Courteous and professional disagreement is a necessary part of most, if not all, negotiations.

5. It's not professional. This is simply not true. There is nothing unprofessional about standing up for yourself and your family and asserting yourself during negotiations. You do not lose the respect of your peers but, in fact, gain their respect and admiration. Being known as a physician who can negotiate well will help rather than hinder your career.

There is no need for physicians to continue to fall into the trap of viewing negotiating as unprofessional. Consider the following example.

Example 1.4 Physician not intimidated
Opponent: (to doctor) You are being very demanding. I have dealt with dozens of other doctors and none of them has ever asked for changes in this PPO agreement.
Doctor: I'm not concerned with other doctors. What I am concerned with is maintaining the highest quality level of care for my patients and making sure that I am fairly compensated for my services.

Lesson: Asserting your right to be treated fairly is simply not unprofessional!

Example 1.5 Physician unafraid to ask for what he is worth
Opponent: (to doctor) This is your first employment contract with this group. You should be ashamed of yourself asking for $160,000 a year plus benefits. Is this what they taught you in medical school—get as much as you can?
Doctor: I am asking for what I am worth and am not embarrassed to negotiate a better life for my family.

Lesson: The successful physician negotiator is neither easily embarrassed nor intimidated by "tough talk."

Chapter 2 Negotiation Basics

Executive Summary

- A good negotiator can be assertive and does not fear confrontation.
- When negotiating long-term relationships, it is best to look for a creative win-win arrangement. This is a cooperative negotiation.
- Building trust with your opponent will make the negotiation process much easier.
- A negotiator's reputation for keeping his promise is a potent tool.
- Stressing that you would like to conduct future deals with your opponent can be extremely helpful in gaining concessions.
- Building goodwill with your opponent is helpful. One easy way to do this is to do favors for your opponent.
- A competitive negotiation involves a "one-shot deal" where the agreement need not be win-win.
- Skillful negotiators can turn competitive negotiations into cooperative ones through forthrightness and the possibility of future dealings.
- Be careful what you say to anyone with whom you may do business. Any communication should be treated as the start of the negotiation.
- When "ambushed" with a request for a deal that you are not fully prepared to consider, take time to think it over by asking your opponent to put the offer in writing and state that you will get back to them.
- Saying "no thanks" is an essential skill. Learn polite ways to do so (see Box 2.3).

Negotiation Defined

The great commentator Edwin R. Murrow once said, "the term *negotiation* implies compromise; painful concessions on the part of both parties." A sterile definition of *negotiation* is to confer and to discuss to reach an agreement. The experts describe negotiation as a more fluid, complex process that involves our most basic needs and desires:

> Negotiation is the field of knowledge and endeavors that focuses on gaining the favor of people from whom we want things. We want all sorts of things: prestige, freedom, money, justice, love, status, security,

> and recognition. What is negotiation? It is the use of information and power to affect behavior within a web of tension....A negotiation is more than an exchange of material objects. It is a way of acting and behaving that can develop understanding, belief, acceptance, respect, and trust. It is the manner of your approach, the tone of your voice, the attitude you convey, the methods you use, and the concern you exhibit for the other side's feelings and needs.[1]

Thus, negotiation is a process that typically involves:

- an exchange of material objects,
- the use of power and information to affect behavior,
- compromise,
- getting what you want without giving too much to get it,
- communication to obtain approval, agreement, or action of another party, and
- gaining the favor of people from whom you want things.

Negotiation is a fascinating and challenging art and skill. It requires the ability to recognize the complexities of human nature and its desires and the ability to satisfy both your needs and the needs of the person with whom you are negotiating. Physicians should use their insight into, and their professional training concerning, human behavior to achieve more favorable agreements. Physicians should not dread negotiation; they should look at it as an intellectual challenge. They can adapt their ability to read people and put themselves in the shoes of others in the negotiation process.

Cooperative Negotiations: Long-Term Relationships

Most negotiation experts agree that the two major types of negotiations are cooperative negotiations and competitive negotiations. This section will explain how physicians can differentiate between these two types of negotiations and why it is crucial to do so.

The cooperative negotiation is characterized by an exchange of information in which there is give and take. A participant in a cooperative

---

[1] Herb Cohen, *You Can Negotiate Anything: How to Get What You Want* (Secaucus, NJ: Carol Publishing Group, 1996) pp. 15, 154.

negotiation asks questions to find out what is important to the person with whom she is negotiating. The search is for a win-win solution or an agreement in which both parties gain and are satisfied with the outcome. Particular emphasis is placed on creating new business opportunities, synergy, and the distinct possibility of future agreements and business if things go well.

This type of negotiation is of particular importance to physicians because they frequently negotiate for the long term (for instance, with colleagues, health-care providers, insurers, and other professionals with whom they will most likely continue to do business). The ability to distinguish cooperative from competitive negotiations and to change a potentially competitive negotiation into a cooperative one are skills of the successful physician negotiator.

When negotiating, we are not looking for a single short-term deal in which we make the most profit and pay as little as possible. We emphasize that we are looking for a way to pay the opponent as much as possible and still make a good profit for ourselves. Using this philosophy, we can gain important concessions from the opponent and establish a long-term relationship in which both parties are satisfied and where multiple future projects are possible. What could be a competitive negotiation is turned into a cooperative win-win agreement by stressing the desire for a long-term relationship and making sure that the opponent gets a good deal.

The cooperative problem-solving approach to negotiations is characterized by a genuine search for the best deal for both parties. It involves the recognition of the fact that your opponent may really need or want some items that you feel comfortable in conceding. What may seem like a minor point to you may be crucial to your opponent. This approach involves being forthright with the disclosure of information, the use of reasonable opening demands or requests, and honest, courteous, sincere dialogue designed to achieve a win-win solution. When this approach is used correctly, the parties do not fight about how to divide the pie, but look for and find mutually agreeable ways to make a bigger pie to divide. Much of the discussion will center around future projects and how both sides can prosper.

BE ASSERTIVE

As a physician negotiator, you face challenges that are not often encountered by other professionals. Your long years of medical training have stressed collaboration, cooperation, and team building. Individualism has been discouraged. The training you received in medical school, your internship, and your residency may have left you deferential to authority, accepting of the standard way physicians do things, unquestioning, trusting, passive, and unwilling or unable to be assertive on your own behalf. If you possess one or more of these traits you will have to overcome them to become a more effective physician negotiator. You must believe and act on the knowledge that just because someone in authority says something, this does not mean that the terms must be accepted as presented.

Example 2.1 Physician must be assertive to avoid life-altering consequences

Doctor: How often will I be on call?
Administrator: Three weekends a month.
Doctor: Why so many?
Administrator: That is the way we have been doing it for 35 years.
Doctor: I appreciate your long-standing policy, but, unfortunately, that does not work for me. My husband and I just had our first child and I cannot give up three weekends per month....

Lesson: For the physician to have any hope of getting better terms than being on call three weekends per month, she could not let the negotiation end on the administrator's statement that that's the way the hospital's done things for 35 years. The doctor's ability to question the status quo was a prerequisite to gaining favorable terms.

Remember that the status quo is often just a starting point and should not necessarily be your final destination. One quick way for you to become more assertive is to think not of what the additional money or time will mean for you, but of what it will mean for your children, spouse, extended family, etc. In a very real sense you are negotiating for them as well. The extra money or time you obtain will go toward education, lessons, family time, vacations, and a safe environment.

You may feel very uncomfortable when your negotiation involves a long-term relationship. This is natural. You will often negotiate with colleagues and you do not want to make an enemy or alienate a person with whom you will have to deal in the future. You want to be a team player and not a troublemaker. Many physicians fear that being too assertive is unprofessional. They are wrong. Your opponents know your fears regarding confrontation and assertiveness and will use them against you.

Example 2.2 Doctor's fear of confrontation used against him
Hospital administrator: Doctor, as I understand it, all the other physicians on staff are on call one night a week, but you feel this schedule should not apply to you.

Lesson: To be a superior physician negotiator, the doctor in this example must not be afraid to say, "Yes. I can't follow the schedule kept by the other doctors." If the doctor doesn't ask, he will never receive.

Example 2.3 Physician refuses to throw herself at opponent's mercy
Employer: (to prospective new physician employee) We all started with these terms. The key is to get you started and on the team. The beginning of the relationship is not the time to rock the boat. So, please sign this seven-year employment contract and we will take care of you in the future.

Lesson: This is a snow job. The doctor needs to assert herself if she is going to get what she deserves. One response the doctor could use would be, "I look forward to formally joining the team, but I can't commit to seven years of employment with your group, or any other group, unless we settle these issues up front. When you say you will 'take care of me' in the future, what exactly does that mean? Can you give me some examples of how you took care of doctors in the past? I'm sure you'd be willing to put that in writing."

The key to success in negotiating long-term relationships is to be assertive enough to suggest a better deal for both parties and to create options for mutual gain. In short, you need to look for a win-win solution.[2] A physician who has become a skilled negotiator will recognize that these win-win opportunities are available but that they need to be searched for and advocated. Once you look for the creative solutions that satisfy the needs of all the parties, you are no longer negotiating "against" an opponent. You are now both working together to find a win-win solution. This is a concept that may be counterintuitive. You can be aggressive and assertive but still build amicable long-term relationships. You need to recognize that many times the potential long-term relationship is as important as the negotiation itself and that you will most likely gain, not lose, respect by being assertive. Physicians will quickly respect that you are a skilled negotiator and will realize that once you join the team, they can benefit from your skill.

When dealing with long-term relationships you need to be concerned with how satisfied your opponent is with the result of the negotiation. There are two reasons for this. First, you want your opponent to be amenable to future agreements and projects. Second, you want her to live up to the agreement enthusiastically and in a timely fashion. (See pages 246–47 on living up to the agreement.)

Win-win negotiation is not a game with winners and losers. It is the first step in building a long-term relationship based on trust, respect, integrity, and agreements that work well for both sides. As a successful physician negotiator you want to expand your business relationships, not waste your time continually searching for new ones.[3] Various ways to expand your existing business relationships are discussed in the next several subsections. Understanding that it is always much easier and cost-

---

[2] "Far too many of us, when we are involved in a conflict, think mainly—or only—of the 'win,' when our best interests would be served if we thought instead of the relationship with the person with whom we are experiencing the conflict." Fred E. Jandt, *Win-Win Negotiating: Turning Conflict into Agreement* (New York: John Wiley & Sons, 1985) p. 135.

[3] "Expanding on an existing business relationship is almost always easier than starting a new one. By creating the right impression you make people want to deal with you over and over again. Achieving that often comes down to knowing how hard to push." Mark H. McCormack, *What They Don't Teach You at Harvard Business School: Notes from a Street Smart Executive* (New York: Bantam Books, 1984) p. 41.

effective to expand existing relationships than to create new ones is crucial. Your opponent will understand the high costs of hiring, training, and turnover. Your opponent seeks stability and successful long-term relationships as well.

BUILD TRUST

Building trust is very important when dealing with long-term relationships. Trust is built over time. If you develop a reputation as a "straight shooter"—a person of your word—this will make your negotiations easier and less stressful. If you can build a mutually trusting relationship, the question will be changed from *if* you can reach an agreement to *how* it will be accomplished.

Example 2.4 Honesty builds trust
Publisher: Can you have the book done by June 1, 2007?
Doctor: No, but realistically I will have it on your desk on July 28, 2007.

Lesson: By being honest, direct, and not promising more than she can deliver, the doctor has built trust with the publisher.

BE ON TIME

It is rare to see high quality work done in a timely fashion. Any reputation you build for this type of performance will be a great asset during the ongoing negotiations of a long-term relationship.

Example 2.5 The power of a reputation for delivering on past promises
Doctor: You don't question the fact that my work will be high quality and delivered on time, do you?
Publisher: Not for a minute!

Lesson: The doctor, by pointing out that both parties agree that her work will be timely and of high quality, has made it much harder for the opponent to argue that the work is not as valuable as the doctor says it is. The fact that the work will be delivered on time is very important and valuable for the publisher. He will not have to waste time "chasing" the author and can plan the most cost-effective schedule based on the "reliable" physician.

BE SENSITIVE TO YOUR OPPONENT'S NEEDS

You should be sensitive to your opponent's needs, desires, and concerns. If you can communicate this sensitivity to your opponents, they will be more likely to trust you. Also, understanding your opponent is critical when you need to obtain a deal that is a "win" for both sides.

Example 2.6 Sensitivity to opponent's needs builds trust
Doctor: (to opponent) What would work best for you? *(or)* Let's see how we can get you what you need.

Lesson: This query should be helpful in building trust and making a win-win deal more possible.

EMPHASIZE THE BENEFITS OF A LONG-TERM RELATIONSHIP

You should almost always stress the fact that a relationship will be long-term. This will accomplish at least two things. First, you will remind your opponent that he has more at stake than this one deal. Second, you can communicate that it is in *your opponent's* best interest to treat you fairly and make sure you are happy.

Example 2.7 Communicating that a long-term relationship is sought
Doctor: (to colleague) Doctor, as you know, it is my hope, if we can work things out satisfactorily, that this is the first of many projects we will work on together.
Colleague: Absolutely. Once we get this project done....

Lesson: By stressing that she seeks a long-term relationship, the doctor communicates that there is more at stake here than the one project. She also communicates that future projects are dependent upon the deal obtained in this project.

How Much Is a Long-Term Relationship Worth?

Both you and the person with whom you are negotiating should consider the value of achieving a long-term relationship. You can use this when determining how far you can and should go to achieve an agreement. You can also directly point out the potential of a long-term relationship to your opponent when attempting to get concessions to put an agreement together.

Example 2.8 Pointing out the value of a long-term relationship
Doctor: If we can agree on a 50–50 deal, the royalties could be as much as $32,000 a year on this project alone. If we could do one project a year for 5 years that would come to….
Opponent: $160,000 gross or $80,000 each.
Doctor: What do you say?

BUILD GOODWILL
In a potential long-term relationship, people want to associate themselves with people they trust and like. If you can establish goodwill, your negotiations will be less stressful and more profitable. A great way to build goodwill is to do a favor for your opponent.

Example 2.9 Doing people favors builds goodwill
Doctor (employer): I see here that you're a golfer.
New physician employee: Yes, it's my third passion after medicine and my family.
Doctor: Have you played the Mountain View Club?
New physician employee: No, that's private. I've been dying to get in there.
Doctor: I'm on the executive committee of that club. Been a member for 28 years. I can sponsor you for membership. I'll give them a call right now….

Lesson: When it's time to renegotiate the physician's employment contract or when it's time to buy into the practice, the new employee will remember the doctor's unsolicited act of kindness regarding the country club. The negotiations will be easier.

Example 2.10 Being nice feels good and can have business benefits
The authors put on seminars across the United States. At one seminar a medical book publisher was a paid exhibitor. He was a one-man operation and was there by himself. After the completion of a three-day program we were all exhausted. As we walked out of the door, we spotted this exhibitor struggling to pack all of his books into a truck. We asked if he

needed assistance and spent 20 minutes helping him. He thanked us again and again and has become a friend to this day. Years later we still do business together. With this small favor we showed him (as opposed to telling him) that we were easy to deal with, friendly, and cooperative. When given an opportunity, demonstrating is far more effective than telling someone the same thing.

MAKE A PHONE CALL OR SEND AN E-MAIL

Frequently, a simple phone call or an e-mail to share some information is all it takes to help build a long-term relationship.

Example 2.11 Doing people favors builds goodwill

You want to merge with another group. You have had informal discussions about this merger with the doctor who heads the other group. You know that the group wants to change its office location. The real estate market is very tight. You become aware of some ideal space that is available and call the other group's head to let her know. She really appreciated it. The cost was minimal but the goodwill benefits could be enormous if and when merger negotiations resume. Letting colleagues know about job openings, available projects, news items, advance information, and new competition is an excellent way to cement friendships and build long-term relationships. One e-mail can take you 10 seconds to send but can be invaluable to a colleague.

LET PEOPLE OFF THE HOOK

If you notice that the person you are negotiating with makes an error or if circumstances beyond the person's control have changed, point it out promptly. This is especially true in the short term if it would work to your advantage to say nothing. You should be careful about mentioning these favors later because neither side is likely to forget them and it may embarrass the other side.

Example 2.12 Treating your opponent well builds trust

When negotiating a contract for a series of medical videos, we noted that the physician with whom we were negotiating made a mathematical error that would have worked to our advantage. We pulled him aside and gently pointed out his error. This saved him from a major problem with his employer and, as you might expect, he really appreciated it. Trust was built and we have been dealing with that physician ever since.

Competitive Negotiation: One-Shot Deals

The competitive negotiation is characterized by the desire to win. It usually does not involve a long-term relationship. In a competitive negotiation, your opponent will disclose as little information as possible, show little concern for the other party, attempt to manipulate the situation, and use every negotiation tactic possible to achieve the best result for himself. An example of a competitive negotiation is a onetime purchase, such as an automobile.

In sharp contrast to cooperative negotiations, people involved in competitive negotiations are more apt to misstate the truth and be skeptical about any assertions you make. In competitive negotiations, the opening demands may be unrealistic and every action and statement of the parties is designed to achieve only one thing—to win. The use of threats, posturing, and hardball tactics are frequently part of competitive negotiation.

Successful physician negotiators must recognize quickly whether they are involved in a competitive or a cooperative negotiation. Savvy physician negotiators attempt to move from a competitive to a cooperative negotiation by asking the simple question, "How do we come up with a better deal for both of us?" Once both parties begin this search, they have moved toward a cooperative negotiation. This ability to change negotiations from competitive to cooperative will be especially helpful in building long-term relationships. Consider Example 2.13 in which the doctor converts a competitive negotiation into a cooperative negotiation through forthrightness and the promise of future business.

Example 2.13 Converting a competitive negotiation into a cooperative one

Doctor: I'm interested in that new Toyota.

Salesman: Step into my office and let's do a work up.

Doctor: Okay, but before you do the work up I want you to know a few things. I'm here to buy a Toyota. My family drives Toyotas. I have a wife and two teenage children that I will also be buying Toyotas for over the next couple of years. I have done my homework and I know exactly

what you pay the manufacturer for this model. I can pay you 5% over invoice cost, which is a fair margin for you. I'm not here to get something for nothing; you deserve a fair profit. However, I don't want to haggle or play games here. If you treat me correctly and respectfully you'll have us for customers for years to come. By my calculations 5% over cost is $32,456.
Salesman: I appreciate your candor and forthrightness and look forward to serving your family for years to come. You've got yourself a deal.
Doctor: I look forward to working with you as well. When can I take delivery?

Lesson: Not only did the doctor secure himself a fair deal, but he also defused a potentially hostile negotiation and made his future car buying negotiations relatively stress free.

Negotiation's "Magic" Formula

What is the "formula" for becoming a successful physician negotiator? Unfortunately, it is not as simple as deciphering the fictitious formula in Box 2.1 and applying it to your situation.

Box 2.1

Negotiation Formula

$$I + P + K = SN$$

In fact, negotiation is an extremely complex art. There is no quick, simple, and easy formula for becoming a successful physician negotiator. To be a superior physician negotiator, you need to understand all of the negotiation principles contained in Box 2.2. You will also need to apply the principles to your everyday negotiations. In addition, you will need specific information about complex physician negotiations (see Chapters 16 through 24).

Box 2.2

Negotiation Principles

Agendas	Introduction
Aspiration levels	Listening skills
Authority	Long-term relationships
Body language	Mutual gain
Characteristics/negotiator	Negotiation location
Clarity of language	Objectives
Closings	Opponent's desires
Communication	Opponent's motives
Competitive negotiations	Power
Concessions	Preparation
Control	Principled negotiations
Cooperative negotiations	Questions
Correspondence	Quickie negotiations
Counteroffers	Relationships
Deadlines	Setting targets
Deadlock	Silence
Defenses	Tactics
Emotions	Take it or leave it
Exercises	Telephone negotiations
Goals	Threats
Goodwill	Time as a weapon
Group negotiating	Ultimatums
Habits	What makes people act
Information	Win-win
Interests	

The Beginning of a Negotiation

The most fundamental skill that you will need to develop is to recognize when a negotiation has begun. *Any* communication with another person with whom you may deal in the future should be considered part of a negotiation. This is especially true when information is sought or given. Thus, you need to be very careful about disclosing information that could be used against you by a person who may want to do business with you. Consider Example 2.14.

Example 2.14 Not recognizing the start of a negotiation costs doctor
Setting: A cocktail party
Background: The physician is employed by Group X, hates it, and is desperate to get out. Group Y needs a new physician and is willing to pay up to $195,000/year. The national average salary for the physician's specialty is $175,000.

Head of Group Y: So, how do you like things over at Group X?
Doctor: It's terrible. I'm looking to move.
Head of Group Y: Sorry to hear that. Are they paying you competitively?
Doctor: Not even. I'm about 10% under the national average.
Head of Group Y: Well, I hope everything works out for you.

Epilogue: One week later, the head of Group Y calls the doctor and "starts" negotiations to bring him into the group. The doctor agrees to switch for $170,000/year. The negotiation began at the party. The doctor's revelation of information hurt him later.

Lesson: The negotiation did *not* begin when the head of the group called the physician one week after the party. It began with the disclosure of information by the doctor to the head of the group at the party. In one brief conversation the doctor disclosed the crucial information of what he was paid and that he hated his present job. His opponent disclosed next to nothing. The result was devastating in that the physician accepted a job for $20,000/year less than what he could have received from the new employer. Note that once the damaging information was disclosed by the doctor, there was very little that could be done to repair the damage. If the doctor in this example had been savvy enough to recognize that a negotiation was possibly beginning, he could have withheld the damaging information.

Example 2.15 Recognizing the start of the negotiation pays off
Setting: A cocktail party
Background: The physician is employed by Group X, hates it, and is desperate to get out. Group Y needs a new physician and is willing to pay up to $195,000/year. The national average salary for the physician's specialty is $175,000.

Head of Group Y: So, how do you like things over at Group X?
Doctor: Why do you ask?
Head of Group Y: We're looking for new staffing.
Doctor: Really? What's the pay?
Head of Group Y: Very competitive.
Doctor: Give me a call next week and we can talk more about it.

Epilogue: One week later, the head of Group Y calls the doctor and starts negotiations to bring him into the group. The doctor agrees to switch for $195,000/year.

Lesson: The doctor's negotiating skills, his ability to control the disclosure of damaging information, and his ability to obtain important information from his opponent will make him an extra $105,000 over five years.

AMBUSH NEGOTIATIONS

Many physicians do not properly identify a telephone call, an e-mail, or a casual remark as the beginning of the negotiation process. This is what we call the *ambush negotiation.* You need to understand that once someone has asked you, "Will you be able to...," you are in the midst of a rapidly developing negotiation. Be very careful about agreeing to requests without first determining:

- the effort that will be involved,
- whether the work will have to be done at home and at night,
- if you will have to give up or postpone more important or lucrative work to accomplish the tasks involved,
- if you really have the time to do this project,
- if you will have to give up family time or much needed recreation or vacation time to complete the task, and perhaps most importantly,
- whether you really want to do this project.

The techniques used to ambush the physician into doing long hours of travel, work, research, etc. for little or no pay include the following.

- *Catching the physician when she is too busy* to adequately reflect on the actual work and compensation involved. This is why the telephone call (especially a cell phone call) is the most effective ambush medium. The call can catch the physician off-guard with little or no time to think about the consequences of a quick "yes" or "OK" reply.
- *Flattery*. Massaging the physician's ego frequently smoothes the way to an all-too-quick affirmative reply. For example, "Our research indicates you are the most knowledgeable physician…."
- *Sense of professional duty* appeals to the doctor. Here the physician is asked to do the work to help patients, the public, or mankind in general. For example, "The chapter you wrote on early cancer detection could help save thousands of lives each year."

Recognizing these and similar techniques is essential to help the physician become a skilled negotiator.

Example 2.16 Doctor agrees without thinking or negotiating
Publisher: Doctor, will you be able to write a brief chapter on (fill in the physician's area of specialty or expertise) for the text we are working on?
Doctor: Sure, no problem. Happy to do it!

Lesson: This is an ambush negotiation in which a physician has been taken by surprise. The physician has committed himself to many hours of hard work without any consideration of the time and effort involved, adequate compensation, deadlines, and work or family time that will have to be sacrificed to meet this new commitment.

Just say no
Your ability to say no can save you hundreds of hours a year. However, many physicians have great difficulty in just saying no. Saying no or deflecting and postponing a decision until you are provided with the details and can do a little thinking are crucial to being a superior physician negotiator.

Example 2.17 Doctor says no
Publisher: Doctor, will you be able to write a brief chapter for the text we are working on?
Doctor: I'm sorry, I can't.

Lesson: The ability to say no is imperative. Having this ability will save you time, aggravation, and money.

Ask for it in writing

One technique you can use to avoid being ambushed is to ask for the proposal in writing. This type of reply will accomplish several things. First, it will reduce the time spent on many preliminary requests (i.e., the feeling-out type of requests that just waste physicians' time). Second, it will give a physician time to think about whether he really wants to do the project. Finally, it will provide the physician with the detailed information he needs to make a reasoned, unrushed, and informed decision as to whether the project is financially and professionally in his best interest.

Example 2.18 Asking for a written proposal gives time to think
Publisher: Will you be able to write a brief chapter for the text we are working on?
Doctor: It sounds interesting. Please send me a note with the details—what you are looking for in terms of length, content, original research, time deadlines, format, my compensation, and the compensation of the other authors and editors. If you have a contractual form send it along so I can take a look at it as well.

Lesson: By asking for the proposal in writing, the doctor has avoided a quick, ill-informed decision. He has given himself time to consider the offer after receiving additional information. He has also asked to see the contract, which may contain provisions that make the deal a non-starter.

Gentle excuses

As a busy physician, your colleagues and others often request you to take on additional projects and work. You should develop a typewritten list of 10 gentle excuses to keep on your desk and in your wallet so you can politely decline most of these requests. Remember the business adage that oftentimes the best deal is the one that you do not do. Successful physicians diagnose and avoid projects that drain their time and potential income. Using this list will save you hundreds of hours per year. Make your list and pull it out as soon as you hear the words, "Doctor, will you be able to...?" The authors have placed 10 sample responses in Box 2.3.

Box 2.3

Polite Ways to Say No

1. "I would love to, but my plate is full."
2. "That sounds great, but I'm swamped."
3. "I am honored, but I'm now focusing on other areas."
4. "Sounds interesting. Could you please send me a written proposal?"
5. "I think I understand what you're looking for. I'm going to refer you to my colleague, Doctor Swensen. He is the real guru in that area."
6. "Let me check my travel schedule and get back to you."
7. "I'm sorry, but I have a previous family commitment. I'm (planning a wedding, caring for an elderly parent, traveling to a graduation, moving a daughter to college, etc.)."
8. "I can't. Ever since my (insert medical condition such as hypertension) was diagnosed, I'm under strict orders from *my* doctor not to take on any additional work."
9. "I wish I could, but I'm so busy now that I'm just trying to keep my head above water."
10. "I'm sorry, but that's out of the question. I've been out of the office and I'm just trying to dig out here."

Example 2.19 The cost of not saying no

Q: You are a forty-five-year-old physician with a busy forensic and consulting practice who lives in New England. You have been requested to give a keynote lecture in Australia. The organization will pay for your airfare. You end up staying two weeks on vacation with your spouse. How much has this "free" trip cost you?

A:

Two weeks lost income:	$20,000
Spouse's airfare:	$2,000
Hotel:	$4,800
Meals:	$2,000

Lesson: Your "free" airline ticket cost you $28,800. You may have been better off just saying no.

Note: Based upon their own lives and experiences, physicians are encouraged to come up with more creative and effective gentle excuses/reasons.

Chapter 3 The Best Place to Negotiate

Executive Summary

- In a strategic sense, negotiating at your opponent's location is usually best.
- You can be distracted and interrupted when you negotiate in your own office.
- You are less able to defer and deflect when on your home turf.
- Your opponent can gain valuable information by coming to your place of business to negotiate.
- You are more likely to prepare thoroughly if you have to travel to the negotiation.
- If you go to your opponent's office to negotiate, you are at an advantage. You can gather intelligence and your opponent will most likely be distracted.

The Home Field Advantage

The conventional wisdom expressed by most negotiation experts is that negotiators are best served by holding the negotiation session in their own office. The sports analogy of the home field advantage is used to explain why negotiations should take place in one's own office. The home team feels more comfortable, is well rested, eats and sleeps at home, and has not been worn down by travel. In addition, when you negotiate on your own turf you have access to your files, documents, reference materials, computers, copiers, and fax machines. You can also control the logistics of the negotiation, including seating, temperature, refreshments, and to some extent, interruptions. It is also more economical because you do not incur travel costs or miss additional time from the office due to travel.

The problem with this conventional wisdom from a physician's standpoint is that each advantage listed above can be a distinct and serious disadvantage as well. See Example 3.1.

Example 3.1 Home field disadvantage: doctor cannot plead ignorance

Opponent: Doctor, will you be able to provide 401(k) plans for all of your employees?

Doctor: I don't know. It will be a question of finances. I will have to look into it and get back to you in a few weeks.

Opponent: Well, Doctor, it's good we are in your office because all the information we need is at our fingertips. There's your bookkeeper. Let's run the numbers on Quicken and do some spreadsheets to see what you can realistically afford.

Lesson: The "advantage" of the physician negotiating on her home turf has quickly turned into a disadvantage. This issue could have been avoided by negotiating in a neutral location.

The Home Field Disadvantage

The disadvantages of physicians negotiating in their own offices are substantial. They include interruptions, difficulty in delaying decisions, handling logistics, and the staff time needed for preparation.

Interruptions

If you negotiate in your own office you could be subject to constant interruptions, e-mails, phone calls, or noise from fax machines, computers, printers, staff, patients, and all the other distractions that come with a busy medical practice. This can make it difficult to concentrate and focus on the negotiation at hand. Under a situation such as this, you could become tempted to just get the negotiation over with so you can get back to work. Such thinking could cost you a lot of money.

Example 3.2 Negotiating in your office can reveal costly information
Background: A physician is negotiating the sale of his solo practice. He has invited a prospective purchaser to his office to negotiate terms, especially the price. The purchaser arrives 30 minutes early (always wise) and takes a seat in the waiting room. The doctor is busy seeing patients.

Opponent: (to patient in the waiting room) How do you like the doctor and staff?
Patient: Well, the doctor is great, but it takes three weeks to get an appointment. I almost always see the nurse practitioner. The billing system is often inaccurate. Let me tell you what happened to my friend Pam last week....

Lesson: Important information has been revealed. It is likely that the purchaser will offer less money to the selling physician.

Example 3.3 More problems from negotiating on home turf
Background: A group practice leader is in the process of hiring a new physician to enter the group practice. The prospective new physician arrives 30 minutes early for his final hiring meeting.

Group Practice Leader: (screaming to staff member) I've told you a hundred times: "light" cream cheese on my bagels. What's the problem? Aren't you smart enough to follow this one simple instruction? (soothingly) Oh…Dr. Jones. I didn't see you in the waiting room. Sorry about that.

Lesson: The new doctor has learned crucial information by negotiating in the group practice leader's office. He may be concerned about accepting a job there.

Such problems can be avoided by choosing a neutral negotiating location. Restaurants, conference centers, and the like can be locations with few distractions.

Deflecting Decisions

As we have seen in Example 3.1, when you negotiate in your own office, it is more difficult to use lack of information as a justification to postpone or deflect a decision. This is due to the availability of records, staff, computers, and partners (see pages 35–74 on information). This inability to delay a decision can be a distinct disadvantage. This is particularly true when time is on your side.

Example 3.4 More difficult to defer a response when at home
Background: You are part of a four-person practice and have been approached to sell your practice to a large corporation. You are appointed by your three partners to meet with the buyer at the group's office.

Opponent: We can offer you $500,000 cash and 25,000 shares of unrestricted HealthCo common stock (series A).
Doctor: I need to sit down with my partners and discuss this. We'll get back to you after we discuss it.

Opponent: I just flew in from the West Coast and don't want to have to fly here again. Why don't you discuss it with them now, while we're all in the same building? I'll wait here and you can let me know in an hour or so….

Lesson: It may be harder to delay a decision or to deflect a question when you negotiate in your own office.

LOGISTICS

Having someone come to your office to negotiate will mean that you or your staff will have to clean up and be concerned with refreshments, lunch, making photocopies, and providing support material and staff. It is not uncommon for one or two copies to turn into hours of extra work for your staff. You may want to consider the staff time and office disruption involved in having a negotiation at your office.

PREPARATION AND FOCUS

Negotiating in your office may result in you preparing inadequately. (See pages 109–22 on preparation.) For example, you may be less inclined to focus on organizing your materials, files, and research before the negotiation. When they know they are going to an off-site negotiation, physicians tend to prepare all the materials they need and spend more time getting organized. Even more importantly, when you negotiate off site it is natural for you to focus more on the negotiation at hand because you are removed from the distractions of your own office. This forced preparation may be reason enough to schedule some negotiations in a neutral off-site location.

ADVANTAGES OF VISITING NEGOTIATORS

The advantages of negotiating away from your office can be substantial. They may more than justify the time, effort, and travel involved.

KICKING THE TIRES

Physicians often start a new business relationship with a negotiation. Savvy physicians may want to visit the place of business to "kick the tires."

Example 3.5 Negotiating at your opponent's business venue may help you gain valuable information

Physician: (to new prospective business partner) I noticed that you have only 3 designated parking spots in the lot. I thought you had over 25 employees.

Prospective Partner: Oh, many of our workers are overseas and we have quite a few part-timers who telecommute.

Lesson: Experienced negotiators may want to "kick the tires" by performing a site visit before completing final negotiations. An on-site visit (which may or may not be scheduled) can be very revealing. It may determine if you actually want to do business with the prospective partner.

GATHERING INTELLIGENCE

Physicians can often gather intelligence when negotiating at the opponent's office. While research and preparation are invaluable, sometimes there is no better technique than seeing things for yourself.

Example 3.6 Negotiating at your opponent's location becomes an intelligence bonanza

Physician interviewing for position in group practice: How long do the new doctors usually stay here?

Medical Assistant: One lasted over 6 months.

Lesson: The physician in this example quickly found out a crucial piece of intelligence by going to the hiring partner's office for negotiations. Knowing that new physicians do not last in the group practice may be extremely helpful in deciding how to negotiate and if he even wants the position.

Authors' Recommendation

Physicians are not necessarily best served by negotiating in their own offices. Physicians should strive to negotiate in the location that feels most comfortable, offers them the most advantages, and has the fewest drawbacks. Frequently, it is best for physicians to negotiate in neutral locations or at the offices of their opponents. In this way, you can become and remain focused on your negotiation and can learn valuable information about your opponents without being subjected to interruptions, distractions, and the unwanted disclosure of information. In short, you can prepare and concentrate on the matters under negotiation. Remember, "You don't get what you deserve. You get what you negotiate."[4]

[4] Chester L. Karrass, *The Negotiating Game* (New York: Harper Business, Revised Edition, 1992).

Chapter 4 Controlling and Obtaining Information

Executive Summary

- Information translates into power in any negotiation.
- Limit the damaging information you provide your opponent.
- Gather as much information as you can prior to and during the negotiation.
- Before the negotiation, make sure you are dealing with a person who has the power to make concessions and close the deal.
- To avoid "trickle-down loss," it is crucial to negotiate with the highest level person you can.
- Asking for an opponent's timeframes can give you a good idea of how eager they are for the deal.
- Do not bargain against yourself. Only give concessions in return for concessions.
- Limiting your own authority (for example, needing to check with partners or a spouse) makes it easier for you to avoid the mistake of making a snap decision.
- To gather information, you must ask questions and listen carefully (using active listening skills) to the answers (what is said, how it is said, and what is not said).
- Start off your negotiation with broad questions that encourage your opponent to talk up.
- Trial balloon questions can be useful in gathering information. (For example, "Would flex time be helpful to you?")
- When used skillfully, softly worded questions can raise your opponent's anxiety level and gain you power. (For example, "What are your plans if we can't come to an agreement?")
- How you word your questions is very important. (For example, asking, "How much flexibility do you have in your price?" is better than, "Do you have any flexibility in your price?")
- When answering questions, give as little damaging information as possible, but provide information that strengthens your negotiating position (such as your alternatives).
- You do not have to answer all questions. There are many techniques to professionally and politely decline to answer.
- Observe your opponent's body language and use this information.

- It is crucial to determine your opponent's needs, interests, and desires.
- Build a relationship and goodwill with your opponent by finding and exploiting common interests or a common background.

Introduction

One of the key elements of any negotiation is information. Understanding how to get information from your opponent and how to prevent the disclosure of harmful information to your opponent is crucial for your development as a successful physician negotiator.

Authority

The first piece of information you will need to determine quickly is your opponent's authority. By *authority,* we mean the ability or power to say yes, to compromise on crucial terms, and to enter into a binding agreement. You should negotiate with a "yes person," a person who has the ability to agree and make things happen. The first order of business, therefore, *before* you start to negotiate, is to determine if you are negotiating with the right person. You need to determine if the person you are dealing with has the authority to negotiate and close the deal.

Example 4.1 Communicating with the decision makers
Doctor: As you know, we have four items we need to finalize an agreement today.
Opponent: Let me write down your needs. I will talk to my superiors and get back to you next week.
Doctor: Thank you very much for your offer to convey a message for me, but I need to deal directly with the decision makers. Let's set up a time when I can talk to them directly.

Lesson: The doctor was told up front that his opponent did not have the authority to close a deal. The doctor recognized that he could not gain anything by talking to the powerless information gatherer and correctly demanded to talk to the decision makers. Note how this demand was made in a polite way designed not to alienate the opponent's subordinate.

PREEMPTIVE E-MAIL

Physicians can avoid wasting time going to negotiation sessions with people lacking authority by using a preemptive e-mail or fax.

Example 4.2 Establishing authority with preliminary e-mail
Doctor's e-mail to opponent:
Dear Ms. Jones,
Prior to setting a negotiation session, please advise if you have full authority to agree on terms and negotiate a binding agreement.

Thank you,
James L. Thompson, M.D.

Opponent's reply e-mail
Dr. Thompson,
I do have full authority to reach an agreement.

Lesson: This physician quickly and efficiently determined that his opponent has authority to negotiate. The opponent will be locked into this position and it will be hard for her to try and defer key concessions.

If the person with whom you are dealing is not the person with authority, find out who is. There are several methods to do this. The simplest and most direct method is to ask your opponent, "Do you have the authority to negotiate and finalize the deal *today?*" Anything less than a direct *yes* means your opponent does not have complete and unfettered authority and will have to obtain approval of any proposed deal by a third party or parties, usually at a later date. This person is usually just gathering information and feeling you out at your expense. When confronted with this situation, you can respond as in Example 4.3.

Example 4.3 Responding to an opponent without authority
Doctor: As I understand it, you are merely on a fact-finding mission here today. Who has the authority to authorize compromises and concessions so we can finalize this agreement?

Lesson: You may need to directly ask your opponent who has the full authority.

It is also helpful for you to determine in advance your opponent's decision-making process or procedure and the timeframe in which decisions are normally made. You will need this information so that you can plan on when a deal will be closed or when you will have to proceed to an alternative plan if the deal can't be consummated. (Please see pages 109–22 on preparation.) Consider Example 4.4.

Learning your opponent's timeframe is an excellent tactic or strategic negotiating technique. Obtaining this information will help you assess:

- how eager your opponent may be to reach a negotiated agreement and
- the amount of pressure your opponent is under to finalize an agreement.

Knowing an opponent's timeframe will help the physician negotiator assess who has the true power in the negotiation (see page 77 and pages 87–88).

Example 4.4 Opponent's timeframe indicates eagerness for a deal
Doctor: I am calling to confirm our meeting on Friday at 1:00 P.M., in your office, to negotiate the proposed contract.
Opponent: That's correct. Park in the B lot and take elevator #3 directly to the 26th floor.
Doctor: What is the procedure your company uses to finalize these types of contracts? What is your timeframe?
Opponent: I will finalize an agreement and, subject to the approval of my supervisor, we will be all set. I have never had an agreement turned down yet. I am shooting for next Monday to wrap up this whole deal.

Lesson: The physician negotiator has determined the scope of his opponent's authority and has a fairly firm timeline as to when he will get a final yes or no. If the answer is no, he can make alternative arrangements. In addition, it appears the opponent and his supervisor are fairly eager to resolve all outstanding issues.

The successful physician negotiator should negotiate directly with a person who has full authority because:

- it is easier to obtain major concessions from this person (subordinates are unsure of what the boss might think),
- it avoids delay (there is no need to run it up the flagpole),
- you avoid bargaining against yourself (never a good idea), and
- you avoid trickle-down loss on key points (see pages 41 and 43).

CONCESSIONS

If the person you are negotiating with has full authority, she can make concessions without having to obtain approval from anyone else. Frequently, this is done to close the deal (see pages 241–49 on closing the deal) or as a response to some concessions you have made (see pages 127–35 on concessions). Without this authority, the spontaneity of the negotiation process is lost. You will run the risk of negotiating against yourself and of having your opponent's recommendations overruled by a superior.

DELAY

If the person does not have full authority, key concessions and compromises will have to be run up the flagpole. This means a delay and a break in the negotiation process. A break in the momentum can sometimes increase the difficulty of ultimately achieving an agreement. In addition, it will certainly increase the amount of time and effort you will need to spend on the negotiation. You should, therefore, always strive to negotiate with a person with full authority.

Example 4.5 The importance of finding the "yes" person

You are running a little late for a short meeting with Dr. Lin at the hospital. You pull into the visitors' parking lot and it is full. The only remaining spots are for staff. You ask the security person at the lot if you could leave the car for 30 minutes, explaining your predicament. She says yes. This is an example of negotiating directly with the "yes person." This person has the authority to let you park in the spot. You obtain a quick response to your request because it does not need approval from a higher authority. What if you had called Dr. Lin on your cell phone?

Would the result have been as effective? What if you had not talked to the security person? Would you have been more or less likely to be towed?

BARGAINING AGAINST YOURSELF

Negotiating with a person without full authority will result in you bargaining against yourself. When you bargain against yourself, your opponent can extract your bottom line from you and you will gain nothing in return. You will then be turned over to a person with full authority to start the negotiation process in earnest.

Example 4.6 What happens when you do not insist on a substantive response

Proposed employer: As I understand it, you want $150,000 but would accept $140,000 and you are willing to be on call occasionally.

Doctor: I am trying to be honest and fair.

Proposed employer: Let me get the administrator in on this as she is the one with the ultimate authority.

Administrator: I see you are looking for $140,000 and can work on call when needed. We can offer you $130,000 and will need you every other weekend and one night per week.

Lesson: In the above example, the employer was able to gain substantial concessions from the physician regarding salary and call while the physician gained nothing in return. Bargaining against yourself should be avoided whenever possible. This is done by insisting on a substantive response to any offer or proposal. If such a response is not forthcoming, the skilled negotiator refuses to modify his position.

Example 4.7 Doctor refuses to bargain against himself

Doctor: I usually get $10,000 a day to train attorneys in how to use the AMA *Guides to Permanent Impairment.*

Opponent: (attorney) We are only a small group of attorneys, we can't afford $10,000 for a one-day course.

Doctor: What can your group of "indigent" personal injury attorneys afford?

Lesson: The doctor refused to negotiate against himself. He forced his opponent to come up with a counterproposal. The doctor could then:

- accept the offer,
- reject the offer, or
- continue to negotiate.

Trickle-Down Loss

The successful physician negotiator understands and avoids *trickle-down loss*. To explain what we mean by trickle-down loss, let's suppose that you are negotiating with a company to sell them a new medical device you invented to take splinters out of someone's finger. The CEO decides that she can pay a 5% production royalty. She so instructs the department manager. He wants to look good, so he tells the legal department to offer you 4%. The attorney negotiating with you has authority at 4%. He also wants to look good, so he offers you 3% "firm." This is trickle-down loss in operation. Every time the terms have gone through a person's hands, it has cost you money. Thus, to save money, you need to negotiate with a person as high up the chain of authority as possible.

Your Own Authority

You also need to be concerned with the extent of your own authority. When you are negotiating for yourself, your practice, or even your partners, your opponent will want to find out whether *you* have full authority. If you do have full authority, you are in a dangerous position. When you have full authority, by definition you will be able to make quick decisions and concessions without consulting anyone and without thinking them through fully. This quick and sometimes emotional decision making can be a recipe for disaster.

Example 4.8 Having full authority can be dangerous

Salesperson: You have looked at the equipment three times. We met your price of $27,000 and your payment terms. You do have the authority to purchase the equipment, don't you?

Doctor: Yes, of course. It is my practice.

Salesperson: Great! Here's the contract. Please sign on pages 4, 10, 12, and 15.

Lesson: It is frequently in your best interest to not have complete authority to negotiate and finalize agreements. If you don't have full authority, or if you profess to have limited authority, it will be easier for you to negotiate slowly and deliberately and to continue to look for better terms before agreeing to a deal. Some good ways to profess to have limited authority are listed in Box 4.1.

Box 4.1

Ways to Profess Limited Authority

1. "I will have to check with my partner, supervisor, spouse, lawyer, accountant, or tax advisor." (Who is unavailable.)
2. "I have another deal pending. Finalizing this agreement depends upon my successfully completing the previous deal."
3. "I will have to see if this creates any conflicts of interest for me."
4. "I want to avoid even the appearance of impropriety."

Intentionally limiting your own authority when negotiating is an excellent strategy. Savvy physician negotiators understand how to use their own lack of authority as an offensive tactic. By intentionally limiting your own authority, you can avoid making a quick agreement that has not been methodically evaluated. It will also help stop you from being pressured into deals you are not sure of and will help you overcome any tendencies you might have to "give away the store."

Example 4.9 Lack of authority cleverly used to gain significant concession

Salesperson: This is our best offer: $27,000 for the computer equipment and one year of service.

Doctor: Our partnership agreement prevents me from signing any contracts in excess of $25,000 without the written approval of my 14 partners. The next time we will be having a full board meeting is three months from now. I can try and put this on the agenda and hopefully we can get to it at that time. If we don't get to it then....

Salesperson: If I take $2,000 out of my commission and cut the price back to $25,000, will you sign the contract today?

Doctor: Let me see the contract, please....

Lesson: The doctor cleverly used his professed lack of authority to extract a concession of 7.4% ($2,000) off the seller's "best" offer.

Example 4.10 How to avoid making a snap decision

Q: You are negotiating the sale of your four-physician practice. The potential buyer makes a serious and fair offer to you and is pressing for an on-the-spot decision. What can you say to her to buy time without jeopardizing the offer?

A: One response is, "I'm going to need a couple of days to consider your proposal. Let me talk to my husband and partners and I'll get back to you in a couple of days."

Lesson: During the two-day delay you can talk things over with others and, more importantly, take the time necessary to consider the proposal.

Example 4.11 How to avoid trickle-down loss

Q: You are negotiating your employment contract with a group practice. You have been contacted by the business manager to sit down and "hammer out the terms." What should you consider doing before agreeing to this meeting? Why?

A: Find out whether the business manager has full authority to bind the group to a contract. If she doesn't, politely request (and insist on, if need be) a meeting with a person in the group who has full authority. You need to avoid negotiating against yourself and the trickle-down effect. Be prepared to respond, "I'll have to check with my spouse...." This will give you time to carefully consider the proposed agreement. You will, of course, want to continue your due diligence inquiry to determine the reputation of the group, physician turnover, the percentage of physicians who make partner, etc.

Example 4.12 Preparing for a negotiation setting

Q: A managed care company wants to come to your office and negotiate your contract with them. They will be sending their representative. What action steps could you take to control the setting and the negotiation process?

A: Make sure your partners are unavailable so that you can claim lack of full authority. Consider whether you want to change the location of the meeting to their office or a neutral location (for example, your private club where you can wine and dine them). Verify that the representative has full authority to make changes to the contract. Ask the representative to fax or e-mail you the proposed contract in advance so you can study, research, and think about the terms. If not, suggest that you travel to his office to meet with someone with full authority. If you meet with a representative without full authority, use the meeting solely to extract information from that person. Do not disclose any information or negotiate against yourself.

Once you have determined the extent of your opponent's authority, you will need to determine other information about him. This information includes his needs, desires, interests, deadlines, pressures, and motives. Such information is best obtained by asking questions, using active listening skills, and by observing body language.

Asking Questions

The key to gathering information successfully in a negotiation session is to obtain as much information as quickly as possible. At the same time, you want to reveal minimal key confidential information. The simplest, most direct, and most efficient method of gathering information in a negotiation session is to ask the right question at the right time. Physicians are often reluctant to ask questions that may be considered personal, impertinent, or too aggressive. It is important to remember that there are very important benefits to asking questions during a negotiation session. Asking good questions will help you discover key information quickly and can help you control the negotiation session flow and momentum. In addition, asking questions might be the only way to obtain certain pieces of information.

General Questions

Early questions

Before the formal negotiation takes place is the best time to start to ask questions. Your opponent is more likely to be forthcoming while responding to a "pre-negotiation" request than he will be when sitting across from you in a formal conference room.

Savvy physician negotiators often send an e-mail to their opponent before the negotiation formally begins. For example:

> John,
> Look forward to meeting with you next week. Please let me know what your goals, objectives, and timeline are and how you propose that we can best work together. This will help me prepare for next week.
> Thank you,
> Steve

Frequently, a simple e-mail can result in detailed answers with crucial information that can set the tone for the entire negotiation.

In addition, the above technique plays on many people's perceived need to respond quickly to their e-mails. Frequently, in their haste to empty their inboxes, opponents may respond without giving the same thought they would to a letter or a fax. (See pages 163–72 on e-mail negotiation.)

You should start the negotiation session with general, open-ended, broad questions. These will help you elicit a good deal of information right away. Open-ended questions encourage your opponent to open up and talk about his job, work, program, or product.

It is important for you to be a student of human nature to be a successful physician negotiator. You need to appreciate that, generally speaking, people like to talk about themselves and show how much they know about a particular subject. The more they talk, the more information they are giving you. This is a technique that the authors have used very successfully when taking depositions.

Example 4.13 Effectiveness of an open-ended question
Background: You have been offered a job at a group medical practice. After the head physician gives you your offer and excuses himself, you have a private chat with the office manager as you head back to your car.

Q: How do you think I should respond to the job offer?
A: Well, the offer is solid, the salary is competitive, and the fringes are okay. Now, as for the personalities of the physicians, that is another thing.…

Lesson: By asking an open-ended question, you tapped into the office manager's natural desire to help and show how much he knows. You were able to find out key information that might not have been obtainable through another source.

Another way to gain valuable information is to appear to be ignorant of certain matters. People love to teach and show off their knowledge. Let them. As one expert puts it:

> In negotiation, dumb is often better than smart, inarticulate better than articulate, and many times weakness can actually be strength. So train yourself occasionally to say, "I don't know," "I just don't understand," "You lost me some time ago," "Help me," when these phrases suit your purposes....Moral: Don't be too quick to "understand" or prove your intellect at the outset of an encounter. Watch your listen-talk ratio. Learn to ask questions even when you think you know the answers.[1]

Understandably, this tactic is often difficult for physicians to master. You don't often hear a doctor say, "I don't understand" or "Help me." You should not feel ashamed to use this technique. As trial lawyers, the authors often had to master technical areas that were beyond our training and scope of expertise. We were able to do so because we were not afraid or embarrassed to ask for help from someone with more knowledge than ourselves, such as our expert witnesses. You will need to develop the same attitude if you would like to be a successful physician negotiator.

Example 4.14 Asking questions to gain information
Background: You have been asked to write a screenplay for a movie about the inner workings of a hospital. You have been offered 10% of the profits. This is the first time you have been offered compensation for your creative writing.

Opponent: We can offer you 10% of the profits.
Doctor: I'm sorry. I'm kind of new at this. What exactly do you mean by profits?
Opponent: Well the accountants figure that out.

---

[1] Cohen, pp. 40, 42, 43.

Doctor: Well, do you know how it works?
Opponent: On a basic level, sure.
Doctor: Could you explain it to me?
Opponent: Sure. You take the total revenue generated from the movie and subtract out the expenses.
Doctor: What are the expenses?
Opponent: Production costs, distribution, allocated overhead, and some others.
Doctor: How are the production costs calculated?

Lesson: By asking questions indicating that he was not an expert in film contracts, the doctor was able to gain valuable information concerning the value of the offered contract. Had he been uncomfortable doing this, he never would have learned that by the time all the expenses are taken out, 10% of profits can and often does amount to 10% of nothing.

SPECIFIC QUESTIONS

After you have obtained as much information as possible by using general questions, it is best to move into more specific, pointed questions. These specific questions are most effectively asked once you have determined the exact information you need. For example, if an employer was worried about call coverage, she could simply ask, "If we were able to offer you this position, would you be willing to work one night a week and one weekend per month?"

One of the reasons for starting with general questions and moving to specific ones is that your opponent is likely to answer the general questions more freely. This is true because it is less likely that he feels that he is being led or prodded. You need to keep in mind that once you start asking specific questions your opponent is more likely to be on guard and to be more careful about his responses.

One technique you can use to take advantage of the above-described phenomenon is to dispense with the pleasantries and easy open-ended questions and ask your most difficult pointed question at the start of the negotiation. This will often catch your opponent off guard. Your opponent is probably expecting general open-ended questions and may be unprepared to answer the "hard question" in a deceptive way. The authors call this technique "the Brooklyn approach."[2]

Example 4.15 Trying to catch your opponent off guard by starting off with a difficult, pointed question
Doctor: We are both very busy professionals. Let's cut to the chase. How much money are you offering?
Opponent: Well, I have authority to offer up to $2.5 million.

Lesson: This is the Brooklyn approach. A direct question will sometimes catch your opponent off guard and make him reveal valuable information.

To employ the Brooklyn approach, you as a physician will have to overcome any aversion you have to asking direct, pointed, and possibly difficult questions. To soften the blow to your opponent you can always follow up your question with a statement such as, "I apologize for being so direct, but I don't have any time to waste on preliminaries."

WHAT'S IN IT FOR ME?
Another direct approach question that can be extremely effective at the start of a negotiation is, "What's in it for me?"

Example 4.16 "What's in it for me?"
Opponent: (to doctor) We would like you to appear in a 30-minute video on chronic pain. We know you are the world's leading expert doctor.
Doctor: What's in it for me?
Opponent: (taken aback by the directness of the question) Well…you would get great exposure and then…

Lesson: The doctor in the above example has cut to the chase by asking one simple yet direct question. The person making the offer is immediately put on the defensive and will have to come up with attractive reasons to get the doctor involved in the project. If she is still interested, the savvy physician will follow up with questions about what precisely is involved in making a 30-minute video: scriptwriting, rehearsing, travel, filming, editing, etc.

---

[2] Mr. Babitsky being brought up in that borough.

Four additional types of questions for gathering information are leading questions, suggestive questions, successive questions, and "what if" questions. *Leading questions* are questions in which statements of fact are turned into questions that contain the essence of the answer you are seeking. This type of question permits the proponent of the question to maintain control over the information flow, the momentum, and the negotiation itself. Leading questions are typically used by attorneys during cross-examination. The problem with leading questions is that they can sometimes be offensive. Furthermore, they do not produce much information that you don't already know or suspect. Leading questions typically must be answered with a yes or a no. They can be particularly useful in pinning a person down on a point by making it much more difficult for them to be evasive. Some sample leading questions are provided in Box 4.2.

Box 4.2

Sample Leading Questions

Q: She has already exceeded her budget, hasn't she?
Q: You are looking for a three-year agreement, correct?
Q: You don't have a problem with..., do you?
Q: Isn't it a fact that you have no other offers outstanding?
Q: Isn't it true that you don't have complete authority to close this deal?
Q: You do have some flexibility on the price, don't you?

Suggestive questions contain a suggestive course of action. These can also be useful during a negotiation. The best suggestive questions give your opponent limited choices and make it awkward for him to raise a third option. For example, you could ask, "Would X work better for you or Y?" As long as both of the proposed alternatives are favorable to your position, the suggestive question is a good method of obtaining closure on a particular point during the negotiation process.

Asking a series of *successive questions* can also be useful. The series of questions should point to a logical conclusion. This technique is often used by trial attorneys and is useful in controlling the negotiation process and building momentum toward your ultimate goals.

Example 4.17 Successive questions can make a persuasive argument
Background: A doctor works for a group practice and is seeking a raise.

Doctor: Haven't I been an excellent employee?
Opponent: Sure.
Doctor: Don't my patients love me?
Opponent: The feedback has been tremendously positive.
Doctor: I am among the top three income producers in the practice, am I not?
Opponent: This year, yes.
Doctor: Who picked up the slack when Dr. Jones was out on maternity leave?
Opponent: We appreciate you pitching in.

Lesson: The successive questions lead to the inescapable conclusion that the physician is entitled to a raise!

"What if" questions can also be useful. These questions are trial balloons in which you elicit responses to less-than-concrete proposals or suggestions. These questions have the added advantage that they are generally not adversarial in nature.

Example 4.18 Trial balloons can help gather information
Doctor: What if we were able to offer you flex time? Would that help you?
Prospective employee: Yes, if I could make my own hours the salary could work.

Lesson: The doctor has gained valuable information without committing herself to anything.

"What if" questions can also be used as a tactic or strategic technique.

Example 4.19 "What will you do if we can't agree?"
Doctor: (to opponent) What will you do if we can't agree?
Opponent: I am not really sure. I guess we would have to start our search over again….

Lesson: The doctor in this example has used a simple "what if" question to do several things.

1. Raise his opponent's anxiety level.
2. Force his opponent to concede that he does not have any available alternatives.
3. Face the specter of failure. The opponent will be forced to think about how he will report this to his superiors and if this will adversely affect his own employment situation. It will also subconsciously push him toward being more "reasonable" to avoid this failure. (For more on tactics, see pages 173–93.)

How you ask your question can be of crucial importance. For example, let's say that you are trying to get a quick read on how firm a price really is. You could ask, "Is that price firm?" As you might expect, almost uniformly the reply will be the same: "Yes." Why is that? Because you have made it too easy for the person to turn you down. What if you asked the question a little differently? "Do you have any flexibility in the price?" Again, it is too easy to say no, and that is what you will probably hear. What if you asked the question as follows? "How much flexibility do you have in the price?" The most common response is, "Not too much." This is a lot better than no and it opens up the matter of the price. From there you are up and running and can discuss how much is "not too much."

In the course of thousands of negotiations, the authors have asked one simple question—"How much flexibility do you have?"—many times. The majority of the time the answers have been very helpful: "a little," "some," "not too much," "quite a bit." When you obtain any of these responses, the door has been opened and you can begin to negotiate the final terms. You will want to actively listen to the precise reply as it may give you some indication of the true amount of flexibility. (See pages 58–68 on active listening.) In the rare case in which the answer is "none at all," you have still gleaned important information quickly. If your opponent is being forthcoming, you may not be able to reach an agreement. Successful physician negotiators cannot be timid or afraid of asking these types of questions in this kind of way.

Asking the right questions during a negotiation is an art as much as it is a science.[3] How to properly respond to your opponent's questions is equally, if not more, important.

Answering Questions

When you use questions effectively, you can expect that your opponent will ask you a series of questions as well. How you respond to these questions is as much an art as knowing which questions to ask. "The art of

---

[3] As an art, we can learn a lot from studying the "masters." McCormack lists the five questions that need to be answered during the negotiation:

What, When, Where, How Exclusive, and How Much?
All five of the questions asked above should be answered during the course of negotiation.
A. <u>The What</u>
What is it, precisely, that you are selling?
B. <u>The When</u>
This means how long, from "one contiguous eight-hour period," which can be used to define a workday, to "forever."
C. <u>The Where</u>
"Territory," which can range from "the world" to "South Cincinnati."
D. <u>The How Exclusive</u>
To what degree does the buyer wish (and are we willing) to shut out the rest of the competition?
E. <u>The How Much</u>
This means money, but not necessarily money alone. It can also mean stocks, securities, or other forms of equity.

Mark H. McCormack, *What They Don't Teach You at Harvard Business School: Notes from a Street Smart Executive* (New York: Bantam Books, 1984) pp. 142–44.

Furthermore, Donaldson lists handy guidelines for asking better questions during a negotiation:

- Plan your questions in advance.
- Ask with a purpose.
- Tailor your question to your listener.
- Follow general questions with more specific ones.
- Keep questions short and clear. Cover only one subject.
- Make transitions between their answers and your questions.
- Don't interrupt. Let the other person answer the question.
- Avoid leading questions.

Michael C. Donaldson and Mimi Donaldson, *Negotiating for Dummies* (Chicago: IDG Books Worldwide, 1996) pp. 138, 139.

answering questions in negotiation lies in knowing what to answer and what not to; when to be clear and when not to. It does not lie in being right or wrong."[4]

It is important that you not let your training as a physician influence the way you respond to questions. You have been trained to respond to queries with complete, responsive answers. As a physician negotiator you should remember that *just because your opponent asks you a question does not mean that you have to answer it or answer it fully.*

When answering questions, keep your answers as short as possible. Don't volunteer information. Make sure that you do not disclose any confidential information. Preparation and planning are extremely important if you want to be able to deal effectively with difficult questions. As part of your preparation you need to decide what information you will disclose and under what circumstances you will disclose it. You need to weigh how the disclosure of information will assist the negotiation process or impede it. You will also need to judge how much the disclosure or nondisclosure of information will affect your credibility and integrity in the eyes of your opponent.

When dealing with difficult questions, you should remember the four Ds: deferring, deflecting, delaying, or declining to answer the question. Politicians use these techniques when responding (or, more appropriately, *not* responding) to difficult, pointed questions. Note that none of the responses involve untruths. Box 4.3 provides examples of the four Ds.

Box 4.3

The Four D Methods

Defer: "That's an excellent question. Let's hold that for now and get back to it after we have some more information."
Deflect: "I appreciate your concern. What I am worried about is…."
Delay: "That question gets to the heart of the problem. I need some time to think that over."
Decline: "I don't know" *(or)* "Let me look into it."[5]

---

[4] Chester L. Karrass, *The Negotiating Game* (New York: Harper Business, Revised Edition, 1992) p. 193.

[5] For additional declining techniques in highly sensitive areas, you can:

- rule the question out of bounds as improper or inappropriate,

Ilich suggests some other techniques that you can use to deal with difficult questions. Box 4.4 provides these techniques.

Box 4.4

More Techniques to Deal with Difficult Questions

Plead ignorance: "I just don't know" *(or)* "I'm not familiar with that."
Plead irrelevance: "That's irrelevant" *(or)* "That's not important. What *is* important is…."
Personal: "That's just too personal, I'm not going to get into that area."
Answer with a question: "I haven't determined that yet. How much are *you* looking for?"[6]

"THAT IS PROPRIETARY"
One final technique that can be employed to refuse to answer questions is the reply, "that is proprietary."

Example 4.20 Citing proprietary information
Opponent: (to physician entrepreneur) Who are your largest distributors?
Physician: That is proprietary. I can't discuss that.

Lesson: When the information sought is (or reasonably appears to be) confidential, the "that is proprietary" refusal is frequently respected. The technique is equivalent to the Defense Department classifying information and always erring on the side of caution.

Negotiating can be a time-consuming process. You do not want to waste your time on a potential deal unless your opponent has something of value to you.

- ignore the apparent inquiry,
- answer a different question,
- answer only the beneficial part of a complex question,
- respond generally to a specific inquiry, or
- respond specifically to a general inquiry.

Charles B. Craver, *Effective Legal Negotiation and Settlement* (Massachusetts Continuing Legal Education, Inc., 1996) p. 23.
[6] John Ilich, *The Complete Idiot's Guide to Winning through Negotiation* (New York: Alpha Books, 1996) p. 69.

Example 4.21 The importance of gathering fundamental information
Q: You are the physician owner of a series of health clinics. While flying to the West Coast you meet a mergers and acquisitions expert who says he can make you a lot of money and help you "cash out" of your business. You get very excited and agree to fly to Seattle (from New York) the following week to discuss details. What have you done wrong?
A: 1. Your excitement has disclosed the confidential information that you are over-eager to sell. This will be very detrimental to any terms you could obtain, especially price. 2. Before you commit the time and expense of entering into negotiations 3,000 miles from home, you need to find out where your opponent is coming from. Is he interested in buying you out via cash or stock in a high profile, publicly traded company or is he offering stock in a start up company (which could be next to worthless)? This question should be asked up front.

As a successful physician negotiator, you need to obtain crucial information from your opponent quickly and efficiently. This can be done by asking the right questions at the right time, in the manner most likely to result in a complete and accurate response. At the same time, you need to closely guard your confidential information and defer, deflect, delay, and decline to answer difficult questions that could harm you.

Example 4.22 The absolute importance of gathering information
Q: You are the managing partner of a six-person orthopedic practice in Longview, Texas. On January 4, 2007, at 5:00 P.M., a twenty-five-year-old law student, Jamie Curtis, tripped over a parking divider in your parking lot and sustained a fractured ankle (posterior malleolus). She was treated by your office by reduction and fixation, physical therapy, and had a walking cast for three months. She has made a good recovery. She incurred medical expenses of $4,950 of which $4,250 was paid for by her health insurer. You will be meeting Ms. Curtis in five minutes to discuss "settling" her claim against your office for inadequate lighting in your parking lot. Ms. Curtis has some residual stiffness on rainy days and says if the matter is not settled today, she will retain her uncle, Gerry Spence, to represent her. Your office manager let your general liability policy lapse without renewing it on December 3, 2006. You have no insurance coverage for this accident. You have consulted with your attorney, who would be pleased to defend your group for $350 per hour with a $15,000

retainer. He tells you that you have a 40% chance of winning at trial. He estimates that defense costs would run between $15,000 and $25,000. If the case were lost, a judgment would likely be between $45,000 and $125,000 depending on how things "break" at the trial. He mailed you a blank "full and final release form" and urged you not to try and resolve this yourself. You feel that Ms. Curtis appreciates the excellent medical care she was given and will be reasonable. Your partners, after blaming you for not having insurance coverage, asked you to settle the case as quickly and as cheaply as possible. Ms. Curtis has thirty minutes to meet with you before she has to get to her class on medical malpractice. In the spirit of negotiation, she has agreed to answer your questions. What will you ask her and why?

A: You need to find out very quickly what this woman is looking for. Is she just looking for her $700 in unpaid medical expenses? She's a law student. She probably has a very good idea what her claim is worth if she pushes it. The crucial question is, does she want to push it? After this trip and fall she was treated by your office. You think she is satisfied. The authors would start this negotiation with pleasantries and ask her how she is doing. You need to get a read on her desires and motives. Look for body language and tone. Is this woman looking for a pound of flesh? You would then apologize for any pain that she has been in and tell her how much you've enjoyed helping her get better. You want her to like you and to keep this from turning into an adversarial situation. You would then ask if there was anything you could do to help her recover financially from this tragic accident and ask her about the $700 insurance deficiency. If all she is looking for is the $700, that is all the doctor should offer. (The doctor should also mention to this law student that the group has no insurance for this claim. She'll then understand that the offer is from the group's pocket and that if she pushed her claim, any money would come out of the group's pocket as well.)

Example 4.23 Information generates power in a negotiation

Q: Joseph Stevens, M.D., age 34, is an internist and is interested in joining a professional corporation of physicians, Falmouth Associates, Inc., in his hometown of Falmouth, Massachusetts. Dr. Stevens is licensed in both Massachusetts and Connecticut. Falmouth, Massachusetts is a rural community on Cape Cod with 35,000 year-round residents and 500,000 summer visitors. It has one hospital, the Falmouth Hospital, and has affiliations with the Cape Cod Hospital twenty-five miles away and Massachusetts General Hospital seventy-five miles to the north. Falmouth Associates, Inc., is one of only two groups of internists in Falmouth, Massachusetts. Joseph Stevens, M.D., is Board Certified and Falmouth Associates, Inc., is well thought of in the community. The average salary for internists nationwide is $174,000. The average salary for internists in rural areas is $124,000. Falmouth Associates, Inc., has four full-time physicians, ages forty-nine, fifty-four, fifty-six, and sixty-three, who are all partners. It also has two physician assistants, ages forty-four and fifty-three, and a support staff of twelve. The clinic has 4,500 patients in Falmouth and the surrounding area. You, as managing partner, are extremely busy and your staff and partners work long hours. Each partner is on call three nights a week and one weekend per month. The partners are earning $259,000 per year, but they are complaining bitterly about the toll the long hours are taking on them, their health, and their families. You have had to turn away new patients and have a long waiting time for patients to get an appointment. You are concerned about hiring a "local" because he may quit the practice and go out on his own. You want someone willing to work hard. You feel that you must hire a good internist quickly. You do not mind training a new doctor as long as he or she will be a team player and stay with the practice. Due to the rural nature of Falmouth, it is hard to get high quality young doctors. Your partners were impressed with the CV of Dr. Stevens and have told you in no uncertain terms that if you do not hire him, they will be very upset and may want to break up the practice and go to work elsewhere. As you were leaving, they also said, "Make sure you don't give away the store." What questions will you ask him at the beginning of the negotiation? What other questions might you ask him as the negotiation progresses?

A: You need to find out at the outset *how badly* this person wants to come to work in Falmouth. Is he entertaining offers from Connecticut and other parts of Massachusetts? Does he have his heart set on Falmouth? If he does have his heart set on Falmouth (his hometown), you may be able to hire him for much less money than otherwise because there is only one other group of internists in Falmouth. You will also need to find out his willingness to be a team player, work hard, and take call. Note that any deal you strike will need to contain a covenant not to compete that will protect the practice.

Active Listening

To gather as much information as possible, the successful physician negotiator needs to develop active listening skills.[7] This is one of the skills that all good negotiators have. The savvy physician negotiator intuitively watches and listens very closely to the person she is negotiating with. This includes the tone of the voice, inflection, what he says, the words he chooses and emphasizes, and what he does not say. Experienced negotiators combine this information with their innate ability to look at the face of the person they are negotiating with for revealing clues, like a poker player looking for "tells."

> The clues we need to make sense of someone or some social situation are right there on the faces of those in front of us…when someone tells us "I love you" we look immediately and directly at him or her because by looking at the face, we can know, or, at least, we know a great deal more—about whether the sentiment is genuine…we make these kinds of complicated lightning-fast calculations very well. We make them every day, and we make them without thinking.[8]

While active listening may not be a hard science, the FBI and other law enforcement agencies have used active listening to resolve volatile

---

[7] "The ability to listen, really to hear what someone is saying has far greater business implications, of course, than simply gaining insight into people....The bottom line is that almost any business situation will be handled differently, and with different results, by someone who is listening and someone who isn't." Mark H. McCormack, *What They Don't Teach You at Harvard Business School: Notes from a Street Smart Executive* (New York: Bantam Books, 1984) p. 8.

"The need for listening is obvious yet is difficult to do; listen well, listening enables you to understand their perceptions, feel their emotions, and hear what they are trying to say. Active listening improves not only what you hear, but also what they say." Roger Fisher and William Ury (Bruce Patton, ed.), *Getting to Yes: Negotiating Agreement without Giving In* (New York: Penguin, 1991) p. 34.

"Active listening is more difficult than most people realize.…You must be alert to listen.…Active listening involves all the senses and many listening devices." Donaldson and Donaldson, p. 118.

[8] Malcolm Gladwell, *Blink* (New York: Little Brown Company, 2005) pp. 2, 3, 214.

confrontations. They have incorporated and emphasized active listening skills in their crisis negotiation training.[9]

Active listening skills can often help you obtain the information that you need. In a negotiation your opponent might not repeat key information. Frequently, physicians and many other professionals ask questions and do not carefully and actively listen to the answers. This happens because the physician is fiddling with papers, being interrupted by phone calls, pagers, PDAs, or is thinking of something else. Prior to negotiating, you should clear your desk and instruct your staff not to allow any interruption. Consider Box 4.5.

Box 4.5

Five Key Active Listening Mistakes

1. Anticipating or assuming (even worse) what the opponent will say.
2. Finishing the opponent's sentences.
3. Thinking about or starting the next question.
4. Trying to impress the opponent or other parties participating in the negotiation with your general intelligence or grasp of the topic.
5. Second-guessing the statements being made.

The three specific active listening skills you need to develop to be a successful physician negotiator are the ability to hear all that is said, the ability to hear what is omitted, and the ability to listen and hear equivocal statements and verbal leaks.

When you are presented with a request, demand, or statement that will affect the negotiation, you need to hear it fully. You also need to understand what your opponent means. Do not be too proud to ask for clarification of a term that is vague, that is technical, that you might not understand, or that your opponent *may* be interpreting differently than you are.

[9] Noesner, Webster, "Crisis Intervention: Using Active Listening Skills in Negotiations" (*Law Enforcement Bulletin* 8: August 1997).

Example 4.24 Asking for clarification of a word open to interpretation
Educational provider: Doctor, we would like you to develop a high quality two-day educational program.
Doctor: When you say "high quality," what do you mean specifically? I want to make sure we are on the same page before we talk cost.

Lesson: The physician negotiator is clarifying what his opponent means. He is not *assuming* that he knows what is meant by the term "high quality." The details of a deal and what is meant by certain terms are critical. It is important not to agree to something before you know—in no ambiguous terms—what the details are.

Example 4.25 Not asking questions leaves the physician in a weak position
Publisher: Because you are the world's leading expert on impairment and disability, we would like you to do "the" book for us.
Doctor: Great! When do you need the book finished by?

Lesson: Now the doctor cannot negotiate effectively on price, compensation, editorial help, marketing, or budget. He has agreed so rapidly to a deal that any further negotiation on terms will be difficult.

Example 4.26 Question asked also sends a message of power
Publisher: Doctor, because you are the world's leading expert on impairment and disability, we would like you to do "the" book for us.
Doctor: That sounds interesting. As you know, I am quite busy. But I am still interested. Please send me a note with the details, length, style, editorial help, compensation, advances, royalties, deadlines, etc., and I will get back to you.

Lesson: The doctor has "heard" the publisher—she wants a book. The publisher no doubt has "heard" the doctor—she will have to work hard to get him. The author will not come cheap, but if there is a fair deal, the publisher can get the author she wants.

Active Listening Techniques

Active listeners use several techniques to encourage an opponent, to send clues that the listener understands, and to encourage the opponent to keep talking. Keeping the opponent talking is crucial to get him to reveal as much critical information as possible.

MINIMAL ENCOURAGEMENT

A brief and well-timed comment can demonstrate you are following what the opponent is saying. "Yes," "OK," or "I see" may be sufficient to convey the message and keep the person talking.[10]

To prevent misunderstandings, you can paraphrase your opponent's statement and restate it in your own words. As the negotiation proceeds toward closure, misunderstandings can lead to deadlock. (See pages 241–49 on closing.) Paraphrasing your opponent's statement will give her an opportunity to correct any false impressions. In addition, you can condense a long, complex proposal into a short, clear statement. For example, you could say, "So, as I understand it, what you are saying is that your bottom line is $150,000 a year plus the fringes we discussed, correct?"

A similar technique you can use is to reframe your opponent's statement by putting it into a different form, size, or scope. The five reframing techniques that the successful physician negotiator should strive to master are listed in Box 4.6.

Box 4.6

Reframing Techniques

1. *Ordering:* The active listener sorts the content elements into a logical sequence based on such things as importance, size, timing, and amount.
2. *Grouping:* The active listener organizes the content elements according to common ideas and issues.
3. *Fractionating:* The active listener breaks a large and complex problem or idea into smaller parts that can be more easily understood and managed (or ordered or grouped).

[10] *Crisis Intervention,* p. 4.

4. *Expanding:* The active listener expands or elaborates on an issue or idea that is stated in generalized terms and offers it for verification for accuracy.
5. *Generalizing:* The active listener identifies the general issues or ideas, omitting the details that expand or elaborate and may confuse this general theme.[11]

It is just as important to appreciate what is *not* being said as it is to hear and understand what *is* being said. Consider the following example.

Example 4.27 The importance of "hearing" what is not being said
Background: A physician and his two partners were invited to a two-hour dinner meeting with a physician in Hawaii. The Hawaiian physician spent most of the evening extolling the virtues of new diagnostic testing equipment he and others had developed. The mainland physician and his two partners were attempting to obtain a contract for help in marketing this new device. After the meeting, the three partners met and debriefed each other. While two of the partners were discussing the terms of the marketing agreement, the other partner said, "You know, I think he was trying to get us to invest in his equipment." The other two partners disagreed strongly. They pointed out quite correctly that the physician from Hawaii never mentioned investments or made any reference to investing any money. At a subsequent meeting, the pointed question was finally asked:

Q: Would you like us to invest in your new equipment?
A: Yes.

Lesson: The physician from Hawaii was not looking for a marketing partner or contract at all. He was looking for an investor. This true story is a good example of listening to what is *not* being said and appreciating a message that is not verbalized. A good active listener understands that what is *not* verbalized is often more important than what *is* said actively. This is because many times your opponent is trying to get you to draw

[11] U.S. Army Corps of Engineers, "When People Complain: Using Communication, Negotiation, and Problem-Solving to Resolve Complaints" (IWR Report 91-R-4, 1991) p. 35.

your own conclusions or come up with the idea yourself. In the above example, the three partners would have been more likely to invest if they concluded that this was a good idea themselves and were drawn to ask the question "are there investment opportunities available?" Thus, leaving out the specific request for money was in fact intentional and an excellent strategy to solicit funds.

Example 4.28 Connecting the dots
Background: After talking to a hotel general manager about his work and hobbies, the authors had different impressions. One felt that they would need a new contact person because the general manager was clearly going to quit. The other author disagreed, pointing out correctly that he "never said" he was quitting. The general manager quit shortly after the conversation.

Lesson: By actively listening to what *is* being said and to *how* it is being said, astute negotiators can hear what is *not* being said as well.

EQUIVOCAL STATEMENTS AND VERBAL LEAKS

Many times your opponents will, intentionally or unintentionally, tip you off as to their negotiating position or bottom line. This is done through making equivocal statements and verbal leaks. You need to be able to pick up on these.

Example 4.29 Listening carefully to every word is critical
Doctor: Do you have any flexibility in the budget for my compensation package?
Employer: The hospital is not *inclined* to offer any more *at this time.*

Lesson: This equivocal statement tells you that the hospital does have flexibility. It will probably offer more money at some point if the doctor keeps negotiating.

Example 4.30 Great question to ask regarding price
Doctor: How much flexibility do you have in the price?
Supplier: Not much.

Lesson: The doctor has asked an excellent question and has received a reply with the unspoken message, "We have some flexibility, you just need to keep negotiating."

As a successful physician negotiator you must be actively aware of all verbal leaks. Such leaks occur with regularity and must be appreciated if you are to obtain the best possible deal. Until you get an unequivocal response, such as, "Under no circumstances can we even consider more money," your opponent may in fact be saying to you, "There is more money to be had." You need to listen hard enough to hear what is being said. To do this, you will need to devote your full and undivided attention to what is being said, practice your active listening skills, hear what is not being verbalized, and listen for verbal leaks and equivocal statements.

BODY LANGUAGE

You need to seek information from all available sources. One frequently overlooked source of information is body language. There is valuable information to be gleaned by interpreting behavioral cues.[12]

You need to be aware of the cues your opponent gives you. It is like being on second base in a baseball game and picking up the signs that the catcher is giving to the pitcher. It is all part of the game. Many physician negotiators do not recognize these cues either because they do not look for them or because they are distracted by something else.

Example 4.31 Failure to observe body language costs the doctor
Doctor: Do you have any flexibility in the price?
Opponent: (small smile) No.
Doctor: That's too bad!

[12] "A cue is a message sent indirectly whose meaning may be ambiguous and require interpretation….Behavioral cues are the language of the body as displayed in posture, facial expressions, eye contact, and hand gestures…." Cohen, p. 106.

Lesson: During the smile, the doctor was not looking at the opponent because she was typing in her BlackBerry. By not concentrating on what was important (the opponent's body language), the doctor missed the opportunity to obtain extremely valuable information.

The above example shows a lost opportunity. It also shows how crucial it is for you as a physician negotiator to not be distracted and to carefully observe your opponent. This is especially true when your opponent is going to answer a crucial question. You will miss most nonverbal cues if your head is buried in a BlackBerry or notepad. Only about half of what you need to know will be delivered in the words your opponents deliver. The other half will be in their body language, such as facial expressions, smiles, frowns, head nods, and crossed arms or legs.

A successful physician negotiator looks for the smallest indication of interest or disinterest in the face or actions of an opponent and uses that information successfully. Consider the following example.

Example 4.32 Picking up and using verbal cues to your advantage
You are attempting to convince a prospective physician employee that he should accept a position in your group practice. You make point after point and the young physician sits there, impassive. Finally, you mention that your town has an excellent school system. The physician, for the first time, pulls out a pen and jots down "excellent school system." You pick up on this interest and explain the school system and extracurricular activities. You picked up on a cue given during a negotiation session and used it to your advantage.

When interpreting the body language of your opponent, it is important to remember that this is an imprecise science and that your opponent may be intentionally incorporating certain gestures to disguise his true feelings.[13] With this in mind, several of the most common gestures and their accepted meanings are listed in Box 4.7.

---

[13] For an excellent text with a detailed look at the "science" of body language and how facial expressions may be involuntary yet extremely revealing, see *Blink,* Malcolm Gladwell (Little Brown Company: 2005).

Box 4.7

Gesture Meanings

Casual touching of person	Sincerity
Clearing throat often	Untruth
Closed fists	Anger
Cocking the head	Receptiveness
Crossing arms and legs	Not receptive to idea
Crossing, uncrossing legs	Impatience
Fidgeting with pen or pencil	Lack of confidence in position
Gritting one's teeth	Anger/trying to control anger
Leaning back in the chair	Confidence
Locking ankles	Resistance
Looking at watch	Impatience
Looking person in the eye	Sincerity
Mirroring body position	Telling opponent that "we are the same"
Nervous laugh	Unexpressed concerns
Open-handed expressions	Sincerity
Rolling eyes	Impatience/disbelief
Shifting eyes	Deceit
Sitting on the edge of chair	Interest in discussion
Staring	Aggressive, controlling behavior
Sudden raise in vocal pitch	Untruth
Touching one's face, collar, tie, etc.	Not telling the truth

It is equally important to be aware of and control the nonverbal messages *you* unintentionally give off during the negotiation session. You should maintain a poker face and not reveal what you are feeling or thinking.[14] If you do not, you could give valuable information to your opponent.

[14] "When you are negotiating the gestures you don't make can be as telling as those you do make....a gasp, a flinch, or a smile can speak volumes about your position. Remember, your opponent is reading your attitude, your facial expressions and your tone of voice just as sharply as you are watching his." Ilich, p. 49.

Example 4.33 Nonverbal leak costs physician

You are negotiating with a potential purchaser of your home. Each time the purchaser asks you about your electric, sewer, or garage systems, you smile and immediately and enthusiastically respond, "Great." When you are asked how you like the neighbors, your smile disappears, you pause for a moment, and say that they're great as well. Your opponent picks up on this change of attitude and becomes worried. The sale falls through.

Lesson: By not maintaining a poker face, the physician unintentionally revealed the information that the neighbors are a potential problem. This nonverbal leak of information lost the deal.

Needs, Interests, and Desires

You must determine the needs, interests, and desires of the party with whom you are negotiating. This is not easy. Most physicians feel that they know or can figure out what their opponent needs and/or wants. Often, nothing could be further from the truth. Physician negotiators make a serious mistake when they assume that due to their intelligence, education, and experience they can sit in their office and figure out the needs, desires, objectives, motives, and interests of their opponents. You cannot necessarily take at face value what your opponent says he or she really wants. You will need to determine this information through research, inference, and deduction. Most importantly, you will need to determine this information as early in the negotiation process as possible.

All negotiations involve the needs or perceived needs of the person with whom you are negotiating. The noted psychologist Abraham Maslow categorized the needs of most people into a hierarchy: self-fulfillment needs, status needs, social/company needs, security/housing needs, and physical needs—water and food. The theory is that once a person satisfies the basic needs of water, food, security, and housing, he then aspires to the higher needs of status and self-fulfillment.

You must know and understand your opponent's needs before you can attempt to satisfy them. To do this, you need to ask her what she is looking for. The entire field of marketing is based on this premise. Surveys, polls, needs assessments, questionnaires, and focus groups are all methods used by marketing professionals to determine what people need.

As a physician, you are or should be familiar with the needs of your colleagues. Physicians may look for financial security, respect, success, professional recognition, challenging work, autonomy, and the opportunity to help their patients and to make a difference. Typically, your colleagues are worried about limited or reduced incomes, not spending enough time with their families, failure, malpractice suits, managed care, risks, the quality of their work, being second-guessed, and being taken advantage of. When negotiating with nonphysicians, you must determine as quickly as possible what they "need" to be successful.

Example 4.34 The importance of finding out what the other person really wants

You are looking for a part-time receptionist to cover your office two afternoons per week. You are about to interview a sixty-seven-year-old woman who worked for thirty-seven years as a legal secretary at a large law firm. She seems like she'd be a great asset. You are concerned, however, that she'll require too much money or that she'll leave to find a more challenging job. At the interview you ask her why she is applying for the receptionist job. You find out that she is retired and her husband, a Wall Street investment banker, recently died. She is looking for a way to get out of the house into an environment where she is useful and helps people.

Lesson: You were able to hire an eminently qualified employee at a reasonable rate because you determined what the employee was (and was not) looking for.

Determine Your Opponent's Needs

Negotiators make a serious mistake when they use logical but faulty assumptions in determining their opponents' needs.

FAULTY ASSUMPTION #1: EVERYONE WILL ACT LOGICALLY

Many negotiators assume that they can sit in their office and, based on logic, figure out what an opponent wants.

This assumption contains several mistakes. Many opponents you negotiate with will not logically arrive at their positions. They may be influenced by bias, prejudice, and emotion to act in a manner that seems illogical to you.

Example 4.35 Sometimes your opponents do not act logically
Background: The authors produced a series of instructional videos that were marketed exclusively by one distributor. When the exclusive contract term was up, the authors sought permission to sell the videos to a completely different market. This was explained in detail and in writing to the distributor. The distributor was so upset about what he saw as a breach of good faith that he refused to sell any of the authors' products. This emotional response cost both the distributor and the authors a substantial amount of money.

Lesson: Not all of your opponents will operate logically.

FAULTY ASSUMPTION #2: EVERYONE WE NEGOTIATE WITH WILL OPERATE AS WE DO

Many negotiators consciously or subconsciously assume that the quickest and easiest way to figure out the needs of their opponent is by putting themselves in their opponent's position. Just because you would do something, act in a certain way, or have certain needs does not mean your opponent will act the same way.

Example 4.36 Why you should not assume what your opponent wants
When a contributing author was about to start working on a book project, the authors asked her a key question: "What do you want to get out of this project?"

We assumed that she would be looking for royalties and financial compensation. This was completely incorrect. What she *was* looking for was recognition as a co-author to assist her with a tenure application.

Lesson: Do not assume you know what your opponent wants or that she would want what you would if you were in her shoes. In essence, this is negotiating with yourself.

Example 4.37 If you want to find out what somebody wants, ask them
For 15 years, the authors met and figured out the products that physicians and other customers *should* want. This technique was somewhat successful.

However, once the authors began to *ask* the physicians what they wanted (with detailed needs assessments), the success of the authors increased dramatically.

Lesson: Do not try and figure out what your opponent might want, should want, or what you would want. Ask directly what he wants and what is important to him.

After you determine the needs of the person you will be negotiating with, you next want to determine what she is interested in; that is, what is it that makes the person tick? The successful physician negotiator sincerely wants to understand her opponent's values and what her opponent feels is important. Look for two things: first, an insight into your opponent and second, a method of bonding with that person. Areas to probe gingerly include the following.

- Values: What does she find important?
- Family life: Children, pets, and spouse (in that order)
- Professional achievements: The living CV
- Art
- Films
- Hobbies
- Athletic achievements
- Volunteer work
- Travel
- The X factor

In almost every negotiation, you can find compatible interests to build upon.

Example 4.38 Look for something to help build a relationship
A physician from the South meets an attorney from Massachusetts at a conference in San Francisco. They are both looking for something to help build a business relationship and friendship on. After fifteen minutes they

discover they both grew up in Brooklyn, New York, around the same time. The bond is formed. One sends another a gift "from one Brooklyn boy to another."

Lesson: The personal relationship that has been formed will be useful during negotiations.

Example 4.39 Putting your opponent at ease by tapping into your knowledge of his interests
You are negotiating the sale of your practice to another physician. You are at an impasse. You know that the other physician is a devoted skier. You suggest that negotiations be reconvened in Vail, Colorado, so that everyone can be more focused.

Lesson: You will be more likely to gain concessions from your opponent when he is distracted and relaxed by his interest in skiing.

While all of us are familiar with most of the factors listed previously, the X factor merits further discussion. The X factor is that one single factor that is the driving force behind your opponent's personality. It is the answer to the question, "What makes Sammy run?" It is the single most important thing that interests or drives your opponent. If you can tap into this X factor, it will be a tremendous advantage in any negotiation.

Example 4.40 Stroking the opponent's ego
You determine that the person you are dealing with prides herself in her creativity and ingenuity. You congratulate her on her great new ideas, ask her how she got to be so creative, and ask if there is any way one can learn to be creative. Her personal needs (i.e., ego gratification and recognition of her creativity) have been satisfied. It is likely that she will be very receptive to your questions and to your negotiations.

Example 4.41 Tapping into the X factor
An excellent representation of discovering someone's X factor is in the movie *The Silence of the Lambs*. In the film, Hannibal Lector is incarcerated in a high security cell but demonstrates a killer's instinct for quickly getting to the heart of his opponent's personality. Clarise is the FBI agent who comes to the cell to question and match wits with him. He

questions Clarise about her upbringing, her father dying when she was very young, and her going to live with an uncle on a farm. The killing and screaming of the lambs are what drove her. She could still hear it and had nightmares. Hannibal Lector got into her psyche. He found out what drove her to a position of authority.

Example 4.42 Using the X factor

You go to your opponent's office to negotiate and notice she has numerous framed pictures of her grandchildren on her desk. After the initial negotiation session you send her a set of picture frames for her beautiful grandchildren.

If you can tap into your opponent's X factor—the single most important factor that drives her, you will know how to prepare for your negotiation sessions.

What is the object of all this psychological delving? There are five important reasons to consider psychological factors.

1. You want to create a *comfortable relationship.*
2. You want to *bond* with the other person.
3. You want to develop *trust* and *respect.*
4. You want to discover and develop *shared compatible interests.*
5. ***You want the other person to like you.***

The last point is the most important and cannot be overemphasized. The people you negotiate with will go to extraordinary lengths to help and assist you if they truly like you. Thus, you will get better deals and terms.

When you tap into the X factor you can often convert your opponent into an ally. If this happens, you will have found someone who is willing to go to bat for you, to work for you, and to make a case for you. What you really have is a friend who is championing your position. Your opponent's prestige becomes tied to the negotiation, to the deal, and sometimes even to his position in his company. He is no longer an opponent but is more like a partner.

Example 4.43 Creating anxiety to help your position
You are negotiating with a salesperson. You start talking casually about sales quotas and determine that the quarter end is in two days. You tell the salesperson that you will do everything you can to help her meet her quota and to get her a commission.

Lesson: The salesperson appreciates your trying to help and you now know that she needs to close the deal. You can get favorable terms.

Example 4.44 Doing favors for your opponent can be effective
You will be negotiating a lease renewal for your group's office space in a few months. Your landlord is an acquaintance whose son is very interested in professional football. You own season tickets to your local professional team. Two days before the biggest game of the year, you offer your tickets (free of charge) to the landlord. You state that "something came up" and you can't use the tickets yourself.

Lesson: By tapping into your landlord's strong desire to take care of his family, you have helped to build a very positive relationship that will be useful during your upcoming lease negotiations.

Example 4.45 Going the extra mile to do a favor for your opponent
Some years ago we were building a relationship and friendship with a new client. She casually mentioned one day over dinner that as a child her favorite book was *The Land of the Lost Buttons.* She wanted to show a copy to her children but was unable to find it. After returning to our office, we made an all-out effort to locate this book, which had been out of print for 35 years. It took us six months, but we finally located it. We sent the book along to her with a note that said: "The difficult we do routinely, the impossible takes a little longer." As you might expect, she was overwhelmed and will never forget our small kindness.

Example 4.46 Be prepared to respond to what your opponent wants
Q: You are entering into an employment negotiation with a hospital administrator. As part of your preparation you will make a list of things that he may try to achieve with this negotiation. Name ten general things he may try to accomplish.

A:
1. Look like a hero with the Board.
2. Seek additional power.
3. Hire a team player.
4. Come in under budget.
5. Get the best qualified physician.
6. Hire someone he bonds with.
7. Hire someone who is willing to take a lot of call.
8. Hire a person with a lot of relevant experience.
9. Hire the most highly intelligent physician.
10. Hire someone with local roots.

Lesson: In preparing to negotiate, you will need to fashion responses addressing each of these potential desires of your opponent.

As a successful physician negotiator, you need to develop fully your potential for identifying the needs, interests, and desires of your opponents. You can often satisfy these needs without sacrificing your own goals. Successful physician negotiators determine what their opponents' needs, interests, and desires are and act accordingly.

Chapter 5 The Best Time to Negotiate

Executive Summary

- Timing affects the negotiating strength of the parties.
- The best time to negotiate is when you need the deal the least and your opponent needs the deal or agreement the most.
- Plan ahead so that you are not desperate for a deal.
- Appear patient during the negotiation or risk signaling that you are in a rush to conclude.
- Make it a habit to "sleep on it" before finalizing a deal.
- Build in time to complete the negotiations.
- Deadlines make things happen. Use them to your advantage. Set a deadline to force your opponent's hand. The most credible deadlines have an objective reason that supports them (such as a partner's meeting).
- Use accelerated deadlines to spur an opponent to action.
- Do not be afraid to extend a deadline if this helps you.

Successful physician negotiators realize that timing plays a crucial part in most negotiations. In fact, timing may be everything in certain negotiations. The four key elements of timing in negotiations are: when to negotiate, when to pause, setting and dealing with the acceptance time, and the use and abuse of deadlines.

When to Negotiate

The best time to negotiate is when you need the deal the least and your opponent needs the deal or agreement the most. It is a poor time to negotiate for snow tires when the first snowstorm of the season is on its way. You must plan ahead. You should avoid having to negotiate when you desperately need a deal.[1]

[1] Of course, if this is not possible and you are forced to negotiate, you need to avoid revealing to your opponent the fact that you are desperate to make a deal.

Example 5.1 Timing affects the negotiating leverage each party can bring to bear

Q: You will be interviewing for a new position at a growing group medical practice. You have a comfortable position but would like to improve your financial situation. Your prospective employer is short two physicians and is working seven days a week to keep up with the workload. His partners have told him to hire someone *now* or they will also leave. In this example, who is negotiating at a good time?

A: The physician who seeks to improve his situation has a much stronger bargaining position. He doesn't need to accept a position. He can choose to accept it if it meets all his requirements. The group is in a disadvantageous situation. It needs to hire someone as soon as possible. If the group tries to hold out for its best terms, it risks not hiring someone soon enough.

You should clearly know the time pressures that you are under in a negotiation. What you do not know, however, is what time pressures exist for your opponent. This is information that you need to determine. One technique that is frequently used to do this during out-of-town negotiations is the *flight back gambit.* Consider the following example.

Example 5.2 Flight back gambit

Q: Doctor, what time is your flight back out of O'Hare tonight?

A: 5:30 P.M. on United.

Q: Don't worry. You can leave from downtown at 4:45 P.M. and still make it.

Lesson: With this innocent-sounding question, the opponent has learned the extent of the doctor's time pressure for the day's meeting. At the same time, she has gotten him thinking about the last-minute, impossible race against time to O'Hare Airport. With this seemingly innocent question, the opponent has made it difficult for the doctor to concentrate on the negotiation session.

A second time gambit consists of simply asking your opponent when he needs to close the deal. This obvious technique can be very useful in determining your opponent's time deadlines, gaining you a timing advantage. Consider the following example.

Example 5.3 Asking about an opponent's deadline
Q: Doctor, when do you want to wrap this up by?
A: I need to have this tied down by Thursday.

Lesson: While this gambit might seem obvious, it is still quite efficient and of frequent use. Here the physician's opponent has learned the key timing information (when the physician must have closure). This clearly gives the opponent the timing advantage. Note that it may be difficult for the physician to be dishonest in this situation. If he really needs a deal by Thursday, but states otherwise, the physician risks that the deal will fall through because his opponent will not feel obliged to follow up within the required period.

You need to recognize and avoid being caught in ambush negotiations. (See pages 23–27.) The ambush negotiation is one way an opponent can use the physician time pressure gambit. This gambit is used repeatedly against physicians who are often too busy to argue. Consider the following examples.

Example 5.4 Avoid ambush negotiations
Broker: Doctor, about that sailboat you and your spouse liked. We are down to crunch time. Do you have a few minutes?
Doctor: Not really. I am really backed up. I will not be out of here until 7:00 P.M.
Broker: It's good I caught you then. The sellers are down to $62,500. They need to know by 2:00 P.M. today.
Doctor: It is 1:30 now!
Broker: That's why I am calling. What do you say?
Doctor: Do you think they might take a little less?

Lesson: The physician in this example was ambushed. He was not ready to negotiate, was distracted, and was under so much time pressure that he was not able to practice any good negotiation techniques. In addition, the broker used the veiled threat of an impending deadline to increase the time pressure. This type of call is used repeatedly with physicians. The callers use time limitations to pressure doctors because they know that doctors are frequently too busy to argue. You need to recognize when this technique is being used against you and you need to respond appropriately.

Example 5.5 Turning the tables on an ambush negotiator
Broker: Doctor, about the sailboat you and your spouse liked. We are down to crunch time. Do you have a few minutes?
Doctor: I am sorry, I do not. Please give me your number and I will call you back when I am free.
Broker: 508-555-1911. But I need to know….
Doctor: Thank you. Goodbye.

Lesson: In this example, the doctor recognized the ambush and acted appropriately. The doctor will negotiate at the right time—when he is fully prepared and is not distracted. The time pressure has now been effectively shifted to the broker.

You should not commence a negotiation until you are fully prepared. (See pages 23–27 on ambush negotiations.) If someone attempts to begin a negotiation with you at a time when you are not ready, you need to say, "I'm sorry, but I am not ready to discuss this at this time." This simple but effective policy will keep you from being taken advantage of in an ambush negotiation.

Patience and Pausing

Patience

Physicians are extremely busy people. Many physicians, due to their workloads and hectic schedules, attempt to get the distasteful job of negotiation over as quickly as possible. If your opponent suspects that you fall into this category, you will be at a distinct disadvantage in any negotiation. Consider the following examples.

Example 5.6 Doctor places himself at distinct disadvantage by appearing impatient with negotiation
Opponent: Thank you, Doctor, for joining us. We have several important issues to resolve on your lease and the improvements on the building. We have set aside three hours to work these out. Does that work for you?
Doctor: Three hours? I thought this could be wrapped up in ten minutes. Three hours? Well, I don't know….

Opponent: Well, Doctor, we will do the best we can to get you out of here and back to work where you can make some money. Now what kinds of improvements were you looking for?

Lesson: The doctor in this example has placed herself at a distinct disadvantage before formal negotiations have even started. She has revealed that she has not blocked out enough time. Most importantly, the doctor has revealed a lack of patience. This desire to get it over with can be, and usually is, quite costly.

Example 5.7 Doctor prepared to devote the time necessary to negotiating will most likely make out much better
Opponent: Thank you for joining us. We have several important issues….Does that work for you?
Doctor: I hope we can wrap it up in three hours. We are committed to getting the improvements we need to run a safe and efficient practice. If we have to discuss this in two or three sessions, so be it. Now, here is a list of the 27 improvements we need. Let's start with number one. The parking situation….

Lesson: The doctor is not rushed and has given a clear, unmistakable message—the negotiation will take as long as necessary.

Patience in negotiations is frequently rewarded with success. Parkinson's Law frequently applies to negotiation sessions: the time taken for decisions is in inverse proportion to the amount of money involved.[2] It makes little sense for you to be too busy to spend the time needed to negotiate over issues involving hundreds of thousands of dollars. The authors recommend "fewer patients but more patience" on the day of an important negotiation.

PAUSING

Successful physician negotiators are able to identify when the key point is reached in a negotiation and when they need some time to think over crucial points, concessions, or decisions. When you reach this point in a negotiation session, ***take all the time you need.*** There is nothing

---

[2] Recall the shortest physician negotiation on record (pages xx–xxi).

inherently wrong or embarrassing in saying that you need some time to think something over. Complex negotiation sessions are like a long drive in unfamiliar territory. They contain many forks in the road. You need to make sure that you are on the right road before you proceed. Your opponent will appreciate and respect your taking the matter seriously enough to think things over.

If you need a short break, you might say that you need to use the restroom or call your partner, spouse, or attorney. This five- to ten-minute break in the negotiation session may be all the time you need to collect yourself and your thoughts and come up with a response or plan. If the matter is more serious and/or you need or want a longer break, you may find that your partner, spouse, or attorney is not readily available. A direct and effective method for continuing the negotiation on another date is to reply, "I need to sleep on that." Any businessperson understands that this is a good, accepted practice. We have all learned that things frequently look completely different the next day. What was seemingly an insurmountable problem is sometimes resolved easily the next day with a creative solution. What you as a successful physician negotiator want to avoid is the "I wish syndrome," where you wish after a deal is consummated that you had acted differently. Consider the following examples.

Example 5.8 Physician should have thought about it overnight
Opponent: Well, Doctor, welcome aboard. We have agreed on the salary and fringes. You start next week.
Doctor: Thank you. See you on Monday.
Doctor: (on the way home to himself) I wish I would have remembered to ask for…If only I had said…I could have gotten….

Lesson: This is the "I wish syndrome." When you sleep on a major negotiation decision, you give yourself time to think things over in a stress-free atmosphere and to reflect on whether you missed anything.

Example 5.9 Prudent doctor sleeps on it before final commitment
Opponent: Well, Doctor, welcome aboard. We have agreed on the salary and fringes. You start next week.
Doctor: I think we have most of the points covered. I need to review your offer with my spouse and see if we omitted any major items. I will

be back at 8:00 A.M. to conclude this and I look forward to starting next week.

Lesson: The doctor has given himself a little wiggle room in case a point was overlooked or omitted in the negotiation session.

A pause also increases the value of a concession you may give to an opponent. When you "sleep on it" before you make a concession, the concession will be valued much more than if you assented quickly to a request for the concession. (See pages 127–35 on concessions.) This is another benefit to pausing and sleeping on decisions before deciding key points or making major concessions.

Acceptance Time

All parties in a negotiation session come to the table with their own points of view, ideas, preconceptions, needs, and goals. Negotiation is about obtaining these goals. This can—and often does—take substantial amounts of time. To get your opponent to change his ideas or preconceptions, you will need to allocate adequate time. Building in sufficient acceptance time is part of adequate preparation (see pages 109–22). The successful physician negotiator anticipates the need for adequate acceptance time and builds it into the negotiation schedule. Consider the following examples.

Example 5.10 Letting events preempt your negotiation to your detriment

Doctor: (to partners) I am glad we are all here. I decided to cut back on my work schedule. Starting Monday, I will be working half time. Now, let's see if we can work out the finances.

Partner: (speaking for other partners) Phil, we wish you would have given us some lead time, a heads-up or something. I think I speak for all of us when I say we are not ready to talk money. We need more time….

Lesson: The doctor in this case caught his partners by surprise. It was probably not in his best interest to do so. His switching to part time is a radical change that might take his partners time to accept. He may have been better served by allowing them the time needed to be persuaded that things can be worked out satisfactorily for all parties.

Example 5.11 Building in acceptance time for your opponent may work to your advantage

Doctor: (to one partner) Fred, I want to give you a heads-up. At the meeting in two weeks I will be announcing that I will be cutting back to half time. Could you tell the partners? At the meeting, I want to work out scheduling, finances, any loose ends….

Partner: That's quite a surprise. I will let everyone know today. We hate to lose you even half time. But let's see what we can work out.

Lesson: The physician has built some acceptance time into the equation. By the time the negotiation session arrives, the parties are more likely to be cool, collected, and accepting of his decision. They will also be more likely to reach an accommodation that works for all parties.

Deadlines

You must fully understand the use and abuse of deadlines during negotiations. There are nine reasons why deadlines are so important during negotiations. These reasons are listed in Box 5.1. Each reason is discussed in the following subsections.

Box 5.1

Nine Reasons Deadlines Are Important

1. Deadlines make things happen.
2. People respond to and strive to meet deadlines.
3. Deadlines are one of the most powerful and effective tools in the negotiator's arsenal.
4. Deadlines play on the fear of your opponent.
5. Deadlines help reduce your opponent's options.
6. The closer the deadline, the more pressure there is to grant concessions.
7. Objective deadlines can be legitimate and are most effective.
8. Few physicians ask for extensions on deadlines.
9. Accelerated deadlines are effective.

DEADLINES MAKE THINGS HAPPEN

An effective way for a skilled physician negotiator to bring a negotiation to a close is to impose a realistic deadline. If you can get your opponent to buy into the deadline, you have made substantial progress toward closure. Setting a realistic deadline will have the added benefit of reducing the posturing, gamesmanship, brinksmanship, and other tactics that negotiators often employ when they are not facing any deadline. (See pages 173–93 on tactics.)

Example 5.12 Agreeing on deadline increases the likelihood of a deal
Doctor: We agree that we will resolve the remaining issues today and we will stay as long as it takes to do so, agreed?
Opponent: Agreed.

Lesson: The agreement on a deadline by both parties will make it much more likely that an agreement will be reached in a timely fashion. In fact, getting your opponent to agree that he will continue to negotiate until an agreement is reached is a major concession (see pages 127–35). The opponent is implicitly agreeing to make concessions and be reasonable in his demands.

NEGOTIATORS RESPOND TO AND STRIVE TO MEET DEADLINES

Nobody wants to be known as a person who cannot meet deadlines. Physicians may be particularly sensitive to the need to meet their deadlines because by their nature physicians are achievers. Many physicians have been "A" students and have received awards for their scholarship. One of the ways you get to be an achiever is by meeting and not questioning deadlines. Your sensitivity to deadlines can be used against you. Consider the following examples.

Example 5.13 Physician should have asked about a deadline extension
Publisher: Your chapter is due June 14 at 5:00 P.M. Eastern Standard Time. It is June 10th. You only have four days left. You know yours is the last chapter we need to send the manuscript to the editor.
Physician: I know…I know…I will have it done. I will work tonight and tomorrow night and have it out to you via an overnight messenger by the 13th. I will not miss my deadline. I am sorry if I have created any problems.

Lesson: The publisher used the physician's sensitivity to meeting deadlines against the physician. The physician should have considered the actual harm likely to be caused by not meeting the deadline imposed by the publisher. The physician could also have asked about extensions or other arrangements.

Example 5.14 Deadlines can often be extended

Publisher: Your chapter is due June 14th…to send the manuscript to the editor.

Physician: I know. I am running a little behind. I will have it to you in two weeks. This way I will not have to kill myself and you will get quality work that will not have to be heavily edited. In the meantime, why don't you send along the rest of the book to the editor so she can get started and no time is lost?

THE POWER OF DEADLINES

The effective use of deadlines requires you to take a step back and focus not only on your own deadlines, but also on your opponent's deadlines. Once you appreciate that your opponent also has a deadline, you can use that deadline as a powerful negotiating tool. Successful physician negotiators do not obsess unduly about their deadlines.

Example 5.15 Setting an artificial deadline can increase the pressure on your opponent to concede or risk losing the deal

Q: You are asked by your partners to lease some office space by March 15, 2007. You are negotiating with an office building owner. It is February 5, 2007, and you are starting to look at the calendar each day. How do deadlines play into this negotiation?

A: How important is your March 15, 2007, deadline? You should talk to your partners and find out whether they really need to move by March 15, 2007. They might give you some more flexibility. The owner says he has no real deadline, but you find out that he is in financial trouble and he needs to rent as soon as possible. You tell him either the deal is completed by February 15, 2007, or you will be forced to go elsewhere. This is an accelerated deadline. If he believes you, he has only ten days to close the negotiation. The more nonchalantly you act, the more nervous he gets. You are using your deadline effectively and can expect increasing concessions from the owner the closer you get to February 15, 2007.

DEADLINES PLAY ON YOUR OPPONENT'S FEARS

The worst fears of your opponent may be that he will fail, not meet his deadline, lose the deal, or will look lazy or incompetent to his employer. By recognizing and playing to these fears, you can use deadlines to your advantage. This can be done quite effectively by phone, e-mail, or fax. Consider the following examples.

Example 5.16 Putting your deadline on the record
Doctor: (to opponent by phone) If we can't wrap this up by Thursday, I will be looking for another supplier. Thank you.

Lesson: This call puts the deadline "on record" and gives your opponent time to react.

Example 5.17 The "closing my file" technique
Doctor: (to opponent by e-mail) Because you have not responded to my calls and letters, I will be closing my file on this matter. Thank you.

Lesson: You as a physician negotiator can use this technique to prod your opponent, raise her anxiety level, and make her respond to your deadlines. This technique has worked well for the authors and in many cases has resulted in the immediate response, "Don't close the file. I was just about to call you...."

Example 5.18 The "Is he still working there?" technique
Doctor: (to opponent's supervisor by fax) Please advise if ___________ is still employed at your company. I was wondering, as I have been unable to reach him for two weeks. Thank you.

Lesson: This technique can be used to increase the pressure even further on a non-responsive opponent and to play on his *worst* fear—that he may be disciplined by his superior. To comfortably use this technique, you need to remember that the goal of negotiation is not to be liked. The goal is to get what you deserve. This technique is only appropriate for one-time competitive negotiations because your opponent will not be happy with you when his supervisor receives the message.

Procrastinators

DEADLINES HELP REDUCE YOUR OPPONENT'S OPTIONS

Frequently, your opponent will attempt to put off decision making. This is especially true if the decision requires work, commitment, or risk taking. The good physician negotiator is a student of human nature. She realizes that many opponents are procrastinators and wait until the last minute to do almost everything.

Example 5.19 Tell-tale sign of a procrastinator
Conference coordinator: (to doctor) When can you get your course outline in, Doctor?
Doctor: When is that last possible day I can submit it? When's the drop-dead deadline?

Lesson: The savvy physician negotiator quickly recognizes when she is dealing with a procrastinator, gives him accelerated deadlines (see pages 90–91), and does not hesitate to use his problem with procrastination against him.

Example 5.20 Deal with a procrastinator by giving a deadline
Letter from conference coordinator to procrastinating physician:

Dear Dr. Jones,

As you know, you have missed the last 3 deadlines for submission of your materials. You are the last of 30 physicians to submit your materials. Please e-mail them to me no later than 5:00 P.M. today.

Thank you for your cooperation.

Paula Wilson

To be successful, you need to simplify an opponent's decisions and make them seem like "no brainers." When your opponent has too many options, decision making and agreement will often be put off.

Example 5.21 Giving your opponent too many options risks a loss of control and delay
Doctor: You have the option of coming on full time, part time, being a consultant, a contractor, or operating on a fee-for-services basis. What do you think?
Opponent: I will have to weigh the pros and cons of each. I will get back to you in a few weeks.

Lesson: The doctor has lost control of this deal. Closing will be delayed while the opponent considers responses to the variety of options offered.

Example 5.22 Effectively using a deadline and limited options
Doctor: We are offering you half-time work at the salary we discussed. We need to have an answer before the board meeting, which is Tuesday at 10:00 A.M. Remember that sometimes the riskiest course of action is to do nothing.
Opponent: I will get back to you on Monday at the latest.

Lesson: Simplifying the deal, reducing the options, and employing a tight deadline has two benefits. First, you control the direction of the negotiation. Second, you speed up the closing of the deal. These are effective techniques.

THE PRESSURE OF CLOSE DEADLINES

An effective negotiating technique is to find out your opponent's time pressures and to delay the tough negotiating until a short time before that deadline. This technique uses the accepted negotiation principle that the pressure to grant concessions increases as you get closer to a deadline.[3] (For a full discussion of concessions, see pages 127–35.)

---

[3] The closer the deadline looms, the *fewer* concessions the skilled physician negotiator will make.

Example 5.23 Using time pressure against your opponent
Physician: (to prospective employee opponent) Your flight leaves in three hours. We have yet to discuss your proposed salary and fringe benefits. I have your demands. As time is short, what is your bottom line? What can you live with? The traffic to the airport will be murder. Maybe you should leave a few minutes early....

Lesson: The doctor is playing off his opponent's time deadline in an attempt to gain concessions.

THE EFFICACY OF OBJECTIVE DEADLINES

An experienced opponent may be somewhat skeptical of your deadlines. She may question whether they are real or just posturing. One way to increase the legitimacy and credibility of your deadline is to make it an "objective" deadline that is difficult or impossible to question. The more concrete, objective, final, and legitimate the deadline, the more likely your opponent is to take it seriously. If your opponent believes the deadline is real and, even better, that it is beyond your control, it may push her to action. Some examples of this are provided in Box 5.2.

Box 5.2

Objective Deadlines

1. The board is meeting at 3:30 P.M. on Tuesday.
2. The lease is up on Friday.
3. I leave for vacation on Wednesday.
4. The flyer will go to the printer at 4:00 P.M.
5. The deal needs to be closed for accounting purposes by Wednesday.
6. We need to resolve this before the weather turns bad.
7. We have other bids we need to respond to by 3:30 P.M.
8. Our fiscal year ends on June 30.
9. I am currently in negotiations with your competitors. If we don't have your proposal by tomorrow, we're going with the competition.
10. For tax reasons, this needs to be done by December 31.

THE EXTENSION OF DEADLINES

Few physician negotiators ask for extensions. They should. By failing to do so they effectively accept their opponent's deadlines and become trapped by their parameters. Opponents will use your preoccupation with the deadline against you. Do not let them. In the rare cases in which the deadline cannot be extended, figure out what will happen if you miss the deadline. You should then perform a quick mental cost-benefit analysis. You need to determine whether meeting the deadline is as important as obtaining your goals. Frequently it is not. Consider the following examples.

Example 5.24 Buying into opponent's deadline can be problematic
Opponent: Well, Doctor, I know you have a few additional items you would like, but we have only 45 minutes left. Why don't you cut down your wish list to its bare essentials and let's see what we can do.

Lesson: You will not lose face or damage your reputation by requesting a deadline extension. When you need or want an extension of a deadline, you should ask for it as soon as you suspect you need it. You should also make sure the extension is long enough.

Example 5.25 Deadlines can be extended
Doctor: (to opponent) We have four or five more items to cover. I am committed to trying to resolve these issues and reach an agreement. I am willing to stay two hours beyond the 3:00 P.M. deadline. Does that work for you?

Lesson: The doctor put subtle pressure on the opponent by questioning his commitment to reaching an agreement. She did *not* accept her deadline as inviolate. An agreement by the opponent to continue to negotiate is an important psychological concession.

When the stakes are high and the negotiators committed, no deadline, no matter how firm or absolute, cannot be changed, modified, or worked around. The request to extend or modify a deadline may play into the question of who truly has the power in the negotiation (see pages 93–108 on power).

Example 5.26 Deadlines can often be extended
During the 1998 peace negotiations in Northern Ireland, after years of negotiations, the parties were running up against their absolute "drop-dead" deadline. They were so close to an agreement that facilitator Senator George Mitchell and the other parties agreed to "unplug" the clock to give themselves the extra 24 hours they needed to reach the Good Friday Agreement.

Lesson: Almost all deadlines can be extended. The questions of whether to seek an extension and when to ask for one are part of the art of negotiation.

THE IMPORTANCE OF ACCELERATED DEADLINES
An accelerated deadline occurs when you tell your opponent that you need the issue resolved prior to when it actually needs to be resolved. Accelerated deadlines are important because your opponent will normally wait until the last possible moment to act. If you do not give yourself an adequate buffer of time, you might not have enough time to explore and close alternative deals.

Example 5.27 Doctor should have accelerated his deadline
Q: A doctor needed an organization to give him some documents he required for tax purposes. He needed them to claim a charitable donation of royalties. There was an intense negotiation going on. Finally, in September 2007, the doctor gave the organization a deadline: "Either I have the documents from you by December 31, 2007, or the deal is off."

What is wrong with the deadline employed in the above example?
A: The doctor failed to give an accelerated deadline to build in time for problems that could be reasonably anticipated. The doctor should have given a much shorter deadline. The deadline permits negotiations until midnight December 31, 2007, and it allows no time for mistakes, snowstorms, acts of God, clerical errors, or review by counsel. This doctor will be helpless if his opponents fax him a letter on December 31, 2007, at 4:00 P.M. He has boxed himself in unnecessarily. An accelerated deadline of November 24, 2007, would have been more appropriate. The doctor here was not a good student of human nature. He failed to factor in the effect of holidays, procrastination, and the need to have many players

sign off on the deal. Unfortunately, the deal was not accomplished in a timely manner.

Conclusion

The successful physician negotiator understands the proper use of deadlines. He will research his opponent's deadlines, set his opponent's deadlines as short as possible, not obsess about his own deadlines, request an extension when necessary, and use accelerated deadlines liberally.

Chapter 6 How to Gain Power in a Negotiation

Executive Summary

- Knowledge is power. Gain knowledge through research, preparation, asking questions, and active listening.
- Having alternatives gives you power. Shop around.
- Citing industry standards and precedents can help gain power.
- The more unique what you have to offer is, the more power you will have because your opponent will have fewer alternatives.
- The more your opponent invests time, emotional energy, and money into a negotiation, the more power you will have.
- If you are somewhat flexible and open-minded, you will have more power in the negotiation.
- Persistence is an invaluable attribute that generates power. The best negotiators are persistent.

Introduction

To be successful, you need to identify the sources of power in your negotiations and use these sources effectively. *Power* in negotiating means the ability to exercise authority and influence. The ability or perceived ability to get things done is also power. The sources of power or perceived power of physician negotiators are numerous and are limited only by the negotiator's creativity and imagination. Lewicki describes the sources of power in the following manner.

Sources of Power	*Description*
Information and expertise	The accumulation and presentation of data intended to change the other person's point of view or position on an issue; and (for expertise) an acknowledged accumulation of information, or mastery of a body of information, on a particular problem or issue.
Control over resources	The accumulation of money, raw material, labor, time, and equipment that can be used as incentives to encourage compliance or as punishments for noncompliance.
Position	Power derived from being located in a particular position in an organizational or communication structure; leads to two different kinds of leverage: • Formal authority, derived from occupying a key position in a hierarchical organization. • Access to or control over information or supply flows, derived from location within a network.[1]

If you can convince your opponent that you are in control, you will have gained power.

Knowledge Is Power

Preparation and information will greatly increase your power. (See pages 109–22 on preparation.) You will be at a distinct advantage if you have done your homework. You should have at your fingertips all of the pertinent statistical, financial, and historical data. You will also need to know about your opponent's needs, desires, and pressures, as well as her business organization and its structure. The most important knowledge for you to obtain is the real, as opposed to the expressed, needs of your

[1] Lewicki, *Essentials of Negotiation,* 3rd Edition (New York: McGraw Hill, 2004) p. 150.

opponent. This knowledge can rapidly shift the balance of power in your favor.

Finding out information requires research. As part of this research, you may want to consider talking to physicians who have already gone through similar negotiations. You will also need to ask a lot of questions. Often, the answers you need will not appear in print anywhere and must be obtained by talking to people. Timid, shy, and unquestioning doctors will not be good negotiators. Knowledge is power. Obtain it and use it to your advantage.

Example 6.1 Doing homework pays off

Opponent: We know you would like to sell your practice and we can offer you one-and-a-half times gross in stock in our company with a one-year employment agreement. We will need a five-year covenant not to compete in this state.

Doctor: As a publicly traded company your financial and acquisition history is a matter of public record. We have checked your SEC form 10Q and your annual report. After reviewing these documents and talking to the heads of the last five practices you acquired, we know that you have paid up to two-and-a-half times gross with 50% cash and 50% stock. The one-year employment contract is considerably shorter than the one you offered *x, y,* and *z,* and the covenant not to compete is twice as long as Dr. Hardball signed. In addition, we are concerned about the way you treated Drs. Smith and Cohen after their acquisition.

Lesson: This is a doctor who has done her homework. She has thoroughly researched her opponent and is therefore in a strong position to obtain more favorable terms.

Example 6.2 Knowledge is power

Background: A physician we know was negotiating to sell his practice to a multi-state group. The negotiations were stalled until he found out that this new company was planning to go public shortly and needed to quickly acquire the licenses his practice maintained. After some tough negotiating, he obtained an excellent offer for his practice of six times his gross revenue.

Lesson: Knowledge is power. By determining that the opponent needed to purchase his practice, the physician was able to obtain very favorable terms.

Example 6.3 Gathering priceless intelligence by asking around
Background: (a young physician is negotiating to join a group practice)

Young physician to former physician employee: I am thinking about joining the XYZ group medical practice and know that you worked there for 2 years. Any words of wisdom you could offer me would be greatly appreciated.
Physician: (former employee) Well, when I started they told me they would take care of me. They never did. I guess it was my fault for never getting it spelled out in writing. Did you know they have had 12 new physicians go through there the last 14 years?

Lesson: The young physician gathered invaluable intelligence by seeking out a former employee. He is in a much better position to evaluate the prospective employer and decide if and how he might negotiate with them.

Alternatives

You should *always* walk into negotiations with several options. You can then compare these options to your opponent's proposal, use them as a benchmark, and, when helpful, show them to your opponent to obtain a better deal. You also need to be aware of your opponent's possible options. You gain power in negotiations when you have more alternatives at your disposal than your opponent does. You are at a tremendous disadvantage when you have no alternatives and absolutely need to make a deal with your opponent.

The experts talk about your BATNA (Best Alternative to a Negotiating Agreement). As Fisher and Ury explain:

> The reason you negotiate is to produce something better than the results you can obtain without negotiating. What are those results? What is the alternative? What is your BATNA—your Best Alternative to a Negotiating Agreement? *That* is the standard against which any proposed agreement should be measured. That is the only standard which can protect you both from accepting terms that are too

unfavorable and from rejecting terms it would be in your interest to accept.

Your BATNA not only is a better measure but also has the advantage of being flexible enough to permit the exploration of imaginative solutions. Instead of ruling out any solution which does not meet your bottom line, you can compare a proposal with your BATNA to see whether it better satisfies your interests.

The insecurity of an unknown BATNA. If you have not thought carefully about what you will do if you fail to reach an agreement, you are negotiating with your eyes closed. You may, for instance, be too optimistic and assume that you have many other choices: other houses for sale, other buyers for your secondhand car, other plumbers, other jobs available, other wholesalers, and so on. Even when your alternative is fixed, you may be taking too rosy a view of the consequences of not reaching agreement. You may not be appreciating the full agony of a law-suit, a contested divorce, a strike, an arms race, or a war.[2]

The key points to remember regarding your alternatives and your BATNA are as follows.

- You should have more than one BATNA.
- The more alternatives you have, the greater your power in the negotiation.
- You need to commit to putting in the requisite time to find viable alternatives.
- Do not be afraid to communicate to your opponent the alternatives you already have in hand.

If you have written alternative contracts or proposals, do not hesitate to show them to your opponent. This is an extremely effective tactic to force your opponent's hand.

---

[2] Roger Fisher and William Ury, *Getting to Yes,* 2nd Edition (New York: Penguin Books, 1991) p. 100.

Example 6.4 Mentioning better options gains the negotiator power
Doctor: As you know, we would like to book our medical convention for 2008. We need 400 sleeping rooms and meeting rooms for 800 (classroom style). We will have continental breakfasts and lunches and maybe another food and beverage function.
Hotel sales manager: We can accommodate you. We need you to sign a $100,000 cancellation clause and an attrition clause indicating that your organization will agree to pay for all the rooms not rented. Here is our standard form....
Doctor: We know about the medical conventions you lost last year and the trouble you had. We do not sign $100,000 cancellation clauses and do not sign any attrition clauses. Here are two proposed contracts from four-star hotels in this area. If you meet their terms we can talk. If not...By the way, this will be an annual event. We will be making a decision in 48 hours.

Lesson: A combination of techniques was used successfully to attempt to negotiate a better contract. They include knowledge of lost meetings, research on the opponent, developing options, having information readily available, and knowing exactly what the options were. It is hard for an opponent to argue against a written contract proposal from a competitor. You need to define your options clearly so that they can be used at the negotiation session.

Obtaining bids or requests for proposals (RFPs) and using them in a negotiation is a standard, yet effective, negotiating technique. Even if you do not go with the lowest bidder, the alternative proposal can help drive the price down.

Industry Standards

It may be useful to demonstrate that your proposal or terms are the industry standard or accepted practice. You can use this fact to gain power in the negotiation. The result can be that your opponent is no longer negotiating against you, but, instead, against the industry. Knowing your opponent's actual cost and usual mark-up or profit can be a great advantage. It is best to bring in the documents, facts, and figures and to have them available on the table. If your opponent was unaware of the industry standards or unaware that you *were* aware of them, your power will be increased.

> Normative leverage is the skillful use of standards, norms, and coherent positioning to gain advantage or protect a position. You maximize your normative leverage when the standards, norms, and themes you assert are ones *the other party views as legitimate and relevant to the resolution of your differences.*[3]

Example 6.5 Opponent's use of industry standards works against the physician

Doctor: I would love to write and edit a national newsletter for you on medical ethics. I understand it will be published bimonthly. How about $4,500 an issue?

Publisher: With your national reputation the newsletter will be great! Doctor, we publish twelve other medical newsletters. We pay a straight 10% royalty payable annually. Here are the contracts for the other newsletters. The 10% is standard in the industry. Feel free to check around. If you are not interested....

Doctor: The 10% will be fine. When do I start?

Lesson: The publisher's knowledge of industry standards increased her power.

> Skilled negotiators use a host of ploys to combine the use of standards with our willingness to defer to authority. They present us with dense, authoritative-looking standard form contracts written in unintelligible legalese and resort to other expert talk in explaining what they call the routine aspects of a transaction...this is a standards-based argument that gains additional power from being combined with an authority ploy.[4]

INDUSTRY STANDARD AS A STARTING POINT

When industry standards are used against you as a negotiation tactic, you can take the position that the standard is only a good starting point. If you have something more to offer, the question you want to pose is how far beyond the starting point will your opponent go to get you signed.

---

[3] G. Richard Shell, *Bargaining for Advantage: Negotiation Strategies for Reasonable People* (New York: Penguin, 2000) p. 43.

[4] Shell, p. 53.

Example 6.6 Industry average is good for the average physician, you deserve better

Some time ago, one of the authors gave a negotiation presentation to resident gastroenterologists who were about to sign their first employment contracts.

A physician speaking for management gave a lengthy PowerPoint presentation citing all of the statistical information about how much the average new gastroenterologist could expect to make broken down geographically.

When it was the author's turn to speak, he turned to the crowd of young residents and asked all of the doctors who were "average" to raise their hands. Only a few hands went up. Then the author posed a second question: "How many of you are *better* than the average doctors?" Almost all the hands went up.

Lesson: Why settle for the average salary or industry standard if your ability and work ethic distinguish you? The industry standard can be just a starting point for the savvy physician negotiator.

Expertise

It may be useful to portray yourself as an expert. If you do, your opponent could have a tendency to treat you respectfully and to defer to your expertise. To appear to be an expert, you need to give the perception that you have superior knowledge, expertise, experience, information, or technical skills. Note that if you need to obtain information directly from your opponent, making yourself out as an expert could make this more difficult. (See pages 46–47 on playing dumb.) Also note that when this technique is used against you, you should cite your own experts and refuse to buy or sign anything you don't understand. Consider the following examples.

Example 6.7 Sell yourself by characterizing your qualifications as rare or unique

Doctor: As I understand this proposal, you would like us to set up a telemedicine service for your multinational company to increase quality of service and hold down costs. Is that correct?

Entrepreneur: Yes. In essence, that's it.

Doctor: I assume the reason you are here is because we have written the text on telemedicine and have developed the standard in interactive computer services.
Entrepreneur: Yes. You are the experts.
Doctor: To make this happen and run a high quality service, we will need the following computer equipment…; the following staff…; and a budget annually of….In the long run, you will increase the quality of medical care and hold down costs.

Lesson: The doctor/expert has used her acknowledged superior technical expertise and experience as powerful negotiating tools. If there are few other doctors with the requisite expertise, the doctor should capitalize on this situation.

Example 6.8 Get technical assistance when negotiating in an area where you lack technical expertise
Salesperson: As you know, Doctor, we developed the fax-on-demand system. What your practice needs is the supercharged 179 system that costs $29,400. Should we draw up the contract?
Doctor: We have retained Ms. Hartley as a consultant. I am sure you have heard of her. She recommends the 119 system and told us not to spend more than $14,500. Before we even get to which model to consider, I have a simple rule of life. I do not purchase or invest in anything I do not fully understand. Can you break this down so someone without a Ph.D. in computer science can understand it? I have set aside ten minutes for this meeting.

Lesson: By employing her own expert/consultant, refusing to sign anything that was not understood, and setting a tight deadline, the physician in the above example neutralized the salesperson's expertise and regained control over the negotiation.

Investment

The more effort, expense, time, and emotional energy your opponent invests in the negotiation, the more your power increases. Such an investment of time and effort indicates your opponent's strong desire to close a deal. After hours, days, or weeks of ongoing negotiation, your opponent does not want to go back to his boss and tell her that he could not reach an agreement. Psychologically, once your opponent has sensed, decided, or in the best case, informed his superior that a deal is close, it is very difficult for that person to walk away. In such a case, he has invested psychic energy and can almost taste the agreement. Anything less is seen as a personal and professional failure.

This is the psychological point of no return or tipping point for your opponent. This may result from the money and effort expended, the periodic favorable reports he has given his supervisors, or the fact that he badly needs to make this happen. A savvy physician negotiator can sense his opponent's desperation and knows when he has reached his point of no return. Some experts call this investment "commitment."

> **Commitment.** Researchers have long recognized that once people have decided something, they can be remarkably persistent in their beliefs. This process has been labeled *commitment to a position,* and it relies heavily on the common need that people have to appear consistent, both to themselves and to others. Most people are familiar with the bait-and-switch sales technique. Unscrupulous organizations advertise merchandise for sale at an incredibly low price but "run out" of stock by the time you arrive at the store. They then try to sell you alternate merchandise at a higher price. Why does this work? One reason is that once you have made the decision to purchase a product (a commitment), you almost automatically follow through with the commitment (even at a higher price).[5]

Once your opponent reaches his point of no return, he will do almost whatever it takes to close the deal. This provides the physician with power to get an excellent deal. You need to recognize this power of investment and use it to your advantage.

Example 6.9 Being prepared to walk away results in a better deal for the physician

Doctor: This is your third and, as far as I am concerned, your final sales call. The $72,000 system you are trying to sell us is priced too high. I know you put a lot of time and money into your presentations and demonstrations. I am sorry. I have to run.

---

[5] Lewicki, p. 170.

Computer salesperson: (sensing a sale slipping away) I hate to see this fall through over a few dollars. What if we reduced the price 5%?
Doctor: Maybe we can reconsider this next year. Thanks again.
Salesperson: (a little more desperate) What will it take to make this sale?
Doctor: A 10% price reduction, two years free service, and the software we discussed. We would need installation within one week.
Salesperson: Give me five minutes to call my sales manager.

Lesson: The physician used the fact that the salesperson was more invested in the deal than she was to her advantage.

Legitimacy and Precedents

You should use precedents and/or legitimacy to increase your power during negotiations. For example, people generally do not question hotel check-in policies of 2:00 P.M. and checkout policies of 11:00 A.M. This is a result of the power of precedents and legitimacy. This policy is printed on the official notices on the inside of the hotel doors and is the way "everyone" does it.

When you receive a standard form, set price, usual and customary mark up, 16% service charge, or penalty for early withdrawal, you see the power of legitimacy and precedents in action against you. Frequently your opponent will utilize pre-printed "standard forms" or "contracts" to drive home the psychological point that there can be no negotiation. Just because a physician is presented with a pre-printed fill-in-the-blank form does not mean that negotiation is not possible.

Example 6.10 Standard practices can be modified, but only if you ask
Doctor: (to hotel employee on phone) I need an early check-in as I will be arriving from the East Coast on Jet Blue at noon. Can you accommodate me please?
Employee: No problem. I put you down for an early check-in.

Lesson: If you do not *ask* for special treatment, you will never get it.

The power of legitimacy and precedents is unquestioned and self-perpetuating. If the reason you pay X is because it has always been X and everyone else pays X, you and everyone else will always pay X. You need to use this technique to your own advantage. You also need to effectively respond to it when it's used against you. The best way to do this is to make your situation appear unique, thus meriting special consideration.

Example 6.11 Doctor uses precedent to his advantage
Corporate sponsor: We would like to be a corporate sponsor for your upcoming medical meeting.
Doctor: Fine. That will be $25,000 and we will need you to pay for the lunch as well.
Corporate sponsor: Well, we didn't really plan on spending that much.
Doctor: The $25,000 fee is set by the Board. Here is the resolution. It has been unchanged for three years. As a matter of fact, it is less than the sponsorship requirements of these three comparable medical conferences (handing him documents). We do have another party interested.
Corporate sponsor: Let me make a few calls. I will get back to you this afternoon.

Lesson: The physician effectively used precedents, legitimacy, knowledge, alternatives, industry standards, and time pressure. As in many cases when this power technique is used effectively, the discussion never turns to whether $25,000 plus the food and beverages was a fair price because it was *the* price.

Example 6.12 An argument to break precedent—your situation is different
Doctor: Our rate for capitation compensation is $1,200 per patient.
Opponent: I'm sorry, Doctor, the set price in our standard contract is $1,000 per patient.
Doctor: Our standard rate is $1,200 per patient. We are currently receiving that from companies X, Y, and Z. We are the most prestigious practice in this part of the state. Without us, you'll never have a strong following here.
Opponent: I appreciate that, Doctor, but $1,000 is our standard rate.
Doctor: Standard service rates a standard rate. Our practice delivers exceptionally good care. Have you had a chance to read the 100 letters of recommendation from our patients that I sent to you? If your doctors give standard care in this industry you'll never get anyone to sign up for your

plan. Our practice is proven to be of the highest quality and, as such, our rate is $1,200 per patient.
Opponent: You may have a point. Let me talk to my boss and get back to you later.

Lesson: The physician successfully set his practice apart from others that received the standard rate. He employed other precedents and used his own standard rate, which he justified, as a way to gain movement on his opponent's set price.

Example 6.13 Everything is negotiable if you ask
Background: A doctor and his wife go away off-season to a beach resort community to have a romantic Saturday night. They prefer to stay at Inn X. Inn X's large parking lot is empty when they arrive.

Doctor: I'd like to get a room for the night, please. What's your rate?
Innkeeper: Our standard rates are published on this card…$119 per night.
Doctor: Wow, that's pretty steep for January. I was quoted $69 per night at Inn Y and that place has a Jacuzzi. Listen, this place is nearly empty. We'd love to stay here and give you the business, but we need to get a rate of $69 per night.
Innkeeper: Fine. We'd love to have you. Let's do it for $69. I'll need to see a major credit card.

Lesson: *Everything* is negotiable. This is especially true of standard rates or prices.

Coping with Uncertainty

You need to be able to cope with uncertainty and react appropriately to unforeseen events. Such flexibility increases your negotiation power. If you follow a script or plan strictly, no matter how well-thought out and well prepared, you will be at a distinct disadvantage and will decrease your negotiation power. This is true because your inflexibility will be perceived as a sign of weakness and a lack of expertise and sophistication. If your opponent senses your inflexibility, he may start to throw you curve balls, red herrings, or negotiation bombshells to see how you react.

Example 6.14 Inflexibility and failure to pause and think hurt the physician

Real estate agent: We can rent this space to you for $4,500 a month.
Doctor: We need to get a long-term lease, medical upgrading so we don't get invoiced, buildout costs, and the right to sublet or assign.
Real estate agent: We can work with those requirements as long as we get a triple net lease.
Doctor: We have never signed anything like that before. It will not be acceptable.

Lesson: The doctor has potentially lost a very good deal. He obtained all the terms he was seeking. However, his inflexibility in not even considering the triple net lease has worked strongly to his disadvantage. The doctor needed to be more flexible and to prepare for the unexpected. He might have been better served by asking a few more questions and at least considering the triple net lease as a possible alternative.

Persistence

Persistence pays off. Physicians who are relentless, who do not back down or give up, and who continue to come back to their central points increase their power in negotiations. Once you are able to convince your opponents that you will not give in, they start to think, "What is it going to take to get this person to sign off?"

Successful physician negotiators are not worn down and do not give up on their central points because a negotiation is taking too long. They know a negotiation will take as long as necessary. When you feel you are right and project the sincerity of your belief to your opponent, you start to raise his anxiety level and increase your power in the negotiation process.[6]

Example 6.15 The best negotiators are persistent

Attorney: Doctor, we have been over this three or four times already. We cannot get you the $189,000. Be reasonable. Compromise and let's be done with it. We are both losing more time and money than this is worth.
Doctor: I don't care if we go over this 44 times. I do *not* back down when I am right. And I am right. You know it and I know it. I will

---

[6] Remember, "persistence is to power, what carbon is to steel." Cohen, p. 83.

continue to stick to the price unless I am convinced otherwise. As to wasting time and money, unfortunately I cannot bill $250 an hour like you do.

Lesson: Persistence can give you power and it often pays off.

Example 6.16 Persistence generates power
Attorneys are professional negotiators. The top negotiator at one of Boston's largest law firms has been described to the authors as the best for one overriding reason: his relentless persistence. He has been described as follows, "Absolutely relentless, will not move on and come back to a difficult point later. Always has another persuasive argument ready to go."

When one of the authors was helping his child with a class project, it became rapidly evident that to get the project done correctly would require renting several pieces of equipment and a substantial amount of time and effort. When he explained this dilemma to his child and suggested a possible new and easier project, she looked him right in the eye and said, "We don't give up just because it is hard. Right, Dad?"

Lesson: This is the attitude you need to be a successful negotiator.

Sole Source

In nearly every physician's life there will be one or more golden business opportunities when she is the only game in town. She may have expertise, knowledge, programs, or products that are unavailable elsewhere or at least are perceived as difficult, if not impossible, to replace. The successful physician negotiator will actively pursue putting herself into this position and will capitalize on this when it occurs. When you are the sole source of information, products, programs, and expertise, many of the standard negotiation rules do not apply. You should no longer concern yourself with or be bound by industry standards, legitimacy, and precedent. The truth is quite simple. Number one, you have what they want. Number two, you are worth whatever they are willing to pay and whatever you are willing accept. Nothing else matters!

Example 6.17 The sole source is in the driver's seat
Attorney: As the leading expert on the AMA *Guides*, we want you to fly down to Texas to testify on the issues of its fairness and constitutionality.
Doctor: No, I am too busy.
Attorney: We will pay you $300 an hour.
Doctor: I am too busy.
Attorney: We will pay you $400 an hour.
Doctor: I am too busy.
Attorney: OK. What will it take?
Doctor: $500 an hour portal to portal, airfare, and out-of-pocket expenses with a $15,000 retainer.
Attorney: But the testimony with travel will be three days…72 hours at $500 an hour.
Doctor: Exactly.
Attorney: OK.[7]

Lesson: The doctor was uniquely qualified. He was the sole source. As such, he was able to command extremely favorable terms. All that was required was that he ask and hold out for them.

Conclusion

Acting as if you have power will increase your opponent's perception of your power in any negotiation. Emphasize and demonstrate your knowledge and expertise. Develop your options and alternatives. Use industry standards, the power of investment, legitimacy, persistence, and flexibility to your advantage. Position yourself whenever possible to become the sole source. If you can, don't be afraid to capitalize on it. Perception *is* reality in negotiation. When you act as if you have power, your opponent will perceive that you actually have power. When your opponent perceives your power, you will be able to negotiate better deals.

[7] This example is based upon an actual event.

Chapter 7 Preparing to Win

Executive Summary

- Thorough preparation greatly increases the likelihood of success.
- Recognize when a negotiation has begun and refuse to take part unless you are sufficiently prepared.
- Find the time necessary to prepare properly.
- Sketch a negotiation plan and decision tree prior to the negotiation.
- Gather as much information as possible from as many sources as possible.

Introduction

Proper preparation is essential. Thorough and well thought-out preparation increases the likelihood of success. Preparation requires you to properly execute a negotiation plan. This plan should identify the issues, your goals, and the likely goals of your opponent. The three preparatory stages are:

1. information gathering,
2. analysis, and
3. planning.

The planning process in negotiations includes the following.

- Defining the issues
- Assembling issues and defining the bargaining mix
- Defining interests
- Defining limits
- Defining one's own objectives (targets) and opening bids (where to start)
- Defining the constituents to whom one is accountable
- Understanding the other party and its interests and objectives
- Selecting a strategy
- Planning the issue presentation and defense
- Defining protocol—where and when the negotiation will occur, who will be there, agenda, etc.[1]

---

[1] Lewicki, p. 43.

Recognize When You Are Negotiating

The single biggest mistake physicians make is not adequately preparing for negotiation. The reasons why physicians frequently do not properly prepare are not dissimilar from why they often do not bother to negotiate at all. (See pages 6–7 on why physicians don't negotiate.) In many cases, the unsuccessful physician negotiator is not prepared because he does not even recognize that he is involved in a negotiation. The physician negotiator who fails to identify when he is, or should be, negotiating cannot prepare for the negotiation. (See pages 23–27 where we discuss ambush negotiation.) Consider the following examples.

Example 7.1 Doctor pays price by not recognizing that a negotiation has begun

Media advance person: Doctor, we would like to interview you for an hour for our cable show on informed consent on June 1, 2007. For your convenience, we will come to your office at 1:00 P.M. Okay?

Doctor: Fine. Should I wear a blue shirt and a solid tie?

Lesson: The physician never bothered to prepare because he failed to identify that he was involved in a negotiation. When he replied "fine," the negotiation was over before it began.

Example 7.2 Doctor correctly identifies that a negotiation has begun and acts accordingly

Media advance person: Doctor, we would like to interview you.…Okay?

Doctor: This sounds interesting, but I am quite busy. Please fax me the names and phone numbers of the last four doctors you interviewed, as I will need to talk to them. I will need you to include in the fax how long this taping will take, what preparation I will need to do, what you intend to do with the interview, and what my compensation will be for my participation. I will call you this week to see if we can reach an agreement.

Lesson: The doctor identified the negotiation opportunity and bought some time to investigate and properly prepare for the negotiation session. This doctor can then call the other doctors who were interviewed and see how they were compensated, if the advance person's time predictions were accurate, and if the interview was a pleasant experience.

Physicians Are Too Busy to Prepare

Many physicians do not bother to prepare for negotiations because they do not have the time to do so. These physicians are too busy seeing patients, filling out paperwork, dealing with insurance companies, getting treatment approvals, and dealing with office staff, etc. The resulting lack of preparation puts these physicians at a distinct disadvantage in the negotiation. It is a chief reason for their poor results. In any significant negotiation, the time you spend preparing will *save,* not cost, you money. If you do not have the time to devote to the preparation, get some help or have someone else negotiate for you.

Example 7.3 How to prepare when pressed for time

Q: You are about to negotiate to buy a new Volvo. You know where the available information is available on the Internet regarding what the dealer pays for them, but you don't have time to play with the computer for an hour and then crunch all the numbers. What should you do?

A: Delay your visit to the showroom until you do have the time to do the research. Alternatively, assign someone else, say a teenage child, to do the research for you and present it to you in an easy-to-understand format.

How to Prepare

Recognizing the need for preparation and setting aside the time for it are only the first steps. You next need to know *how* to prepare. You should first identify the issues to be negotiated and then set your goals and anticipate the likely objectives of the opponent.

ISSUES

You will need to fully and completely identify the issues. This task should be accomplished promptly. Doing so in a timely fashion will leave you adequate time for further preparation. As the following example shows, it can often be advantageous if you position yourself, as opposed to your opponent, to define the issues to be discussed.

Example 7.4 Setting the agenda makes negotiator more powerful
Doctor: Jim, I am faxing you the agenda for our meeting next week. As I understand it, the issues are annual salary, medical and dental benefits, vacation, hours, and coverage. Did I miss anything?
Prospective employee: No, that covers it. Fax it along. Thank you.

Lesson: The physician seized control of the negotiation by preparing the agenda. The order of issues and time allocations in the agenda can be important in maintaining control over the negotiation session. If they are ever reached, issues placed at the end of the agenda with short time allocations will be discussed only briefly. Drafting and setting the agenda is an effective negotiation strategy. It is remarkable how closely parties will adhere to an agenda. If your opponent asks to add items to the agenda, this is a clear signal of what she wants or thinks is significant. Sessions with agendas are usually more productive than unfocused sessions.

GOALS

A negotiation goal is "your highest legitimate expectation of what you should achieve".[2] Successful physician negotiators recognize that they need to set realistically high goals. It is a well-accepted axiom that negotiators who start with high aspiration levels (but not so high as to be unrealistic) achieve better results than those who aim lower. High aspiration levels that are logical, dependable, and make sense are often extremely effective in a negotiation. Unsuccessful physician negotiators may set their goals too low because they are afraid to lose and afraid to fail.

Before you can achieve your goals, you need to set them. Once you have laid out your goals and the likely objectives of your opponent, you can begin information gathering in earnest.

In setting goals, it is best to identify what you are trying to achieve, the least you can offer (and still be realistic), the most you can offer (and still be satisfied with the result), and your best alternative. It is also very important for you to put yourself in the shoes of your opponent and attempt to anticipate what she sees as her goals, lowest offer, best offer,

---

[2] G. Richard Shell, *Bargaining for Advantage: Negotiation Strategies for Reasonable People* (New York: Penguin, 2000) p. 27.

and alternatives. Determining what the opponent really wants is a crucial part of the preparation process. Sometimes a direct approach works very well. For example: "Before we start negotiations, what are the things you really look for?"

You will be more convincing if you honestly believe that your position is reasonable. As Shell notes,

> Optimistic goals are effective only if they are feasible; that is, only if you believe in them and they can be justified according to some standard or norm.[3]

In other words, first convince yourself. It will then be easier to convince your opponent. You should use research, information, objective data and statistics, and precedents to help convince yourself about the correctness of your position.

Example 7.5 Sample negotiating plan
Background: A physician is preparing to negotiate for the purchase of a group medical practice. She makes the following plan.

Goal	To acquire successful specialty practice in geographic proximity to current practice to increase income and compliment practice.
Least can offer	One times their gross annual receipts
Most can offer	Two-and-a-half times their gross annual receipts
Best alternative	Acquire similar practice 30 miles away. (Tentative offer to sell at one-and-a-half times gross revenue.)
Other	They need to sell more than we need to buy.

<u>Opponent's anticipated position</u>

Goal	To sell their practice. (The doctors want to retire.)
Most will demand	Four times gross
Least will accept	One times gross
Best alternative	To find another purchaser in same area with same specialty focus. (Difficult to locate.)
Other	Desperate to sell.

---

[3] Shell, p. 32.

Lesson: The physician has thoroughly thought through the anticipated negotiation. This is preferable to looking for divinely inspired answers to difficult questions you have never thought about before. By putting all the important information in front of her, the physician can rationally determine how much she should offer and how she should respond to the demands of the seller.

Information Gathering

The five Ws of journalism are *when, who, what, where,* and *why.* These five Ws are a good guide to the type of information you should gather prior to a negotiating session.

WHEN

Start to gather information as early as possible.[4] This should begin well before the formal negotiation session starts. The closer you get to the negotiation session, the harder it is to obtain information. You also need to leave yourself a little extra time in case the information you sought turns out to be harder to gather than you anticipated.

Example 7.6 Why it is best not to wait until the last minute to prepare
Q: You have scheduled a negotiation session to discuss employment with a large health insurer. You realize that you should review the company's SEC filings published on the Internet prior to the negotiation. One hour before the meeting you go online to get the company's latest annual report and proxy statements. Unfortunately, the server is down and the information cannot be retrieved. What have you done wrong?
A: By waiting until the last minute to gather information, you cannot respond to the contingency of the server being down. If you had tried to obtain the information one week ahead of time, there would have been ample time remaining to secure it.

[4] "How do you gather information? You start early, because the earlier you start, the easier it is to obtain information. You can always get more information preceding an acknowledged, formal confrontation, because people willingly let their hair down…once…their attitude becomes defensive, they say, 'Come on…I can't tell you anything now. It's negotiation time.'" Cohen, p. 102.

WHO

Talk to *anyone* who can help you gather information. Do not be shy. Do not be an elitist. Start from the bottom up. Talk to clerks, janitors, secretaries, assistants, patients, colleagues, former partners, business associates, spouses, and former spouses. Do not ask inappropriate questions and try, where appropriate, to maintain anonymity. Be aware that some of your questions may find their way back to your opponent. It is often appropriate to ask for an information package directly from the person with whom you will be negotiating. Don't be afraid to ask for any and all information. You will often be pleasantly surprised at what you will get.

Example 7.7 Using an "alternative" source for information
You are negotiating an employment agreement for yourself at a group practice. You want to know how busy the practice is. You call up and tell the receptionist that you are a new patient and would like to get an appointment. She informs you that it will take five weeks.

Lesson: By going to the receptionist for information, you have learned that the group is very busy. This is important because it means that they may be desperate to make a hire. It is also important because you may suspect that you will be overworked if you take the job.

WHAT

Seek out any type of information that can help you prepare. For example, if you are dealing with public companies, seek out on the Internet, or elsewhere, their public filings, annual reports, SEC filings, etc. The company will, if requested, send you a catalog, advertisements, and press releases. Getting on their mailing list can be very beneficial. Searches on the Internet can provide a wealth of information, ranging from your opponent's CV to the company's business plan.

Example 7.8 Why research is crucial
A small, publicly held corporation is negotiating with you for the acquisition of your practice. They have offered you 20,000 shares of their company's stock. You research the company's stock performance record through the Internet. You learn that five years ago their stock was trading

at 90, that it fell to a low of 2, and it is now up to 6. They state that the stock is "going places."

Lesson: Your research indicates a shaky performance for the company's stock. You should strongly consider insisting upon cash.

WHERE

There are few limits on where you can seek out information to prepare for your negotiation. The only true limits are the imagination and tenacity of the negotiator. As a successful physician negotiator, you or a member of your staff can use specialized business or medical libraries, online services, inside reports, or articles written by or papers delivered by your opponent. The depth of your information gathering should depend upon the amount at stake in the negotiation. When lawyers prepare for a significant case, they frequently obtain and read everything their opponent and/or experts have ever written or delivered orally. While much of this information is not directly "on point," it may reveal important personal, professional, or other information about your opponent. In negotiations that include substantial amounts, the successful physician negotiator should do no less.

Example 7.9 Newspaper article provides critical information about opponent

You are considering selling your practice to a company headed by "Chainsaw" Al Smith. You would like to stay on at the practice for five more years, then retire. You perform a literature search on Mr. Smith. You learn from old *Wall Street Journal* articles that he is called "Chainsaw" Al because he has a reputation of taking over businesses and firing most of its high-level employees.

Lesson: After conducting this research, you may want to consider demanding an airtight five-year employment contract. You might also want to consider finding a job somewhere else or not selling to this buyer.

WHY

The more you know about what motivates your opponent, the more likely you are to achieve your negotiation goals. (See pages 70–74 on what makes your opponent tick.)

Example 7.10 Using research to provide a favor for your opponent
You are negotiating a business deal with the CEO of a mid-sized company. One day, when talking with his secretary, you discover that he is an avid golfer. You send him a case of highly prized golf balls from "one straight shooter to another."

Lesson: This act of goodwill, based on information regarding the opponent's passion for golf, can only help facilitate the upcoming negotiations.

Analysis

A careful analysis must be made once all the information is gathered. You need to analyze the facts and arguments and then challenge the underlying assumptions upon which they are based. You should not assume to know what the other party wants, desires, or thinks is important in a negotiation. Physicians frequently assume that:

1. their opponent will act as they would if they were in the same situation,
2. their opponent will act logically, and
3. their opponent will do what is in his best interest.

Each of these basic assumptions is flawed.

Assumption #1: Your Opponent Will Act as You Would

Do not assume that your opponent will act as you do. If you do, you will essentially be looking in the mirror and negotiating with yourself. Making this assumption can lead to poor results.

Example 7.11 Assuming you know what your opponent wants and poor listening skills are major mistakes
Doctor: We appreciate all your hard work and will take care of you during bonus time.
Colleague: I appreciate it, but that doesn't solve my problem. The traveling I am doing is wreaking havoc on my spouse and kids. I am never around on weekends. I missed the last three soccer matches,…I was

the only parent that wasn't there during the annual show at school. Instead I was stuck at an airport hotel. I am very close to leaving.

Lesson: The doctor is wrong in assuming that money, in the form of a bonus, will resolve the problem. This is a common mistaken assumption. Many studies show that lifestyle issues, quality of work, and personal satisfaction may be more important than money. This could be a very costly assumption. What his colleague may really be concerned with is the time away from his family. A bonus will not fix this problem. The doctor needed to employ better active listening skills. (See pages 58–68 on active listening techniques and pages 62–63 on hearing what is *not* being said.)

ASSUMPTION #2: YOUR OPPONENT WILL ACT LOGICALLY

Frequently, physician negotiators assume they know what their opponent will do because it is the logical thing to do. This assumption is dangerous. *People do not always do what is logical.* (See pages 149–55 on emotions.) You also need to consider that when your opponent is under pressures or stresses of which you are unaware, actions that would seem illogical to you may seem very logical to your opponent.

Example 7.12 It might seem crazy to you, but it's perfectly logical for your opponent

Doctor: Phil, are you telling me that you are going to give up the practice of medicine, move to Cape Cod, and open a few bagel shops?

Partner: That's right—less hassles, more family time, less pressures….

Doctor: Phil, that's crazy. Your lost income, the goodwill, the patients….

Partner: I am forty-nine. It is now or never. I will be having some fun.

Lesson: What seems illogical to you may seem very logical to someone with different values. Just because your opponents are doing something that appears to be illogical, it doesn't mean that they are being illogical in their own minds. In fact, this action may be the "right" one for them. The key is not to try and figure out what they want, but to ask them directly. Open-ended questions such as, "What do you dislike the most about practicing medicine?" can result in very revealing replies. Again, find out what makes your opponent tick.

ASSUMPTION #3: YOUR OPPONENT WILL DO WHAT IS IN HER BEST INTEREST

Even when it is clear to you what is in the best interest of your opponent, she may still not take that course of action. This fact is difficult for physician negotiators to accept. It occurs because often your opponent assumes different things than you would assume if you were in her position. It also occurs because some people simply make flawed and, in some cases, emotional decisions.

Example 7.13 Illogical, emotional decision costs

The authors had a set of medical videos placed exclusively in a catalog. The videos were selling well. At the end of the exclusivity period, we informed the catalog owner that we would start to market the videos ourselves to a completely different market. The catalog company owner could continue to sell the videos in his catalog at the same terms. The catalog owner was insulted by our lack of confidence in his catalog and no amount of logical argument or proof would change his mind. He dropped the set of videos. This was truly a lose/lose conclusion, because both parties lost money for no logical reason. It seemed to us that it was clearly in his best interest to continue to sell the videos. That is the reason why we did not renew the exclusive arrangement.

Planning

Once you have set your goals, anticipated the likely objectives of your opponent, and gathered all the information available and analyzed it, you are ready to move to the final preparation stage. This stage involves the preparation of a negotiation plan. The successful physician negotiator carefully plans each aspect of the negotiation session from the location (see pages 29–34) to the tactics to be used (see pages 173–93). You need to think of yourself not only as the actor, but as the producer, director, choreographer, and stage director as well. Your negotiation plan needs to be well thought out. The authors use the decision tree model as an effective negotiation planning device.

As former trial lawyers, we always prepare our case *and* the other side's case. We put ourselves in the other lawyer's shoes. What will she argue? How should we respond? What are our weak points? There are four elements we concentrate on. These elements are listed in Box 7.1.

Box 7.1

Preparation Points

1. What is the opponent's *position* likely to be?
2. What is the opponent's *rationale* likely to be?
3. What are the opponent's *weak and strong points*?
4. Where is the opponent most *vulnerable* (on the opening position, the fall back, or the bottom line)?

A decision tree can be very helpful in avoiding surprises. It allows you to prepare to react "spontaneously" to events in the negotiation. In reality, however, you have had time to think through the logical consequences of your response. Successful physician negotiators who effectively employ their decision trees are like chess grand masters. Like grand masters, they are prepared for every move of the opponent and have played the game out several times in advance before their next move.

Example 7.14 Sample decision tree
A decision tree for a simple negotiation follows.

Employment negotiation

Salary

If they offer less than $150,000 a year: sticking point (must meet this base salary or else catch early flight back).

If they meet or exceed $150,000 a year: move to health and dental insurance.

Insurance

Malpractice:	Mandatory: nonnegotiable
Health Insurance:	Mandatory: nonnegotiable; full family coverage
Dental Insurance:	Negotiable: (get if can)

Length of contract

Ideal:	2 years (for flexibility)
Lowest:	1 year (security)
Highest:	3 years (do not want to be boxed in)

[NOTE: If they demand more than three years, revisit salary and ask for cost of living increases: A) based on rate of inflation and B) other standards.]

<u>On-call status</u>

Ideal:	1 day per month
Highest:	3 days per month

[NOTE: If 2 days or more, ask for compensatory pay to discourage additional coverage time. Propose sliding scale downward with passage of time for on-call dates.]

<u>Vacation</u>

Ideal:	5 weeks per year
Minimum:	3 weeks per year

[NOTE: Fight hard: "rationale"—need to stay fresh and not "burn-out." Tie into length of contract if less than 4 weeks, no more than 2-year contract.]

<u>Perks</u>

Moving expenses:	Ask for $4,500; take $2,500
Sick days:	Ask for 10; take 5; if need be, talk "team player"

Income from other sources:	Ask to keep 100% (can cap at $20,000 if need to).
Noncompetition clause:	"Talk trust" and give away as little as possible. Have attorney check. Blame her if need be.

Lesson: The decision tree forces the physician negotiator to prepare and anticipate problems. Once prepared, the physician has persuasive arguments and rationales readily available. The decision tree also enables the negotiator to see the big picture and to demonstrate how all the terms in an agreement are interdependent. The key for the prepared physician is that she has thought through the many scenarios that may be played out. The physician has come up with the minimal acceptable terms that would make her happy and the rationales, research, and objective reasons why she should get more than the "average" physician. The more prepared the physician, the less she will have to deal spontaneously with the unexpected.

Chapter 8 Silence Is Golden

Executive Summary

- Let your opponent talk first.
- Let your opponent do most of the talking.
- Your silence can raise your opponent's anxiety level.

Introduction

You will need to be able to keep silent when necessary. Silence is a potent strategic weapon. It can also be an excellent method of communicating. It can, however, often be one of the most difficult communication skills for physicians to master.

Strategic Weapon

You should let your opponent talk first and let her do most of the talking. This requires self-discipline.[1] If you are able to listen more than you talk, you will accomplish a chief aim of the negotiation because you will get more information than you give. (See pages 114–17 on gathering information.) Just as nature abhors a vacuum, a weak negotiator abhors silence. You need to realize that silence may make your opponent very uncomfortable. The longer the silence, the more excruciating it can be for your opponent. Your opponent will frequently talk to fill the void and keep the negotiation going. The more your opponent talks to fill the void, the more likely she will be to inadvertently disclose information you can use or to make a key concession. Consider the following examples.

Example 8.1 Silence can be an effective weapon
Seller: We are asking $395,000 for the office building.
Doctor: (long silence)
Seller: We do have some flexibility. How much are you looking to pay?

Lesson: Silence can immediately raise the anxiety level of your opponent. He could be thinking to himself, "Am I too high? Am I off base? Have I angered my opponent?" The doctor's silence directly resulted in the concession of flexibility on the issue of price. It also demonstrates where

---

[1] Above all, you need to avoid the temptation to prove how smart you are by continuously talking.

the power lies in the negotiation. If after one minute the seller is backpedaling, it is clear the true power resides with the buyer.

Example 8.2 Keeping silent takes discipline but can pay great dividends
Consider the movie *The Caine Mutiny.* In the film, José Ferrer cross-examines the Captain (Humphrey Bogart) to try and prove that he was mentally unstable and unfit for command. He questions the Captain until he goes off on a long and disjointed verbal tirade about the missing strawberries and other topics. At the end of the tirade, the Captain proved through his own conduct that he was unfit for command. This gambit worked only because José Ferrer's character was disciplined and sophisticated enough to keep silent and let his opponent hang himself. The more the Captain rambled on, the clearer it became that he was in fact mentally unbalanced.

Silence is also an effective way of increasing the significance given to what you eventually do say. When you do not speak often, your words take on heightened significance. Consider the following example.

Example 8.3 The less you say, the more weight every word you say will be given
At a recent negotiation session, there were eight doctors, three insurance representatives, and one attorney in attendance. All of the physicians and others at the meeting fully expressed themselves about the matter at issue. For forty-five minutes the attorney sat silent. At the end of forty-five minutes, one of the doctors said, "We have not heard from Steve. Steve, what do you have to say?" The room quieted and the attorney's comments were singled out. They were treated with more attention and respect than they probably deserved. Silence was used to amplify what was eventually said in the negotiation session.

Method of Communication

Remaining silent after your opponent has made an offer or proposal can be effective. This technique may quickly reduce your opponent's aspiration levels. In addition, remaining silent gives you the added protection of not making any verbal information leaks. Consider the following examples.

Example 8.4 Silence can be an effective response
Insurer: Doctor, your outstanding medical bill is $3,892. As you know, we are disputing coverage and the services rendered. We will offer you $2,000 to settle this bill today.
Doctor: (silence)

Lesson: Although the doctor has said nothing, he has quickly and decisively communicated his displeasure with the offer made. In addition, it is much harder for his opponent to read the doctor. There are no verbal cues or leaks. (See pages 63–64 and 196–97 on verbal leaks.)

Example 8.5 Verbal response less effective than silence
Insurer: Doctor, your outstanding bill is $3,892. We will offer $2,000 to settle this bill today.
Doctor: I think that is a little low.

Lesson: The verbal response in this example may be less effective than the silent response above. The verbal response gives the opponent the information that, although low, her offer seems to be in the ballpark.

Tempo

Silence can control the tempo of a negotiation and it can shift the momentum from your opponent. The physician negotiator can sense the momentum in a negotiation. The experienced negotiator can use one or more tactics to completely change the momentum. This is especially true when his opponent makes a tactical or strategic mistake.

Example 8.6 Silence expresses displeasure and gains concessions
Hospital administrator: So, Dr. Smith, your salary will be $150,000 a year.
Doctor: Fine.
Hospital administrator: You will have medical and malpractice insurance.
Doctor: Good.
Hospital administrator: You will have four weeks paid vacation.
Doctor: As we agreed.

Hospital administrator: You will be committing to six years full time and then if you need extra time for maternity leave or flex-time, we will work it out.
Doctor: (long silence)
Hospital administrator: (flustered, recognizing the mistake) I didn't mean to imply that…obviously, under the FMLA…you are certainly within your rights to….
Doctor: (after another long pause and silence) Let's move on for now to life insurance, office space, and coverage terms.

Lesson: The physician used silence to communicate her intense displeasure at what was said. She has also effectively masked her future intentions and completely seized the control, power, and momentum of the negotiation. She will be more likely to gain concessions.

Example 8.7 Changing negotiation dynamics by accusing opponent of insult
Physician to opponent: That project will take me approximately 20 hours of research and analysis.
Opponent: That's hard to believe.
Physician: Are you calling me a liar? (starting to get up…) If you don't trust me maybe you should get someone else.
Opponent: No—I am sorry. I didn't mean to suggest that you were lying. I have the highest regard for your reputation and integrity….

Lesson: The physician here used a minor unintentional slight to put his opponent completely on the defensive and change the momentum of the negotiation.

Conclusion

Recall the Miranda warnings a person receives when he is arrested. That language is, "You have the right to remain silent. Anything you say can and will be used against you." This is equally true in negotiations. Also remember the authors' advice: "Anything you *don't* say can and will be used to *benefit* you."

Chapter 9 How to Gain Valuable Concessions

Executive Summary

- Leave yourself room to negotiate. Don't paint yourself into a corner.
- Do not negotiate against yourself. When giving a concession, gain one in return.
- Plan to give concessions that cost you little, but that are very valuable to your opponent.
- Characterizing your demands as relatively minor can help.
- Try to get your opponent to make the first major concession.
- As time goes on, your concessions should get smaller and smaller.
- The rate and timing of your opponent's concessions can be a good clue as to how badly she wants a deal.
- Make your opponent look good in front of his boss. This will pay dividends in future negotiations.

Room to Negotiate

Concessions are an important part of any negotiation. The first rule to remember is to leave yourself adequate room to negotiate. A *concession* is giving something up, granting a request, or yielding on a point in a negotiation. This increases your flexibility. It also gives you the ability to react to your opponent's reasoning, facts, figures, and arguments. In short, you can concede on certain points in order to get something in return and to close the deal.

Example 9.1 Backtracking to give yourself a little more room for negotiating

Prospective employee: Your offer of $32,500 is low. I would love to work with you, but I need $35,000.

Doctor: Well, I gave you all I had….I guess I could talk to my partners. We would hate to lose you for $2,500.

Lesson: The doctor has left himself a little wiggle room. He communicated that he may very well not go any higher, but he has left himself the option to agree after talking to his partners.

Recognizing Concessions

In almost every negotiation there will come a time when you have to give up something to make progress. It is crucially important, therefore, that you leave yourself adequate room to negotiate. During your preparation you should consider possible concessions you might make, their cost to you, and their value to your opponent. When you give up *anything* during a negotiation, you are making a concession. This includes granting your opponent's request or yielding on a point. This also includes the situation where your opponent introduces a significant demand, unexpected request, or trial balloon. Your not dismissing it out of hand is a concession and should be viewed as such. For example, even just agreeing to consider a request can be an important concession. You need to minimize what you give up (in terms of its cost to *you*) and maximize what you receive. At the same time, you should try to maintain or develop a good ongoing working relationship with your opponent.

Example 9.2 Missed opportunity to get a return on a small concession
Opponent: This negotiation session is scheduled to go until 2:00 today. We cannot finish by 2:00. Can you stay until 6:00 P.M.?
Doctor: Okay.

Lesson: Everything you give up is a concession. The doctor has made a concession but has handled it poorly. He trivialized the value of his concession and has obtained nothing of value in return.

Reciprocity

Reciprocity, the tit for tat, plays a significant role in receiving concessions during a negotiation. The savvy negotiator recognizes the principle and how to use it to her advantage.

> The norm of reciprocity has been studied for years by philosophers, anthropologists, sociologists, and other social scientists. This norm suggests that when you receive something from another person, you should respond in the future with a favor in return. This norm is thought to be pan-cultural in that groups around the world appear to respect it.
>
> The norm of reciprocity plays an important role in negotiations. Negotiators give concessions and expect concessions in return. For instance, negotiator A does a small favor for negotiator B and later asks for a larger favor from B in

return. The net advantage goes to A. Although one may think that the norm of reciprocity should apply only to favors of the same size, this does not appear to be the case. In fact, many sales pitches rely on giving the consumer a small gift early in an exchange and then asking for a large concession from the consumer later.[1]

Example 9.3 Minor concession rates a concession in return
Doctor: I hope my coming to your office to negotiate helps you out. I know you are in the middle of your busy season.
Opponent: Thank you, I appreciate it.

Lesson: Even the minor act of going to your opponent's office to negotiate can be portrayed as a concession which, "in fairness," should be reciprocated at some point. During a key point in the negotiation, the doctor can remind his opponent of this concession to receive a reciprocal concession.

Example 9.4 Preemptive concession
Doctor: Before we even get started, I understand you really want a three-year deal. We were looking at a two-year agreement. To accommodate your needs we are willing to go the extra year.
Opponent: Great. Let's work out the other details.

Lesson: A preemptive concession may be unusual, but it may be worth the risk in light of your opponent's need to reciprocate.

Value

You need to understand the value of any concession to your opponent. The more valuable the concession, the more you can ask for and expect in return. The value that your opponent places on a concession will depend upon how badly she needs the concession, how hard you make her work for it, and the perceived cost to you. The most important thing to remember about concessions is that *what may be a crucial concession from your opponent's point of view may cost you little or nothing.* These are the concessions you should search for and use freely in your negotiation.

---

[1] Lewicki, p. 169.

Example 9.5 Making a small concession appear bigger to gain more leverage

Opponent: This negotiation session is scheduled to go until 2:00 P.M. today. Can you stay until 4:00 P.M.?

Doctor: Well, this was scheduled weeks ago. I would have to try and move things around. Do you want me to make a call to my office?

Opponent: If you can.

Doctor: (five minutes later) I changed the two appointments. I guess I will be working late again tonight.

Opponent: I appreciate it.

Doctor: (seizing the initiative) Now that we have a little breathing space, let's get to the salary issue.

Lesson: The doctor recognized the opponent's need for the extension, made her work for it, and clearly pointed out the cost he paid for the concession. He is now in a stronger position to obtain a concession from his opponent.

Example 9.6 A good concession to make—one that costs you little or nothing, but is worth a lot to your opponent

You are writing a book and you know that it will be done on time. Your publisher struggles with chasing authors for their work and making up production and marketing schedules. Delay costs publishers money. What if you guarantee that your book will be done on time or early? This costs you nothing. To the publisher, it may be valued as a major concession. In return, you might ask for slightly higher royalties if delivered early.

Example 9.7 Concession that cost nothing out of pocket put to good use

During the Arab-Israeli peace talks of the late 1970s, the photo opportunity of Menachem Begin and Anwar Sadat shaking hands was the lead story on the news across the world. This was a major concession from the Israeli point of view and was treated as such by all parties. The Israelis used this concession to their advantage.

Other examples of things that could be very important to your opponent but that cost you nothing are:

- links to your Web site,
- putting out flyers at your conference, and
- making a contributor a co-author of a textbook.

Linkage

You should try to get something of equal or greater value in return for each concession you make. One of the most effective techniques for achieving this is *linkage.* The effective use of linkage requires that you evaluate and have your opponent evaluate each potential concession in the context of the entire proposed agreement. What at first blush seems very significant or insurmountable may, in the context of the big picture, be a relatively minor concession. Consider the following examples.

Example 9.8 Linking a demand with a concession
Prospective employer: Doctor, we are looking for a three-year covenant not to compete within 100 miles of our office. Is that acceptable?
Doctor: No, it is not.
Prospective employer: What is the problem?
Doctor: I am a little taken aback by your lack of trust with the request for a three-year covenant not to compete. It doesn't bode well for a future relationship.
Prospective employer: (backpedaling and attempting to soften the blow) How could we make it work?
Doctor: If I was to get $160,000 for year one and $170,000 for year two, I would consider a 50-mile covenant not to compete.

Lesson: The physician linked his concession on the covenant not to compete with his demand for increased salary. Note also how he quickly put the prospective employer on the defense by raising the "trust" issue.

Example 9.9 Characterizing your demand as minor minimizes the apparent value of the concession you seek
Doctor: What I need is an additional $16,000 to sign this three-year contract for services.
Opponent: I can't do…
Doctor: Jim, we are talking about a $1.6 million contract, a staff member spread over three years. We have tailored the agreement for you. We only need 1% more to wrap this up. Let's not have to start negotiating from scratch.

Lesson: The doctor has emphasized the overall context in an effort to minimize the significance of his $16,000 demand.

Timing

You should always try to get your opponent to make the first major concession. This is true for the same reasons that you would want to get your opponent to make the first offer. The first major concession will frequently tip the negotiator's hand and reveal what she really wants. The concession may also reveal how badly she wants something and, in some cases, what she is willing to give up to get it. Making the first major concession is often perceived as a sign of weakness. Experienced negotiators can sense this weakness and will not hesitate to exploit it to the fullest extent.

Example 9.10 Making the first major concession is a costly mistake
New doctor: We have been going back and forth for three hours. I asked for $135,000 and you offered $100,000. As you know, I have student loans, a family, and other expenses. My spouse is not working. I will drop my request to $125,000. I need to line up employment.
Practice leader: I appreciate your frankness. I am already over budget but I will talk to the powers that be and see if I can get you $110,000. Otherwise, if this is not satisfactory…. (putting papers in file)
Doctor: Thank you. I appreciate whatever you can do for me.

Lesson: By making the first major concession, the physician has lost power in the negotiation and revealed his desire to close the deal. He has also revealed his ability to accept $125,000. The opponent used this information against him.

Size and Rate of Concessions

You should start with making the largest concession first and reduce the size of your concessions as the negotiation progresses. This technique is effective because of your opponent's emotional investment as the negotiations progress. (See pages 101–3 on investment.) After hours, days, weeks, or months of negotiations, it becomes increasingly difficult, if not impossible, for your opponent to walk away from the potential deal. After you have positioned your opponent into this state of mind, it is time to reduce the size of your concessions.

Example 9.11 Decreasing the size of your concessions as the negotiation progresses can improve your results

Health care officer: Kathy, we have been at this for four months. We want to purchase your practice. We started out at $1.5 million, went to $1.7 million, and then to $2 million.

Doctor: We've moved also. We went from $2.8 million to $2.6 million, down to $2.5 million.

Health care officer: We have been "moving" a lot more than you have.

Doctor: You have a lot more money than we have. Was your gross income $54 million last year?

Lesson: In this example, note the rate of concessions of both parties. The health care officer *increased* the amount of his concessions: $200,000 and then $300,000. This incentivized the opponent to keep negotiating because it appeared that there was more money to obtain. The doctor *decreased* the rate of her concessions: $200,000 and then $100,000. This told the opponent that there was less and less to negotiate for and discouraged requests for additional concessions. Continued requests for concessions may be perceived as "nickel and diming" the opponent. By holding fairly firm, the doctor gained major concessions from the purchaser. She correctly determined that her opponent was heavily invested and would not want to walk away from the deal.

Information and Rate of Concessions

There is much information to be gleaned by the rate of concessions made by your opponent. When the increments of concessions are increased as the negotiation progresses, this tells you that your opponent needs the deal more than you do. If you fall into a predictable pattern of concessions, you may tip off your opponent as to what your next concession will be.

Example 9.12 Negotiating against yourself

Doctor: (to owner of building) We can go to $260,000 for the building.
Owner: I can't do it for $260,000.
Doctor: How about $270,000?
Owner: You are getting closer.

Lesson: The owner will keep asking for more and more until the physician reaches his top dollar. A better response would have been, "What can you do it for?" The answer to that question might have been a number less than $270,000.

The Story of Concessions

Almost every opponent will report back to a boss or spouse regarding the negotiation. The story that your opponent reports is significant. This story will help justify the concessions made and will make your opponent look good or bad. Ideally, the story should be worded so that your opponent looks like a hero. You should interweave this potential story into the negotiation. You want your opponents to be able to visualize how they can sell the deal so their concessions come off looking good. The more concessions they can sell, the better they look, and the more they can give you.

Example 9.13 Making your opponent look bad will impede future negotiations
Your opponent leaves her office at 10:00 A.M., meets you at 10:05 A.M., and says that she will offer you $50,000 for your medical invention. You agree and she reports back to her boss at 10:15 A.M. and tells her the story.

Lesson: Your opponent's boss will say, "You should have offered less. You overpaid." The negotiation was concluded too quickly. There was no resistance. This may impede future negotiations.

Example 9.14 Making your opponent look good will help you in future negotiations because your opponent will be more empowered by his employer
The same opponent as in Example 9.13 leaves the office at 10:00 A.M. and calls her boss at 2:00 P.M. to say that negotiations are difficult. The doctor has read a negotiation book and is using everything he has learned. She staggers back to the office at 4:45 P.M., goes through all the demands and problems, but then says she got the signature for $52,500.

Lesson: The boss is likely to compliment your opponent because you were tough and the negotiation was hard fought and protracted. The experienced physician negotiator recognizes this need to report back and look good. When you acknowledge to your opponent that you are in the same boat and also have to look good, you develop an "us against them" negotiating relationship. This us against them negotiation tactic can be very effective because it helps you bond with your opponent because you are in the same boat. Here is how the opening part of the dialogue sounds:

> "I understand that you have a tough supervisor and that he thinks you should get everything for almost nothing. Confidentially, I am in exactly the same situation. The boss sits up in her ivory tower and expects me to work miracles—spin straw into gold. I am not exactly Rumpelstiltskin here. Let's see if we can work together to get a reasonable deal that will satisfy both our supervisors."

Making your opponent look good is important if you will negotiate with that person in the future.

Chapter 10 Using and Breaking Deadlock

Executive Summary

- Appearing willing to walk away from a deal will gain you power and help avoid deadlock.
- Conciliatory language can often help to break deadlock.
- Remaining flexible and leaving yourself room to negotiate will help avoid deadlock.
- A gentleman's agreement to agree will usually help avoid deadlock.
- Suspending negotiations and reconvening at a later time can often help avoid deadlock.
- Changing negotiators may help reinvigorate a negotiation.
- To break deadlock, try to turn a competitive negotiation into a cooperative one.

Appear Willing to Walk Away

When you are unable to reach an agreement after negotiations, you have *deadlock*. The goal of negotiation is *not* to get an agreement. The goal is rather to reach an agreement that is favorable and meets your needs. Many physicians will agree to unfavorable terms to avoid deadlock. Deadlock for these physicians has become synonymous with failure and is to be avoided at all costs. You should not fear deadlock. In fact, you should use the anticipation of deadlock as a negotiating technique. ***Most importantly, you need to give the impression that you are prepared to walk away from the deal.***

Example 10.1 Appearing ready to walk away generates negotiating power

Attorney: Unless we are able to work out this new retainer agreement, our firm will not be able to continue to represent your medical group.
Doctor: I understand.
Attorney: Will you agree to our $350 per hour partner time, $275 per hour associate time, and $200 per hour paralegal time?
Doctor: As I mentioned previously, it is too high.
Attorney: I guess we are at an impasse.
Doctor: (calm and ignoring the last comment) How long will it take you to pull our files together and transfer them to the new firm, Cost-Yu-Less?

We already have a bid from them for all our legal work and according to my calculations by switching we will save $21,000 a year. Over a period of 5 years, that is....
Attorney: Let's not be impetuous. I am sure we can work something out.

Lesson: The doctor did not agree to a bad deal just to get any deal. She was prepared with a real alternative that increased her bargaining power immensely. More importantly, by giving the impression that she was willing to walk away, the doctor will probably gain concessions.

Techniques to Break or Avoid Deadlock

In some cases you will want to attempt to break or avoid deadlock. This can occur if you do not want to jeopardize an existing or potential long-term relationship. It can also occur when you need the deal and have few, if any, palatable alternatives. There are various methods you can use to avoid deadlock. These include conciliatory language, flexibility, room to negotiate, cautious use of deadlines and ultimatums, eliminating the possibility of deadlock, and "change" during the negotiation session.

Conciliatory Language

If you feel close to unwanted deadlock, a simple question or statement may help. It may even put the negotiation back on the right track.

Example 10.2 Conciliatory statement may help break deadlock
Provider: You want us to change our reimbursement for covered services and our payor alternative reimbursement schedule?
Doctor: Correct, we need the slight change to make it work for us.
Provider: No can do. We do not want to rewrite our standard agreement.
Doctor: We appreciate your prior movement and flexibility and your need to maintain a standard agreement. We are a unique facility. One fair way around the problem would be to attach an addendum to the contract. This would be fair to us and would still enable you to deal with your concerns. We would, of course, agree to keep the addendum confidential.

Lesson: The doctor used conciliatory language, employed active listening skills (see pages 58–68 on active listening skills), stressed fairness, and offered a simple, cost-effective solution. Deadlock may be avoided. What the doctor "heard" was that changing the standard contract could impact the provider's other clients and could increase costs across the board.

Flexibility

The successful physician negotiator carefully prepares for the negotiation (see pages 109–22 on preparation) and builds flexibility into her decision tree (see pages 119–22 on flexibility). Flexibility may be needed to avoid deadlock.

Example 10.3 Problem solving, creativity, and flexibility help break deadlock

Prospective employer: (after extensive negotiations) We would love to have you on board, but the most we can offer for salary is $130,000 and, as I understand it, you need $150,000.

Doctor: That's right.

Prospective employer: I wish I could come up with the $20,000, but my hands are tied. We have a salary structure.

Doctor: If I take the $130,000 and am allowed to retain any money I can generate from trauma call, honoraria, royalties, IMEs, and occasionally testifying as an expert witness....

Prospective employer: As long as it does not interfere with your duties. That works for me.

Lesson: The physician used flexibility and her ability as a problem solver to avoid unwanted deadlock. Note that the concession was granted because it cost the employer little, if anything.

Adequate Room to Negotiate

Leaving adequate room to negotiate will help avoid most deadlocks. (See page 127 on room to negotiate.) As part of your preparation, you should "play out" the negotiation scenario by working backward from the desired goal to the starting point. You need to understand and anticipate your opponent's desires, goals, needs, and likely reaction to offers. An adequate physician negotiator reacts well to offers and demands. The sophisticated negotiator will also plan the negotiation so that an opponent will almost have to make the desired concessions.

Example 10.4 Using your opponent's numbers against him
Prospective employer: We are getting close to an agreement. The salary is $150,000 plus a bonus.
Doctor: I need assurances that the practice will be growing and thriving and will not be in financial difficulty like my last practice. What kind of growth are you looking at?
Prospective employer: We anticipate an increase in revenue of $450,000 after you sign on for year one, and $500,000 for year two.
Doctor: I am looking for a 7% bonus on the increase in gross revenue on a consolidated basis, with the right to withhold consent for capitated and reduced contracts, post-termination collections for two years, with a guaranteed base bonus amount of $30,000 for year one and $32,000 for year two.
Prospective employer: (taken aback somewhat) I see you have done your homework. However, we can only go to 5%, and about the guaranteed base bonus….

Lesson: When your opponent attempts to sell an overly optimistic picture with what you consider to be inflated future projections, you can make those numbers work for you while at the same time leaving yourself room to negotiate. Savvy physician negotiators induce their opponents to come up with these rosy, or in some cases, inflated, projections. They then anchor their demands on these projections. When done correctly, it is difficult, if not impossible, for your opponents to move away from these numbers. After all, *they* are the ones who offered them in the first place.

DEADLINES AND ULTIMATUMS

Hard and fast ultimatums and "drop-dead" deadlines (see pages 82–91 on deadlines) can quickly lead to deadlock. They represent inflexibility and may leave you little room to negotiate. The most effective ultimatums and deadlines are ones that deliver the message without completely cutting off the possibility of continued negotiations. Here is where knowing your opponent and the right buttons to push becomes crucial. (See pages 70–74 on knowing your opponent.)

Example 10.5 Negotiating yourself into a corner
Doctor: Unless you agree to sign this two-year covenant not to compete, we cannot hire you!
Prospective employee: (angrily offering his hand) Thank you for your time!

Lesson: The doctor's statement left him no room to negotiate. If his bluff is called, he has lost the opportunity to make a new hire.

Example 10.6 How you ask for something is often more important than what you ask for
Doctor: Tell me what it is like to be an All-American football player.
Prospective employee: A lot of hard work, but the scholarship paid my way all through school and I made a lot of great friends on the team. I am still close to….
Doctor: How many colleges were after you?
Prospective employee: Fifteen or twenty.
Doctor: What made you go to BC?
Prospective employee: It is a great school—great team, good academics—and it was around the Flutie era.
Doctor: That's what we have here: a "great team," excellent medicine. We need you to sign a letter of intent just like you did at BC. We need a level of commitment. The covenant not to compete is our assurance that you will not "jump to Notre Dame" the first chance you get. Are you a team player, Jim?
Prospective employee: Yes, I am.
Doctor: Let's get this contract signed and work on your position on the team.

Lesson: The doctor got the covenant not to compete by pushing his opponent's buttons and attacking around his opponent's flank. He avoided a frontal assault and did not make any take it or leave it demands that may have backfired.

Eliminating the Possibility of Deadlock

The best way to deal with the specter of deadlock is to eliminate it. If you can get your opponent to agree that deadlock is not an option, you have gone a long way to eliminate the possibility of deadlock. This requires recognition by both parties that they *need* to avoid deadlock and reach an agreement. The sophisticated physician negotiator will plant the seeds for this type of commitment early on in the negotiation in case it is needed later.

Example 10.7 Mutual agreement to avoid deadlock
Doctor: Are you really committed to reaching an agreement on the terms of this contract?
Opponent: I have the same level of commitment to reaching an agreement that you have.
Doctor: I am willing to cancel the rest of the day and my dinner plans and agree to stay in this room with you until we reach an agreement.
Opponent: Agreed. Let's take five minutes to make some calls and get back to work.

Lesson: The agreement to avoid deadlock was made well in advance. Although this agreement is not binding, it will help avoid deadlock. This commitment to stay in the room until an agreement is reached is a major concession—both sides are tacitly agreeing to:

- be reasonable,
- not give up,
- make concessions, and
- do everything possible to reach a negotiated agreement.

If your opponent refuses to commit to staying until an agreement is reached, he is saying that he:

- is not that interested in reaching an agreement,
- may not make any additional concessions, and
- "needs" the agreement less than you do.

Example 10.8 Get your opponent to buy into the concept of closure
Doctor: Nancy, we have been negotiating for two hours. You have looked at your watch four times and taken three calls on your cell phone. Are you sure you have time to reach a fair agreement *today?*
Opponent: That's why I came to your office—to reach an agreement.

Doctor: I am willing to cancel out and agree to stay in this room until we reach an agreement.
Opponent: Agreed. Let's take five minutes.

Lesson: The opponent has been positioned to buy into the concept of closure.

CHANGE
Physicians need to recognize when a negotiation is heading for unwanted deadlock. You can use change to avoid deadlock. A change in the timeframe, location, goals, negotiator, and type of negotiation can help avoid unwanted deadlock.

Example 10.9 Reconvening later can help to avoid or break deadlock
Doctor: It doesn't look like we will be able to give each one of the issues you raised adequate discussion time today. I suggest that we schedule another session to complete the job so we are not rushed.
Opponent: Agreed. How does Tuesday at 2:00 P.M. work for you?

Lesson: Putting the issue over to another negotiating session is one way to avoid a deadlock. You and your opponent may have different views during the new session. In addition, circumstances for either party may have changed in the interim. Giving the parties time to calm down and come up with alternatives can be effective.

Example 10.10 Venue change may facilitate the negotiation
Doctor: I feel uncomfortable in this setting. Your staff keeps interrupting us and the noise….What if we continue this in a nice, quiet, neutral environment? I could call and get us a conference room two blocks from here where we will not be interrupted. I think we will make more progress over there.
Prospective employer: (reluctantly) Well, let me pack up my stuff and tell my staff where I will be.

Lesson: The change of location may help facilitate the negotiation.

Part of being a flexible negotiator is being able to roll with the punches. If it becomes apparent that you will not be able to reach the goal you originally intended, you may want to modify your goal so as not to come away empty handed. *Caution:* Do not fall into the trap of being so invested in the negotiation process that you agree to almost anything to avoid coming away without a deal. (See pages 101–3 on investment.) There is nothing wrong, however, with modifying or scaling back your goal so long as the agreement reached is still favorable to you.

Example 10.11 A little flexibility helps avoid deadlock
Doctor: What we are looking for is $24,000 a year to write and edit your new medical-legal newsletter.
Publisher: We can't commit that kind of money. What if the newsletter does not take off?
Doctor: We are confident it will do well. It will fill a much-needed niche. We will agree to write and edit the newsletter on a monthly basis for $2,000 a month with a 60-day notice to discontinue.
Publisher: Make it a 30-day notice to discontinue and you have a deal.

Lesson: The doctor employed the technique of gradualism to salvage a deal headed toward deadlock. While she didn't achieve her original goal, she did achieve favorable terms. Many times if you can start working together on a smaller scale the relationship can later be expanded. Once the newsletter catches on, another attempt can be made to get a longer commitment.

Sometimes negotiation deadlock can be broken by employing a new negotiator. This technique requires an admission that someone else may be more likely to avoid deadlock. An admission that they may not be the best person to achieve a favorable agreement is difficult for many physicians. You must recognize that passing a negotiation to a partner or colleague is not an admission of failure. When there is someone else in a better position to score, it is time to pass the ball. Sometimes the mere suggestion that you may have to change negotiators can itself be used to help avoid a deadlock. Your opponent will be concerned with having to start over and/or dealing with someone who is even more difficult.

Example 10.12 Switching negotiators may facilitate the negotiation
Doctor: We are not really making any progress, are we?
Computer salesperson: We are not. I have tried to explain to you the merits…cost savings…how the system will work for you and not cost you….
Doctor: The problem is that I am probably not the right person to talk to. Let me get Dr. Patton. You two will be able to talk "computerese" without much of the translating you were doing for me.
Computer salesperson: Is she available now?

Lesson: Deadlock has been avoided. Dr. Patton's computer knowledge may help facilitate the process. The doctor was sophisticated enough to realize that turning the process over to Dr. Patton may be helpful and should not be seen as a sign of failure.

Example 10.13 Raising the possibility of passing things off to a different negotiator helps break deadlock
Doctor: I know we have been at this for three hours, but the bottom line is that the $74,000 price is a sticking point.
Computer salesperson: That's the best we can do.
Doctor: Maybe I am completely off-base here. You might be better off if you start *fresh* with my partner, Dr. Hardass. She knows a lot about computers. She is tough but fair. Don't be put off by her abrasive manner….
Computer salesperson: I would rather resolve this with you right now. If I made a call and knocked 10% off the top….

Lesson: The very mention of starting over with a new negotiator has strengthened the doctor's position.

To avoid deadlock, the sophisticated physician negotiator will rapidly change the type of negotiation while it is in progress. Changing a competitive negotiation into a cooperative one is particularly helpful. (See pages 10–16 on competitive and cooperative negotiations.)

Example 10.14 Transforming a competitive negotiation into a cooperative one can help break deadlock

Doctor: Let's forget about my demands for a moment and concentrate on what additional items, terms, or conditions we could add or modify to make this a win-win situation for both of us. Let's stop discussing how to split up the pie and let's concentrate on making a bigger pie where there is plenty for both of us. What do you say?

Opponent: It sounds good to me. If you could....

Lesson: The doctor changed a competitive negotiation to a cooperative one to avoid an unwanted deadlock.

Going Off the Record

One effective technique to avoid deadlock is to go off the record to get more candid assessments of how parties might be willing to modify their positions. Negotiators often fear that if they make a concession, they will get nothing in return and, essentially, end up bargaining against themselves. This can prevent them from making the concessions necessary to avoid deadlock.

By "going off the record," each party can feel the other party out without committing to the concessions.

Example 10.15 Going off the record helps break deadlock

Doctor: I understand that you cannot offer more than $160,000 to settle this claim and I can't accept less than $200,000. Let's put our pens down and go off the record. No future mention of this discussion unless we can reach an agreement today.

Opponent: That's fine with me.

Doctor: Off the record, what could you pay to get this wrapped up today?

Opponent: This is *not* an offer.

Doctor: Understood.

Opponent: I could probably get $170,000 to wrap this up today.

Doctor: If you get $175,000 you have a deal.

Lesson: Going off the record and avoiding any formal offers or demands has broken the impasse and avoided deadlock. Once the fear of bargaining against oneself was removed, the parties quickly resolved their differences.

Conclusion

The successful physician negotiator does not fear deadlock. Instead, she uses the potential for deadlock as an offensive negotiation technique. The use of conciliatory language, flexibility, adequate room to negotiate, deadlines and ultimatums, eliminating the possibility of deadlock, and change are all methods to avoid or to move away from unwanted deadlock. Remember, you need to be prepared to walk away from a deal. This is particularly true when you have a better alternative, if the deal does not meet your needs, when you may be able to get a better agreement at a later time from your opponent, or when the deal violates your professional or personal morals or ethics. Under these circumstances, the deadlock is not unwanted and you should walk away from the proposed agreement.

Chapter 11 Using Controlled Emotions to Your Advantage

Executive Summary

- Control your emotions.
- An angry posture sometimes helps gain concessions because your opponent may (rightly or wrongly) believe that you are angry because he did something wrong.
- Appearing offended can also be used at strategic moments to gain concessions.
- Tap into your opponent's fears (for example, fear of failure) and use this to your advantage.

Introduction

Emotions can play a key role in negotiations. You need to understand how to use emotions to your advantage. Techniques using emotions include playing it cool, controlling anger, personalizing, and tapping into the fear or anxiety of an opponent. These techniques are discussed below.

Playing It Cool

You will sometimes be faced with an opponent who is getting agitated, screaming, or yelling. Your natural reaction is to assume that your opponent probably has a valid point or he wouldn't be screaming. This is a flawed assumption. You need to remember that just because someone is yelling and screaming does not mean that he is right.

It is equally important to try not to lose your temper during a negotiation. Losing your temper could easily result in your saying or doing something that you might later regret. If you feel you are getting close to the edge, ask for and take a break. (See page 80 and pages 201–2 on taking a break.)

Example 11.1 Threatening posture effective in gaining concession

Lawyer: (to doctor's assistant, talking in a loud, threatening voice) The doctor is in big trouble. I am in court. The case is coming up in one hour. The doctor did not fill out the medical-legal report. We ordered it two weeks ago. We will now lose the case. The client will have every right to look to the doctor for damages because of her failure to fill out the report.

Doctor's assistant: Is there anything we can do?

Lawyer: Yes, I will send the client over in a half hour to pick up the report. Get the doctor. Make her sit down and dictate the report and type it up. If you can give the client three copies I will try and postpone the case for one hour. This could solve the doctor's problem.
Doctor's assistant: Okay. We will get right on it. Sorry for the trouble.

Lesson: In this true example, the attorney had *not* previously sent the request to the doctor's office. The attorney used a loud and threatening manner to bully the doctor to help him. The moral of this example is that just because someone is yelling and screaming about a particular point in a negotiation does not make the person right.

DIFFUSING THE OPPONENT

When faced with an emotional opponent, you should attempt to sift through his emotions to the substance of his position. One technique for accomplishing this is to move the opponent from the general to the specific. This will focus the energy of the negotiation on the relevant issues and will help determine how justified, if at all, your opponent's strong emotions really are.

Example 11.2 Responding to anger by getting down to specifics
Opponent: (to doctor, yelling) Your proposal is outrageous. I should just get up and walk out of here. I have never been so insulted in all of my professional career.
Doctor: (in control) I can see you are not happy. Let's take the four key points one at a time and see if we can't get some closure. Okay, on issue number 1….

Lesson: What the doctor is really trying to drive home is that as long as the opponent is yelling and screaming, he can't "hear" her. By moving to the specifics, he can determine if his opponent's anger is at all justified.

Controlling Your Anger

Emotions that are released in a calculated and controlled manner can be helpful. When you feel that your opponent has crossed the line and said something totally inappropriate, it is legitimate for you to get angry. The key is not to go off the deep end with your anger. If you do, you could reveal damaging information or say something that would permanently destroy your working relationship with your opponent.

Example 11.3 Used at the right time, controlled anger gains concessions
Colleague: The reason we are having financial trouble is because of questionable medical competency.
Doctor: That's bullshit and you know it. I don't have to take this shit. How dare you question my competency.
Colleague: I'm sorry, I didn't mean to imply that you weren't competent. Look, we'll find the money for your raise. Again, my deepest apologies.

Lesson: The doctor has used controlled anger to pounce on a point. This use of anger may help him gain power in, and seize the momentum of, the negotiation.

Getting on Your High Horse

Occasionally, you may be faced with an opponent who has said or done something so out of bounds that you are justifiably more than upset. Your opponent will quickly realize that he has made a serious error and must fix the problem whatever the cost.

Example 11.4 Pointing out inappropriate remark gains the doctor power
Prospective employer representative: (to doctor) You will, of course, have four weeks of vacation time and whatever Jewish holidays you people are claiming now.
Doctor: I do not appreciate your anti-Semitic remark.
Prospective employer representative: I didn't mean to imply…what I meant was….

Lesson: When your opponent has made an intolerable remark (for example, something sexist, racist, or regarding your sexual preference), you should immediately point out to him that you will not tolerate such comments. Your opponent should immediately realize the legal and professional jeopardy that the remark has created. He will have to bend over backward apologizing, backpedaling, and, essentially, doing whatever it takes to make this serious problem go away.

Personalize the Negotiation

Personalizing the negotiation may be helpful. People are generally nice and like helping other people out. On the other hand, people generally couldn't care less about helping out a corporation or other business entity. When you personalize the negotiation, you tap into your opponent's natural desire to help out another person. The successful physician negotiator attempts to make each negotiation personal, rather than a negotiation between corporate conglomerates. When this is done, you will be more likely to obtain concessions. If the person you are negotiating with likes you, then personalizing the negotiation is that much more effective. (See page 72 on your opponent liking you.) Note that there is nothing wrong with asking for a personal favor as long as you do not overuse this technique. Consider the following examples.

Example 11.5 Getting the other person to feel sorry for you
Doctor: I will get to the chart dictation as soon as I can.
Medical records charge nurse: You don't really appreciate the situation. I need this done *today*. My credibility is on the line.
Doctor: You are taking this much too personally.
Medical records charge nurse: I have to take it personally. My job is on the line.
Doctor: I'll see what I can do.

Lesson: People generally do not like to see other people lose their jobs. This is because they would never want to lose their own job and thus have compassion for the other person. Here the nurse effectively personalized the negotiation and used the doctor's compassion to her advantage.

Example 11.6 Requesting a concession as a personal favor
Doctor: (to long-time opponent) Just this one time, as a personal favor, I need you to…I will not forget it.

Lesson: The opponent may very well concede. He may be thinking of the time in the future when he really needs to get something for himself. At that point he may be asking for a quid pro quo.

Example 11.7 Mentioning to opponent that you might get in trouble with your boss unless you get a concession
Doctor: I need to obtain the change in the lease that we talked about.
Leasing agent: We did not officially offer that change.
Doctor: Based on your representation, I already told my employer about the change. If you backpedal on this, I am in big trouble.
Leasing agent: Let me work something out.

Lesson: Everyone can relate to getting in trouble with a boss. Noting your situation can gain you sympathy and concessions from your opponent.

Tapping into Fear or Anxiety

You should use your opponents' fears and anxieties against them. Before you can use these fears, you need to understand what they are. (See page 85 on fear and anxiety.) Common fears you can use against your opponent are the fears of failure, loss, and embarrassment. Consider the following examples.

Example 11.8 Tapping into your opponent's fears
Doctor: What are you going to do if we are not able to negotiate an agreement on the terms of your contract?
Prospective employee: Well, I guess I will continue to send out my CV. I do have some other feelers out there.

Lesson: The negative consequences of failure have been put in the mind of the opponent. This should make it psychologically easier for the opponent to grant concessions to avoid failure. Even asking innocent questions such as, "What will happen if you don't bring back an agreement?" can raise the anxiety level of your opponent.

Example 11.9 Psyching out your opponent
Doctor: How many claims are you handling currently?
Insurance adjuster: Two hundred forty-seven.
Doctor: (sympathetically) That's a lot of claims. With that many cases there must be a lot of pressure to resolve them and move on.
Insurance adjuster: I get seven to ten new ones each week.

Doctor: It's Friday. How many have you adjusted this week?
Insurance adjuster: Three, not counting this one.
Doctor: You are losing ground. My good friend was an adjuster. I went up to see him one day and the company had a big GOYA chart on the wall.
Insurance adjuster: GOYA?
Doctor: Yes, Get Off Your Ass (GOYA). They charted the number of cases each adjuster settled and posted the results. Should we try and resolve my claim or should I send a note to the company and tell them we couldn't work it out and put it into litigation?
Insurance adjuster: Let's keep talking.

Lesson: In some cases, the fear or anxiety is not expressly mentioned, but it is subtly talked around. This can be even more effective because it may be harder for your opponent to detect that she is the target of a negotiation tactic. When faced with the specter of real or imagined failure, most opponents will go the extra mile to avoid such failure. The savvy physician negotiator understands when and how to use this to her advantage.

Example 11.10 Inexperienced negotiator makes huge mistake by trusting his opponent
Experienced attorney: This is a straightforward workers' compensation case. The claimant fell at work, triggering her multiple sclerosis. Here are the medical reports on causation and disability.
Novice: Which side of the courtroom should I stand on?
Experienced attorney: Here on the left, farthest from the workers' compensation judge. One point—because you do not have a medical report, when she asks you what you have to say, I wouldn't say too much, just that you are opposing the request, and sit down. You don't want to embarrass yourself.
Novice: Thank you.

Lesson: The fear of being embarrassed is one that can be used effectively by the sophisticated physician negotiator. Your opponent, whether a doctor, lawyer, or other professional, especially if he is inexperienced, may go to great lengths to avoid personal or professional embarrassment. This example is true. The injured worker was placed on workers' compensation for multiple sclerosis due to the trauma of a fall. The fear of embarrassment played a significant role in the pre-hearing negotiation between the experienced and the novice attorney. This type of negotiation is played out routinely at the expense of inexperienced or novice negotiators.

Conclusion

You need to be able to play it cool and control your emotions. You should understand that just because people are yelling and screaming does not make them right. Take your opponent's emotional objections from the general to the specific and use the controlled anger technique when appropriate. Personalize the negotiation and occasionally ask for personal favors. Do not be afraid to get emotional when it is appropriate and can be used to your advantage. Finally, understand and capitalize on your opponent's fears and anxieties.

Chapter 12 Telephone Negotiations

Executive Summary

- Do not allow yourself to negotiate on the phone unless you are totally prepared. Tell your opponent to put it in writing or that you will call him back.
- Prepare just as diligently for a telephone negotiation as you would for one in person.
- Initiate the call—you just might catch your opponent off guard.
- Actively listen to your opponent. That's all the information you will be getting.
- Take good notes and send confirmation letters.

Introduction

Many, if not most, of your negotiations will be conducted over the telephone. There are methods that you can use to gain an advantage during telephone negotiations. These methods include focusing, preparing, initiating the call, setting the agenda, listening for auditory feedback, taking notes, and sending the confirmation letter. Each of these methods is discussed below.

Concentrate and Focus

Telephone negotiations can be just as important, in some cases more important, as in-person negotiations. A negotiation that may have taken hours in person may take only minutes or even seconds over the phone. When things happen that quickly, you really need to force yourself to focus on the negotiation. You must recognize the importance of focusing on your telephone negotiation. Failure to do so can be disastrous.

Example 12.1 Doctor allows himself to be successfully ambushed on the phone

Computer salesperson: Doctor, the service agreement for your computer equipment is running out at the end of the week. Should I put you down for the two-year renewal? The cost is the same.

Doctor: Fine, send along the paperwork.

Lesson: The accelerated pace of phone call negotiations can result in the physician not negotiating at all. The telephone negotiation is the method most used to ambush the unaware or unprepared physician negotiator (see pages 23–27 on ambush negotiations). Even when one or both of the parties has the time to negotiate (see pages 6–7 on time), the result of these "quickie" negotiations can be extreme—with one party winning and one party losing.

Example 12.2 Doctor pays the price when he does not carefully consider telephone negotiation
Doctor: Busy?
Colleague: Swamped!
Doctor: Me, too. I will be lucky if I get out of here by 8:00 tonight. Did you look at our proposed lease? $3,500 a month and you are in our new building.
Colleague: $2,000 a month for year one and $2,500 for years two to four.
Doctor: Done. I will have my attorney send over the lease.

Lesson: Here the doctor conducted a negotiation involving thousands of dollars in seconds. The irony is that this same physician may spend more time comparing and shopping for a $75 dress shirt than he would spend in the lease negotiation. Had he taken more time, he would have saved a substantial amount of money.

<u>Prepare</u>

Telephone negotiations happen quickly. When dealing with such fast-paced negotiations, you need to be fully prepared and organized. You need to have your facts, figures, files, research notes, documents, computer, calculator, and other materials organized and ready to use quickly and efficiently. Many negotiations are lost due to the inability of the negotiator to put her hands on a crucial file or piece of paper.

Example 12.3 Poor preparation hurts the doctor's position
Provider: We can offer you $2,400 for your outstanding bill of $4,900. This is a one-time offer. Is that acceptable?
Doctor: That's less than 50%! Joanne, can you get me that file? This was a difficult and complex case!

Provider: Doctor, we have been through this with your billing clerk already. Your provider agreement clearly states….
Doctor: (rummaging through file) I think we called you for authorization before….If I could only find that phone message. These little pink slips drive me crazy!

Lesson: The doctor needed to be better prepared. If he had been, he would have had the information readily available. If he cannot find the missing document, he should suspend the negotiation and call the provider back after he locates it.

Initiate the Call

The party who originates the call is at a distinct advantage. She has time to prepare, is not taken off guard, can prepare a checklist, and can organize the key files and documents. The initiating party can select a quiet time and call from a distraction-free place. If you initiate the call and catch your opponent "cold," your opponent's surprise and lack of preparation can work in your favor. You can also use your initiation of the call as an opportunity to set the agenda and thus control the issues to be discussed.

You will need to be able to defend against this tactic when you receive a call. First, you need to listen carefully for the purpose of the call. Once you recognize the call as the start of a negotiation, you should obtain as much information as you can. You should then call the party back at a convenient time after you have properly prepared yourself.

Example 12.4 Properly responding to an ambush negotiation
Opponent: (on telephone) Hi, Doctor. How are you?
Doctor: (doing two things in addition to talking on phone) Busy.
Opponent: Let me get right to business then. I am calling to discuss the buyout provision of your equipment lease.
Doctor: When is the lease up? How much is the proposed buyout in the contract? What specifically are you looking for?
Opponent: The lease is up at the end of the month. There is no specific amount mentioned, just the "resale value," but we are looking for $24,000 and the equipment is yours free and clear!

Doctor: I will get back to you later this week. I will pull my file, talk to my office manager, and see if we even want this equipment. It is, after all, three years old. I will call you.

Lesson: The doctor recognized the importance of the pending telephone negotiation. She correctly gathered as much information as possible and stated that she would call her opponent back.

Example 12.5 Initiating the call is advantageous to the doctor
Doctor: (to prospective employee) This is a call to see if we can wrap up the loose ends of you taking the position. I need to get closure on three issues: salary, starting date, and hospital coverage. On the salary, the offer on the table is $160,000. Is that acceptable?

Lesson: The doctor did not ask if this was a convenient time, nor did he ask if the prospective employee had any issues to add to the agenda. The doctor used his initiation of the call as a way to control the agenda and resolve the issues that he wanted to resolve.

Listen for Auditory Feedback

Telephone negotiations do not allow you to read your opponent's body language (see pages 64–67 on body language) and other nonverbal communication. Many opponents will find it much easier to say no over the phone than in person. This is the reason why some experts recommend limiting your phone negotiations to those situations where you suspect that *you* will be saying no. The realities of the workplace make it difficult, if not impossible, to avoid telephone negotiations. Few, if any, physicians are able to fly 3,000 miles to conduct a ten-minute negotiation in person.

The only information you receive from your opponent during a telephone negotiation is auditory in nature. You need to be very sensitive to this auditory feedback. Active listening is required. (See pages 58–68 on active listening.) The pitch, tone, volume, pauses, topic selection, silences, and other auditory cues are your only sources of information. Some experienced negotiators go so far as to close their eyes so they can better concentrate on what is and is not being verbalized.

Example 12.6 Active listening used during a telephone negotiation
Doctor: How does that proposal sound?
Opponent: Well, generally, it sounds good. (long pause)
Doctor: I sense your hesitation. Tell me what you are concerned about. As you know, we are looking for a long-term business relationship. We want to give you the best agreement we can.
Opponent: I have three major concerns.

Lesson: The doctor sensed her opponent's concerns. She also heard the important verbal leak "generally, it sounds good." This is important because the doctor is looking for a win-win deal that will serve as the basis of a long-standing relationship.

Take Notes and Send Confirmation Letters

Telephone negotiations can result in many misunderstandings between the parties. You will need to take legible, comprehensive notes during telephone negotiations. To avoid problems with handwriting, it is best to have your notes typed/transcribed after the negotiation. Taking notes is also an opportunity for you to clarify your opponent's proposal during the negotiation.

You should consider turning your written notes into a memorandum of agreement and sending it to your opponent after the negotiation. The drafting of this memorandum is yet another opportunity to specify the terms of the deal, remove (and control) any ambiguities, and ensure that any oral assurances are specified in writing. For complex or significant agreements or those involving substantial amounts of money, you should consult with counsel *before* sending out the memorandum or agreement.

Example 12.7 Summarizing the offer so that there are no misunderstandings
Doctor: (to opponent) I want to write this down correctly. As I understand it, what you are offering is two years of free service and, if we agree today, you will throw in….Is that correct?

Lesson: By summarizing his opponent's proposal, the physician has eliminated possible ambiguities and pinned down his opponent.

Conclusion

Savvy physician negotiators recognize the importance at excelling at telephone negotiations. These physicians recognize the large amount of negotiating that takes place over the phone. They are able to quickly "diagnose" a negotiation call, obtain the information they need, and then call the opponent back when they are prepared and have time to negotiate.

It is critical to recognize the need to prepare for telephone negotiations as if they were important face-to-face negotiations. Initiating the phone call can be helpful. It is important not to negotiate when you are not prepared. You should have all your tools readily accessible, set the agenda, and listen actively for auditory feedback. To make sure that there are no ambiguities, your notes should be converted into a letter to be sent to your opponent after the negotiation.

Chapter 13 E-mail Negotiations

Executive Summary

- E-mail negotiations may go faster than those on the telephone.
- E-mail negotiations allow you to bypass gatekeepers.
- Use e-mail requests to generate multiple offers and thus gain power in the negotiation.
- Resist the temptation to reply to your opponent without carefully considering your reply.
- Beware that your negotiations can be easily forwarded to other persons—they are not confidential.
- When dealing with a "techie," change the mode of negotiations from e-mail to telephone (where the techie may be less comfortable).

Introduction

With increasing frequency, physicians may be called upon to negotiate with the use of e-mail. Similar to telephone negotiations, e-mail negotiating has its own advantages and disadvantages.

Advantages of E-mail Negotiations

The advantages of negotiating by e-mail include the following.

- Speed
- Direct access to party
- Specific (in writing)
- Encourages prompt and direct response
- Easy to "interrupt" party with an instant message
- Easy to send multiple requests
- Ability to utilize 24/7
- Easy to have multiple "back and forths" quickly without phone tag

Speed

E-mail negotiations are the fastest negotiations in which the physician will be involved. An e-mail is sent in the blink of an eye and a prompt or almost instantaneous reply is expected.

Example 13.1 E-mail negotiations are easy to initiate
Opponent to doctor (e-mail):
Doctor Jones,
Will you be able to speak again this year at the National Conference on Evidence-Based Medicine?
Tom

The above e-mail takes less than one minute to send to the doctor. By custom, most persons sending e-mail expect a prompt reply.

Example 13.2 Prompting a nonresponsive adversary
Opponent to doctor (e-mail):
Bill—
Did you get my e-mail I sent this morning? I am wondering because I did not hear back yet.
Tom

Lesson: Due to the speed of e-mail negotiations, physician negotiators should take care in what they send and should take a time out before they send any e-mail for negotiating purposes. The savvy physician negotiator looks for potential information leaks in e-mails.

DIRECT ACCESS TO OPPONENTS

With e-mail negotiating the physician does not have to deal with the opponent's gatekeeper or assistant. Once the physician has the e-mail address of the opponent, she has direct access.

Example 13.3 E-mails allow you to bypass gatekeepers
Doctor to opponent (e-mail):
Ms. Johnson,
I have been unable to get through your formidable gatekeeper and her assistant on the phone. I would like to speak to you about a new medical video. As you recall, we met at the Las Vegas conference last week and you told me to give you a call.

Thank you,
Dr. Fred Simpson

Lesson: The physician negotiator recognizes the tremendous potential advantage of being able to reach otherwise inaccessible opponents directly by e-mail. Cell phones share this advantage.

SPECIFIC (IN WRITING)
One of the distinct advantages of negotiation e-mails is that because they are in writing they are usually specific and unambiguous. The "misunderstandings" that frequently result from phone negotiations can be avoided.

Example 13.4 E-mail negotiations are usually more precise and can help prevent misunderstandings
Doctor to opponent (e-mail):
Tom—
I will accept your offer of employment as we discussed if I receive $165,000 salary for year one and $175,000 for year two. Do we have an agreement?

Thank you,
Dr. Steven Jobs

Lesson: The precision of e-mail negotiations can be a distinct advantage to firm up loose ends and to avoid any misunderstandings.

ENCOURAGES A PROMPT REPLY
Due to the speed of e-mail, Internet etiquette encourages prompt replies.

Example 13.5 E-mail negotiations may go faster than other types
Doctor to opponent (e-mail):
Tom,
I will accept your offer of employment as we discussed if I receive $165,000 salary for year one and $175,000 for year two. Do we have an agreement?

Thank you,
Dr. Steven Jobs

Reply (45 seconds later):
Done—please drop by Monday to sign the employment agreement.

Lesson: The physician negotiator recognizes that if he wants a prompt reply, he may want to use a negotiation e-mail. The savvy negotiator uses the e-mail to obtain a reply sent without the normal thought and caution.

EASY TO INTERRUPT WITH INSTANT MESSAGES
In certain circumstances, the negotiator will instant message the busy opponent. He hopes to get an even more rapid reply that may be sent with very little thought.

EASY TO SEND MULTIPLE REQUESTS
The negotiator may start the negotiating process with an e-mail to multiple parties as a method to get quick and easy feedback about the possibility of doing business.

Example 13.6 Sending out feeler e-mails to multiple vendors generates power
Physician e-mail to multiple hotels:
I have been selected to head the *2009 National Physician Executive Conference* to be held in Orlando, Florida on 1/7/2009 through 1/10/2009. We anticipate having 1,000 attendees. Please advise if you have meeting space (classroom style) and the availability of 500 sleeping rooms.

Thank you,
Dr. Francis Gray

Lesson: By using multiple e-mails, the negotiator can quickly get feedback before sending formal requests for proposals (RFPs) to potential opponents. The negotiator may or may not let the recipients know who else has been targeted.

ABILITY TO UTILIZE E-MAIL 24/7
With the advent of professionals checking their e-mail almost constantly at home, on the road, and on their PDAs, negotiation e-mails can reach an opponent at night, weekends, holidays, while she is traveling, etc. This

can help to speed the process. Workaholic opponents are easily identified by their 4:30 A.M. responses on holidays or weekends.

QUICK AND EASY "BACK AND FORTH" WITHOUT PHONE TAG

One of the key advantages to negotiation e-mails is their rapid give and take without the inefficiency of phone tag.

Example 13.7 Chief advantage of e-mail is that it avoids phone tag

Opponent's e-mail to doctor:

Have you decided if you would like to develop the CD-ROM we discussed?

Tom

Opponent's e-mail reply:

Tom,

I am interested, but am concerned about the 15% royalty offered.

Sandra

Ensuing e-mail negotiation…

Sandra,

What if we guarantee you a minimum of $25,000 against the 15% royalty?

Tom

Tom,

Make it a $30,000 guarantee and you have got me.

Sandra

Sandra,

Done. $30,000 guaranteed minimum against a 15% royalty contract to follow.

Thank you,

Tom

Lesson: The multiple back and forth that could have taken days or weeks with the delay of phone tag for busy professionals can be accomplished in a few hours with e-mail negotiations.

Disadvantages of E-Mail Negotiations

The disadvantages of negotiating by e-mail are the flip side of the advantages. These include:

- no buffer (i.e., staff/administrative assistant),
- tempting to reply without thinking it through,
- easy to get caught in ambush negotiation,
- lack of confidentiality (easy to forward to multiple parties instantly), and
- e-mails not getting through because of spam filters, mistyped addresses, or accidental deletion.

No Buffer

The physician can expect, and should be prepared for, negotiating e-mails that do not go through her normal gatekeepers. These can be annoying and may come at inopportune times.

Lesson: To reinstitute your gatekeeping system, have your assistant reply to the e-mail. You can then channel the negotiation, slow it down, and give yourself more time to respond when you are properly prepared.

Reply without Thinking

The most serious danger for the physician negotiator is to try and clear his 172 e-mails and reply in haste to a negotiation e-mail. This quick and easy "fix" can cost the negotiator thousands of dollars and/or countless hours of unnecessary and unproductive work.

Example 13.8 Doctor's quick reply to an e-mail puts him at a disadvantage

Publisher's e-mail to doctor:

Dr.—

We need the supplement to your textbook by 2/17/2008. Please send it to me in Word. Please acknowledge that you will be able to meet the deadline.

Alice

Alice,
No problem—will do.
Tom

Lesson: By agreeing without really thinking it through, the physician has committed to 40 hours of work. The savvy physician negotiator is *not* rushed by a negotiation e-mail and will respond only after additional thought and details are provided.

Example 13.9 Doctor who thinks before responding to e-mail makes out much better
Doctor's e-mail reply to publisher:
Alice,
Before I commit to another supplement:

1. I need a $5,000 cash advance to hire a research assistant and
2. I will also need a 20% royalty to make it worth my while.

Please advise.
Tom

Easy to Get Caught in an Ambush Negotiation

Invariably, the physician will review negotiation e-mails when she is very busy. If she replies instantly, she has been ambushed.

Lesson: The authors recommend that in the above instance the physician print the incoming e-mail and reply to it only after careful consideration.

Lack of Confidentiality

One of the very real dangers of e-mail negotiations is the ability of your opponent to quickly, easily, and widely disseminate your reply. This can be very damaging to the physician, to her bargaining position, and, in some extreme cases, to her career.

Example 13.10 Doctor should have kept in mind that anything he writes can be used against him

Attorney's e-mail to doctor:

Doctor Spring,

Would you like to discuss reviewing medical records for our plaintiff's firm? Please advise.

Attorney Donald Mastie

Doctor's reply:

Attorney Mastie,

I limit my work to defense firms as I do not like to deal with plaintiffs, their phony injuries, and their attorneys.

Doctor Spring

Lesson: When the attorney disseminates the above reply, the doctor's career as an impartial medical expert may be seriously affected.

Recommendations

The authors recommend that when physicians sense they are, or know they are going to be, involved in an e-mail negotiation, they do the following.

- Make sure that the person they will be negotiating with has the authority to make a deal (see pages 36–44 on authority).
- Diagnose the negotiation as early as possible (see pages 110–11 on when a negotiation has started).
- Do *not* respond immediately or impulsively. A physician should print the e-mail and respond to it only after he has had the time to think it through and has properly prepared for the negotiation.

Demand Confidentiality

Physicians should *always* be concerned about their replies being widely disseminated. Savvy physician negotiators demand that their replies be treated confidentially. Despite the above, they always assume that their replies will be disseminated. They should *never* say anything in writing that could come back to haunt them.

Change Mode of Negotiation

Physician negotiators recognize that many of their opponents specifically choose e-mail to negotiate with because

- they are not comfortable talking to people and
- they do not do well with confrontation.

This is an opportunity. Wise physician negotiators make the most of this opportunity by changing the mode of the negotiation.

Example 13.11 An opponent who initiates a negotiation by e-mail may be uncomfortable negotiating in person or over the phone

Opponent's e-mail to Dr. Johnson:

Dr. Johnson,

We would like you to speak at our conference on 7/14/08 in Tampa, Florida, on Disaster Planning. Are you available and would you like to do this?

Thank you,

Armond Cuttone

Dr. Johnson's phone call to opponent: This is Dr. Johnson, you sent me an e-mail about speaking at....

Opponent: How did you get my phone number? I mean, I expected....

Dr. Johnson: I just Googled you. Is this a good time to talk about your proposal?

Opponent: Well—could we do it by e-mail? I am more...I mean, it could be more efficient....

Dr. Johnson: No. If you don't want to discuss it with me....

Opponent: No, no. I guess we could talk about it now.

Lesson: The experienced physician negotiator sensed that his opponent would be very uncomfortable with a surprise (ambush) phone call and used it to his great advantage.

Savvy physician negotiators change the mode of their reply to gain a tactical advantage.

Example 13.12 Changing the negotiation's mode to snail mail smokes out opponent

Opponent's e-mail to physician:

Dr. Howard, will you be able to do the consulting work we have discussed?

Dr. Howard's reply:

I mailed you a detailed letter this A.M. with my thoughts. Thank you.

Opponent:

You mailed me a letter? That will take about a week to get out here. Perhaps I didn't sufficiently impress you with the time constraints here....

Lesson: By changing the mode of negotiation and using snail mail to reply to e-mail, the doctor has:

- thrown the opponent off stride,
- learned that the opponent is somewhat desperate, and
- determined that he (and not the opponent) has the real power in this negotiation.

Changing the mode of negotiation can be a very effective and revealing negotiating tactic when replying to an e-mail negotiation.

Conclusion

E-mail negotiation presents unique challenges and opportunities. The physicians who recognize and respond to these will get the best results from their negotiations.

Chapter 14 Defeating Your Opponent's Tactics

Introduction

Physicians must be able to "diagnose" and "treat" the myriad of negotiation tactics used by their opponents. Treatment is possible only when you are properly prepared. This chapter is designed to help you prepare to deal with your opponent's tactics. The negotiation tactics most frequently employed against physicians are discussed in the following sections.

Tactic 1: Let's Split the Difference

Diagnosis

This tactic is usually fairly simple to diagnose. The proponent will suggest, "in the spirit of fairness and equity," that each side offer an equal concession in order to achieve a rapid conclusion to the negotiation. This request has a lot of surface appeal and is difficult, if not impossible, for most physician negotiators to resist. In the end, the negotiation tactic of an equal compromise is difficult to turn down. More money and other negotiables are lost due to this tactic than almost any other single tactic. When your opponent says to you, "Let's split the difference," she is really saying, "I want a 50% concession." Because this is a request for a major concession, it should be considered as carefully and cautiously as any other request for a concession. (See pages 127–35 on concessions.) The response you make to the tactic will usually determine the outcome of the negotiation.

Example 14.1 Splitting the difference

Opponent: (to doctor) Doctor, you were looking for $30,000 for your boat. I offered you $20,000. Let's split the difference and call it $25,000.

Lesson: This statement needs to be diagnosed as a demand for a 50% concession. Such a demand needs a careful response.

Treatment

A strong, reassured response can effectively neutralize the tactic without harming an existing or anticipated long-term relationship.

Example 14.2 Effectively responding with believable justification as to why doctor cannot split the difference

Doctor: (to prospective new doctor) Fred, we can meet most of your terms with regard to insurance, coverage, staff, hours, and vacations. The final stumbling block is starting salary. You asked for $140,000 and we offered $120,000. We are willing to meet you halfway and I am authorized to split the difference and go to $130,000. (offers his hand)

Fred: I wish I could split the difference, but I just cannot afford to with student loans, mortgages, a child on the way….We did our budget….

Lesson: This was a direct rebuttal. It was possible because Fred was prepared to justify why he *required* $140,000. Fred refused to give in but has left himself very little room to negotiate. The sophisticated physician negotiator would have anticipated the use of this tactic and would have left himself more room to negotiate. (See page 127 on room to negotiate.)

Example 14.3 Ready for follow-up after refusing to split the difference

Doctor: (to prospective employee) Fred, I certainly understand about obligations. I do have to go back to my partners. If you can't split the difference, what can you do for us?

Fred: We might be able to make it on $138,000. I would want to check with my spouse before committing to that.

Lesson: The experienced physician negotiator reasonably anticipates the follow-up request after a refusal to split the difference. The concession he offered was less than what his opponent demanded. The above response/concession may be made in order to foster a new long-term relationship and/or to get closure on the negotiation.

Example 14.4 Standing firm is risky

Fred: I probably did not make myself clear and I am sorry. I cannot afford to posture or play games. The $140,000 is my bottom line. I know for the practice $2,000 or $3,000 is not a lot of money, but for us, it is make it or break it.

Lesson: Standing firm (with adequate justification) is an option. Because you have not left yourself any room to negotiate, you should only employ this tactic if you are prepared to walk away from the deal (that is, you have another offer on the table).

Tactic 2: Take It or Leave It

Diagnosis

This is usually a simple tactic to recognize. The proponent will make an offer or demand and make it clear that this is her best offer and it is not negotiable. While the precise words "take it or leave it" are not always used, the result is the same—there is no room to negotiate.

When faced with this hardball tactic, many physicians will accept the dictated terms and not challenge their opponent's rationale or reasonableness. (See pages xx–xxi on the world's quickest negotiation.) You should not cave in to this type of pressure no matter how strongly this tactic is expressed. You should keep in mind your other alternatives. Also, please consider if you'd really want to have a long-term relationship with someone who treated you like this.

Example 14.5 Take it or leave it

Attorney: We are sorry to see that you have been sued for medical malpractice for an amount exceeding your coverage. We would be pleased to defend you. We will need a $10,000 retainer and our hourly rate will be $300 an hour. (See pages 207–23 on negotiating and retaining an attorney.)

Doctor: I would like to talk about the retainer and the hourly rate.

Attorney: (cutting her off, pleasant but firm) Our rates have been set by the management committee. They are nonnegotiable.

Lesson: The message in the above example is clear (although not expressed in these exact words): *Take it or leave it!*

Treatment

You will need to recognize that take it or leave it is a hardball tactic and respond accordingly. What your opponent is really saying is: "I have all the power in this negotiation and will do (and charge) whatever I want." The first thing you need to do is to evaluate the offer on its merits. You should not automatically accept or reject the offer. If you do not decide to reject it, you will need to neutralize the tactic. One good way to do this is to change the balance of power as quickly and as painlessly as possible. This can be accomplished by stressing the desire to establish a long-term relationship.

Example 14.6 Stressing the desire for a long-term relationship can soften many opponents' positions
Doctor: (to attorney) As I was starting to say, we are looking for a firm to represent doctors in my situation. I will be the first case. I will be reporting back to the association, which has many doctors in similar situations. We are looking for a contract with a firm where there is a modest retainer against time—$2,500—and hourly rates for paralegals, associates, and partners. Should I be talking to you about this or one of the senior partners?

Lesson: By stressing the desire to begin a long-term relationship, the doctor has gained power in the negotiation.

You will also need to be prepared to walk away. As we have seen, the ability and determination to just say no is an absolute requirement if you want to be a successful physician negotiator. *Before* you do walk away, however, you need to be sure of what your alternatives are.

Example 14.7 Preparation and options defeat take it or leave it
Attorney: We are sorry that you have been sued for medical malpractice for an amount exceeding your coverage. We would be pleased to defend you. We will need a $10,000 retainer and our hourly rate will be $300 an hour.
Doctor: I have contacted three of your competitors and they say they will only require a $2,500 retainer. Should I go with one of those firms?
Attorney: Well, if the retainer is a sticking point....

Lesson: By doing his homework before the negotiation, the doctor has vastly improved his bargaining power and is much less susceptible to the "take it or leave it" tactic.

Example 14.8 Being prepared to walk away builds power in negotiation

Salesman: We've been going over this for thirty minutes. The price is $5,000, take it or leave it.
Doctor: Thanks for your time, I'll leave it. I can get comparable equipment for less than that. Can you find your own way out?
Salesman: Well, I think we'll still be able to work something out, how about $4,500?

Lesson: You need to be prepared to "leave it." This doctor knew that she could get comparable equipment for less than $5,000 and was, therefore, empowered to decline her opponent's demand. Also, calling her opponent's bluff with the take it or leave it tactic was successful in gaining a major price concession. She was able to respond in this direct way *because she had alternatives.*

You should react to each take it or leave it proposal on its merits and not assume that just because it is the first offer, it is not a reasonable or fair one. You should recognize and capitalize on many situations in which you can avoid unwanted and/or protracted negotiations through the use of a fair preemptive offer at the start of a negotiation. This variation of the take it or leave it technique is particularly effective when used before a negotiation starts. Use of this technique will save you the trouble and uncertainty of lengthy negotiations and can help to build trust in long-term relationships.

Many savvy negotiators recognize the best way to avoid having to give many concessions is to avoid a negotiation altogether. The person with the power in any situation frequently can state the price or the terms in a friendly but firm tone, making it clear there will be no negotiation. This deceptively simple tactic can be extremely effective when done well.

Example 14.9 A polite form of take it or leave it

Opponent: We would like you to write a 1,200-word article for our new textbook. As an author you will be entitled to two free books and we will list your contact information so new clients can contact you directly.
Doctor: Well, I would like to retain copyright and what about….
Opponent: I am sorry. The terms are as expressed in my e-mail. Because we already have 94 physician authors who have agreed, we

cannot start to change the terms now. We would love to have your article and you will be getting massive free publicity.

Lesson: The opponent here was nice but firm. The bottom line was no negotiation—essentially, take it or leave it with a little window dressing.

The person making the pitch for no negotiation may use arguments of precedent and legitimacy (see pages 103–5) to justify the fairness of the deal.

The savvy physician negotiator does not abuse his power and will not try to squeeze every penny out of his opponent. This is not the way to build loyalty or long-term relationships.

Example 14.10 The importance of not taking advantage of someone you will need to work with on a long-term basis

New doctor: I need $150,000 to accept this position. I know I can do a great job.

Hiring partner: We agreed you will do a great job, but, as I stated before, we have never started anyone at more than $140,000. You understand the precedent and potential ill will. (pause) To make this happen I will recommend a $5,000 relocation payment to get you on board, how does that sound?

New doctor: Great. I really appreciate you going the extra mile for me.

Lesson: The hiring partner in the above example knew, or at least suspected, that he could get the new doctor for the $140,000. The "extra" $5,000 was, however, money well spent if it makes the new hire feel good about the negotiation and leaves him with new-found loyalty to his employer.

Example 14.11 Preemptive strike with generous offer avoids protracted negotiations

Doctor: You have done an excellent job these past ten months. Rather than wait for your annual review, we are going to raise your salary by 10% effective the first of the month.

Office manager: Thank you.

Lesson: This preemptive, fair but firm offer combines the element of surprise with a softer version of take it or leave it. Through its use, the doctor was able to avoid protracted negotiations, control the outcome, and build trust in her long-term relationship with her office manager.

Tactic 3: The Estimate: Ballpark Price

DIAGNOSIS

This tactic may be difficult to diagnose. It can be expressed in many ways and disguised quite successfully. Physicians, in their eagerness to help and desire to be liked, are particularly susceptible to this tactic. When this tactic is used, you will be asked for a rough estimate of the cost, time, and effort involved in a project soon to be a matter of negotiation. This rough estimate request is a very effective negotiation tactic. The proponent of the question is seeking the most crucial information of the negotiation; that is, the information to determine what is a fair price for the proposed work. Most importantly, the tactic traps you into setting a price without adequate thought or analysis. (See pages 23–27 on ambush negotiations.) You may be assured that your opponent is just looking for a rough estimate and that no one will hold you to the price or terms. *Do not fall into this trap.* Once you have given an estimated price, it may be very difficult, if not impossible, to distance yourself from that price. Even when you are able to move away from the original figure, it is unlikely that you will reach the result that could have been achieved had you not been tied to the estimate. That is why the savvy opponent will frequently push you hard for your estimate. Consider the following examples where this tactic is employed.

Example 14.12 Rough estimate requested
Opponent: (to doctor) Give me a rough estimate of how long it will take you to do the medical review for our CD-ROM project.

Example 14.13 Approximate charge
Publisher: (to doctor) Doctor, approximately how much would you charge to edit our medical newsletter?

Example 14.14 Ballpark figure
Insurer: (to doctor) Doctor, how difficult will it be for you to set up a protocol for our return-to-work program for our carpal tunnel syndrome employees?

Example 14.15 Agreeing to a price without a precise understanding of the scope of the work can be a costly mistake
Insurance company executive: We admire your work in occupational medicine. We know you pride yourself on your efficiency. I have files I would like you to review. It is the first of what we hope will be a lot of new work. I would like to send you the file to review.
Doctor: That would be fine.
Insurance company executive: Would $500 be reasonable?
Doctor: Yes, send it along. How many other files do you have?

One week later...
Doctor: A messenger just delivered your records. The box weighs 43 pounds. You never mentioned the voluminous nature of the case!
Insurer: You never asked.
Doctor: I can't review this file for $500 and do a good and thorough job.
Insurer: Well, Doctor, I already noted on the file that you agreed on $500. This puts me in an awkward position. We assumed that once you gave your word....But as an accommodation, I will put an additional $250 on the file. You will get $750. Okay?
Doctor: Thank you.

Lesson: The doctor ends up thanking his opponent for paying him about 20% of what a fair price should be. She made a fatal error by agreeing to a price before knowing all the pertinent information. To avoid this problem in a consulting situation you should charge by the hour.

TREATMENT

As a preliminary matter, you need to be able to diagnose this tactic no matter how well it is disguised. You need to insist on being provided *all* of the details of the assignment before even attempting to start to estimate the time and effort or cost involved. Even then, you should proceed cautiously because it is difficult to retract statements once they are made.

You need to appreciate that once a figure is placed on the table, it is often difficult, if not impossible, to move away from it.

Example 14.16 The importance of asking questions to define the scope of the work
Corporate executive: We would like you to do three days of consulting work. Give me a ballpark figure on the cost. We will not hold you to it. I am putting my pen down. I will not even write your answer down.
Doctor: It will depend on the details of the assignment. What is the type of work to be done? Where is it to be done? How soon do you need the results? Why is the work being done?
Corporate executive: Well, it is actually a rush job….We need you to go to Chernobyl this August. It will be fieldwork but not too close to the meltdown. The U.S. government has contracted with us to do this work to see if we can help clean up the radiation any quicker. There are just too many people dying due to the radiation.
Doctor: Just out of curiosity, what is the dollar value of the contract you have received from the government?
Corporate executive: It is not a big job. But the total contract is $210 million.

Lesson: As you can see, frequently the devil is in the details. The doctor was well advised to obtain all the details of the assignment before giving *any* estimate as to the cost. If she had just jumped in and said that her consulting fee is $2,500 a day, she probably would have not been able to successfully free herself from that quick estimate and negotiate a better deal for herself.

Example 14.17 Failure to ask enough questions leads to poor result
Insurance executive: (to doctor) We would like you to lead a one-day course on the AMA *Guides* because we know you are one of the world's leading experts. What would you charge us?
Doctor: Well, for a one-day course I would have to charge you $5,000 and travel….
Insurance executive: You got it. The date is March 17th.

Lesson: What the doctor failed to determine before he gave his "ballpark price" are the crucial details. How many people will be attending (300) and will the insurance company charge admission? (Yes, $300 per person.) Had the doctor known that the insurance company would generate $90,000 gross income, he might have charged more. Giving the ballpark figure without having the crucial details resulted in a negotiating disaster for the doctor.[1]

Tactic 4: Lack of Candor

DIAGNOSIS

This tactic is frequently difficult to diagnose. Your opponent may be shading the truth, not telling you the full truth, failing to correct false impressions you have, or, in fact, lying to you. While we would all like to think that everyone we are negotiating with is telling the full truth, we know that this is not the case. As a matter of fact, the legal system even permits salespeople and others to engage in "puffery" as an accepted business tactic. Thus, many opponents will not even have a legal obligation to tell the truth during negotiations. The sophisticated physician negotiator understands puffery and discounts much of what her opponent tells her.

You need to investigate, research, and fully prepare for your negotiation. (See pages 109–22 on preparation.) The diagnosis of lack of candor is made when the physician catches the opponent in misrepresentations or untruths. This can be verified by research conducted before the negotiation. You should also make a provisional diagnosis of lack of candor when you have a gut reaction or an instinctive feeling that an opponent is not being candid. Consider the following examples.

Example 14.18 Take anything a salesperson says with a grain of salt
Salesperson: (to doctor) That is a bottom-line price on the condo. There is no room to negotiate. A young couple is coming back today to sign a purchase and sale agreement.

Lesson: A classic ploy. You should immediately have a gut reaction that the salesperson is not being candid when he states that someone else is coming later to buy the property. If they liked it so much, why didn't they already buy it?

---

[1] This example is based on a real case.

Example 14.19 The antidote to your opponent's misstatements is doing your homework
Doctor: (to proposed purchaser of practice) You have seen the books, the office, and met the staff. The practice is a turnkey operation. You should be able to do very well here. With a little hard work....

Lesson: The words "with a little hard work" should signal that something may be awry that the seller has not been completely honest about. You will need to do your homework to research the practice as thoroughly as possible.

TREATMENT
You may feel an ethical or moral obligation to walk away from any negotiation in which your opponent has been less than candid. Unfortunately, due to the proliferation of this tactic, this is not always a practical alternative. Frequently, the best way to proceed is to not immediately jump to your feet and call your opponent a liar. While this might feel good, it will rarely advance the negotiation process or assist you in achieving your goals. The best way to proceed is to fully prepare by gathering as much negotiation information as possible and, at the crucial juncture, use it as a sledgehammer. This should allow you to seize momentum and power and achieve your goals.

Example 14.20 Calling your opponent's bluff to attempt to get a lowball price
Proposed purchaser: (to colleague) I know you are looking for $750,000 for your practice. I have checked the books and they look fine. What you failed to tell me is that your HMO status is in serious jeopardy. You just settled your third malpractice suit and a competing practice has been trying to get hospital privileges and move into your area. Normally, I would just walk away from this deal due to your lack of candor. If you really want to sell your practice *today,* give me your bottom-line figure now or your best chance for a sale will be walking out that door in thirty seconds!

Lesson: The doctor has turned his opponent's tactic against him. He has gained power and momentum in the negotiation.

Another technique is not to "call out" the opponent when you suspect he is being less than candid. This tactic uses the opponent's lack of candor against him. In fact, the savvy negotiator will go so far as to "encourage" the exaggeration.

Example 14.21 Using your opponent's exaggerations against him
Opponent to doctor: We will offer you the $150,000 starting salary plus 3% of the profits of the practice. The 3% can be substantial as well.
Doctor: How much are we talking about with the 3% bonus?
Opponent: It could be $20,000–$30,000 per year.
Doctor: I tell you what. I will take $165,000, no bonus. This way you save money and I can make firm plans to repay my loans.

Lesson: The doctor in this example suspected his opponent was painting too rosy a picture with the bonus and mousetrapped him by encouraging his exaggeration. The opponent is in a very awkward position. He does not want to say he lied or exaggerated. Thus, he will be hard pressed to reject the $165,000 offer.

Tactic 5: Outrageous Opening Offer or Demand

Diagnosis

This tactic is usually easy to diagnose. When using this tactic, your opponent takes the advice of "leave yourself room to negotiate" to the extreme and opens the negotiation with a grossly inflated offer or demand.

Example 14.22 Outrageous opening offer
Consultant: (to doctor) We can come in and straighten out your billing, accounts receivables, computer software, your hardware, and your leasing arrangements for the flat fee of $100,000. It sounds initially like a lot, but over two to three years it will more than pay for itself.

Treatment

You need to recognize the ploy and refuse to play into the hands of the opponent by getting into an auction type of negotiation. Alternatively, a response of a ridiculous counteroffer may jolt your opponent back to reality.

Example 14.23 Insisting your opponent negotiate against himself before negotiations can begin
Doctor: (to consultant) Your opening bid is so high it is ridiculous. Why don't you rethink your position and, when you have something in the ballpark, give me a call?

Lesson: This is the direct defense. If your opponent comes back in the ballpark, essentially bargaining against himself, you can start negotiations in earnest. If he does not, you will not be wasting any more time negotiating with him.

Example 14.24 Fighting fire with fire, using your own ridiculous opening offer
Doctor: (to consultant) Your $100,000 figure is ridiculous. We were thinking in terms of $1,000.

Lesson: Another direct defense. She has responded with an equally ridiculous offer. This counteroffer communicates to your opponent the fact that he is far afield and leaves substantial room for future negotiations.

Tactic 6: Belly Up

DIAGNOSIS

This tactic is easy to diagnose. When using this tactic, your opponent puts himself at your mercy and refuses to negotiate. It is a psychological tactic in which your opponents hope to manipulate you to bend over backward to be fair due to their frank admission of their inability or unwillingness to negotiate.

Example 14.25 Refusal to negotiate
Colleague: (to doctor) Fred, you know me. I am a doctor and not a negotiator. Pay me what is fair and let's be done with it.

Example 14.26 Anything that is fair
Colleague: (to doctor) Fred, you know my family situation. You know I am in no position to negotiate. I have to trust you to be fair. We have always been fair to each other in the past.

Treatment

You should not fall for this tactic by giving additional concessions to your opponent because he has gone "belly up." You need to recognize the belly up tactic for what it is, a psychological ploy to wring additional concessions from a sympathetic doctor. To combat this tactic you need to stick firmly with your fair offer.

Example 14.27 Standing firm and not letting emotions and sympathy weaken your resolve

Fred: (to colleague) I try to be fair. I am a doctor also and not a negotiator. What I can offer is…, which is fair to both of us.

Lesson: The doctor turned the situation around by stressing what was fair to *him*. Additional concessions were not given. The doctor had the strength of will to stand firm in the face of his opponent's powerful psychological ploy.

Tactic 7: Anchoring

Diagnosis

This may be the most difficult tactic for the physician negotiator to diagnose. It may be used when your opponent suspects that you do not know, or have not set a price or value on, your service, program, or product. Your opponent knows that if she can throw out a price, you may get psychologically anchored to that price area and fail or be afraid to ask for what the service is really worth. Your opponent also knows that you may be afraid to embarrass yourself by questioning the anchor price.

> Social scientists have discovered a psychological quirk they call the "anchor and adjustment" effect. The term refers to a human tendency to be affected by "first impression" numbers thrown into our field of vision. We tend to make adjustments from these often arbitrary reference points.[2]

The "anchor" can have and very often does have, a powerful psychological impact in the negotiation.

> Cognitive biases in anchoring and adjustment are related to the effect of the standard (or anchor) against which subsequent adjustments (gains

---

[2] Shell, p. 159

or losses) are measured during negotiation. The choice of an anchor (e.g., an initial offer or an intended goal) might well be based on faulty or incomplete information and thus be misleading in and of itself. However, once the anchor is defined, parties tend to treat it as a real, valid benchmark by which to adjust other judgments, such as the size of one side's opening offer. For example, research shows that real estate agents' house appraisals are strongly affected by the asking price. The asking price serves as a convenient anchor to use in appraising the value of the house. Goals in negotiation—whether set realistically or carelessly—can also serve as anchors. These anchors may be visible or invisible to the other party (a published market price versus an uncommunicated expectation), and, similarly, the person who holds them may do so consciously or unconsciously (a specific expectation versus an unexamined, unquestioned expectation or norm). Thorough preparation, along with the use of a devil's advocate or reality check, can help prevent errors of anchoring and adjustment.[3]

Example 14.28 Doctor successfully anchored because he did not research what his services were truly worth

TV producer: Doctor, we have a tentative agreement on a five-part series of ten-minute segments on "You and Your Health." We normally pay $100 for short segments, but because you are a physician, we will make it $150. What day next week is good for you to film the segments?

Doctor: There is no way I will do it for $150.

TV producer: What are you looking for?

Doctor: I will be losing one to two days out of the office. I need to get at least $1,500 for the five segments.

TV producer: You doctors are tough. Okay. You got the $1,500, but keep it confidential. We don't want the rest of the talent to get jealous.

Lesson: The doctor got anchored to the initial offer and did not even look at what his services might really be worth.

The opponent has added a very effective twist when he asks the doctor what he is looking for. When the doctor replies $1,500, he has not seen past the original anchoring area. In addition, he can no longer complain because he is the one who came up with the price. If he should later voice any concerns about the project he will be met with: "But, Doctor, you are

---

[3] Lewicki, pp. 125, 126.

the one who came up with the $1,500 price, which we met in full." That is why this is such an effective and insidious tactic.

TREATMENT

You need to accept the initial offer as just one piece of information. You should not fixate on it when determining value and asking price. You should not be intimidated by the anchor price and should not be embarrassed to question where the anchor figure comes from. You need to determine your value independently and look at the initial offer as merely the opponent's attempt to get you to stick close to the anchor. Do not let the anchor in any way impede your assessment of the true value of your opponent's offer.

Example 14.29 Defeating anchoring by independently valuing the services at issue

Doctor: To do a professional job, I will have to spend a considerable amount of time writing and researching the scripts. I estimate that each segment will take four to five hours to script. My normal consulting fee is $300 an hour, so I will require….

Producer: Doctor, we are not "60 Minutes" here, but we can probably get you….

Lesson: The doctor simply refused to be anchored. His demand was based upon his own independent valuation of his services, not his opponent's opening offer.

<u>Tactic 8: You Have Got to Do Better than That</u>

DIAGNOSIS

This tactic should be easy to diagnose. Here your opponent feigns surprise at your initial demand and requests that you immediately reconsider your position. What your opponent is really asking for is for you to bid against yourself. (See page 134 on bidding against yourself.) Bidding against yourself is one of the biggest mistakes a physician negotiator can ever make.

Example 14.30 "You have got to do better than that" is another way to ask the opponent to bid against herself
Opponent: (to doctor) Doctor, we have your price of $25,000 for the consulting contract. Just because we are a large company does not mean that we throw money around. You have got to do better than that.

Lesson: The doctor has been asked to bid against herself. She should not do so.

TREATMENT

You need to recognize this as another psychological tactic and ploy. Your opponent is trying to intimidate you into lowering your price by playing on your fears that you priced yourself out of the market, failed to consider a crucial factor, or made some other error. What makes this tactic so effective is that your opponent does not specify the mistake you made, but lets your imagination run wild as to all the possible things you could have done wrong. The savvy opponent knows that physicians do not like to make mistakes and will do almost anything to avoid being embarrassed. To combat this tactic you cannot be intimidated and should put the ball back in your opponent's court. Do not bid against yourself!

Example 14.31 Refusal to bid against yourself by asking for a counteroffer
Opponent: Doctor, we have your price of $25,000. You have to do better than that.
Doctor: We took great pains to come up with a fair price. What do you have in mind?

Lesson: The doctor is not intimidated nor does she allow herself to be browbeaten into bidding against herself. A counteroffer is demanded from the opponent. The doctor does not bid against herself.

Tactic 9: Pleading Poverty

DIAGNOSIS

You should normally be able to spot this tactic without too much difficulty. The tactic involves your opponents pleading that they only have limited funds to accomplish the job. It is therefore not their fault, or so they argue, that they cannot pay you more. Consider the following example.

Example 14.32 Crying poormouth
Nonprofit agency executive director: Doctor, we know your time is worth $25,000, but the budget I am working with only has $20,000 allocated.

Lesson: What the opponent is really saying is that some third party/agency has made a mistake in setting its budget unrealistically low and, as a result, you should pay for its mistake.

TREATMENT

You need to recognize that the party who makes a mistake normally should pay for the mistake. You also need to understand that many opponents intentionally come to the table with their "hands tied" as a ploy to strengthen their bargaining positions. To combat this tactic you need to turn the focus of the negotiation back to what you require. You will need to justify your demands to make them more effective. You can also point out to your opponents ways in which they can free up more money.

Example 14.33 Recognizing that you are not a charity defeats the poverty tactic
Nonprofit agency executive director: Doctor, we know your time is worth $25,000, but the budget I am working with only has $20,000 allocated.
Doctor: I appreciate your position, but budgets are not engraved in stone. See if you can get yours corrected to reflect my true value so we can proceed with the project.

Lesson: The doctor correctly refused to accept her opponent's claims of poverty. She suggested to her opponent ways to make more money available and focused the negotiation on her true value.

Tactic 10: Limited Authority

DIAGNOSIS

Diagnosing this tactic requires you to determine the level of authority that your opponent has. (See pages 36–44 on authority.) The best way to do this is to ask early in the negotiation.

Example 14.34 Smoking out someone without authority to negotiate
Doctor: (to executive) As I understand it, you have no final authority to negotiate today. You are on a fact-finding mission.

TREATMENT

You need to insist on the opponent producing someone with the authority to negotiate. You should refuse to negotiate until this occurs.

Example 14.35 Firmly asking to deal with someone with authority to negotiate
Doctor: (to executive) I understand that you are only authorized to obtain my demands and pass them along to management. Before we start to negotiate, we need to get someone in here with the authority to finalize the terms of the agreement.

Lesson: The physician correctly refused to negotiate with the person with limited authority. She correctly demanded to deal with someone in authority before she would begin to negotiate.

Additional Tactics

You may be exposed to other negotiation tactics as well. Following is a list of such tactics, the offensive statements, and brief defensive replies.

The nibble
Offense: "If you throw in the service, I will buy the system."
Defense: "I am sorry, I don't have the authority to do that. You can see the price list on the wall."

False flattery: You're the best!
Offense: "We know you are the best physician for the assignment…."
Defense: "I appreciate the flattery, but I can't pay college tuition with kind words and thoughts."

The screamer
Offense: (screaming) "I need an answer **NOW!"**
Defense: (softly) "I hear that you may be upset. Maybe we should lower our voices so we can hear each other better."

Need to talk it over
Offense: "I would love to agree today, but I need to talk to my partner."
Defense: "Call him now and let's go over it. What's his cell phone number?"

Trial balloon: Would you be willing to accept…?
Offense: "Would you be willing to accept $150,000 for the position as outlined?"
Defense: "Are you offering $150,000?"

The staller
Offense: "I need more time to think it over."
Defense: "Are two days okay? How about one week?"

Brinksmanship
Offense: "Well, we still have three days to the drop-dead deadline."
Defense: "We know the deadline. We don't know if last-minute negotiations will work here."

Bids
Offense: "We are putting this out to bid and then will be interviewing the lowest bidder."
Defense: "We will bid, but we would like you to call us last and give us an opportunity to match any other bids."

Team player
Offense: "Our offer is $125,000. Be a team player and accept it."
Defense: "You would not want an unhappy team member. I need $150,000."

Think of the future
Offense: "We are offering you $95,000 for year one, but as you get more experience, we will take care of you."
Defense: "I need taking care of now—$125,000." *(or)* "Let's put in writing the salary for each subsequent year."

Limited time offer
Offense: "This offer is only good for 24 hours."
Defense: "If you really want me, I am sure you will give me the weekend to think this over and talk to my spouse."

Selection from a limited menu
Offense: "You deserve $120,000. All I can offer is between $100,000 and $110,000."
Defense: "I will take what we both agree I deserve…$120,000."

Renegotiation
Offense: "I need $160,000, not the $150,000 we agreed to yesterday."
Defense: "I cannot negotiate under these conditions. We do not renegotiate terms already agreed to."

Chapter 15 Team Negotiating

Executive Summary

- Choose a good team before the negotiations begin.
- Each team should have one leader.
- Each team member should have a specialized role (such as, research, listening, or note taking).
- Team members need to tightly control information to the opposition.
- Everybody should get on the same page before the negotiation starts. Never negotiate unless the team has the same goals.
- Devise a system of codes or signaling before the negotiation starts so that dissention in the ranks is not telegraphed.
- Find the weak link on the opposing team and exploit it.
- Be prepared for your opponent to try to play you off against each other.
- If there is a weak link on your team, get him off your team or keep him on the shortest leash possible.

Introduction

You will often be forced to negotiate as part of or against a team or committee. Such negotiations require special techniques. These techniques are discussed in the following sections.

Team Size and Composition

The size of the negotiating team is important. When selecting the size of the team, you should consider the size of the opposing team, what each proposed team member has to offer, and the amount of time available to negotiate. To avoid being worn down by the opposing team, your team should be approximately the same size as that of the opponent. Each proposed team member should be evaluated on his ability to help prepare, his specific area of expertise, and his ability to keep silent and to get along with fellow team members. Leaving a person off the team who will later have to approve the proposed deal may make it more difficult to obtain their approval for a deal they have not personally negotiated. The larger the team, the longer the negotiation is likely to take. When your opposition has tighter time constraints than you have, you can capitalize on this by producing a large negotiating team.

Selection of the physician negotiation team leader is a crucial decision. It should not be taken lightly. The physician selected should be the most skilled and experienced negotiator and a physician who is well respected by all the team members. Generally, physicians who are self-confident, flexible, and exercise good business judgment make good team leaders.

Example 15.1 Assigning each team member an important role
Doctor: (to proposed team members) The "opposition" has four team members and so we will go with four ourselves. We need someone to pull together the history of past negotiations and to research the salary structure of other similar groups, a team leader, a number cruncher, and a listener. What are your recommendations? Let's remember they are the ones that need to get a deal quickly.

Lesson: The doctor is thinking of how to compose the team. Team members should be given duties that correspond to their strengths. The researchers should research, the listeners should listen, and the leader should negotiate. If they want to put additional pressure on the other side, they may want to increase the size of their negotiation team. This will slow down the process, which may be helpful in gaining concessions.

Controlling the Information Flow

It is essential to tightly control the flow of information coming from any and all team members. Ideally, the team leader should also act as the sole spokesperson. This will avoid leaks of confidential information or contradictory statements. In addition, information that is not to be revealed should be discussed and agreed to in advance of the negotiation. All team members must be made to understand that even the most innocent-sounding question could be an attempt by an opponent to find out confidential information. When properly prepared and coached, the team members will tightly control the information flow. (See pages 123–24 on getting as much information and revealing as little information as possible.)

Example 15.2 Verbal leaks
Negotiation team member: What time is your flight out of here tonight?
Opposing team member: We are all catching the last flight at 7:00 P.M.

Lesson: The negotiation team now has better information as to the time constraints of the opposing team. Information has been disseminated. A better answer may have been, "I'm not sure. Doctor [team leader] is in charge of those arrangements."

Example 15.3 More verbal leaks
Opposing team member: What's with Dr. Dunlop? Why is she being so difficult?
Negotiation team member: She is under a lot of pressure to get this deal done today.

Lesson: Harmful information has been revealed.

Example 15.4 Answering a question with a question
Opposing team member: What time is your flight out of here tonight?
Negotiation team member: Why, do you think we will finish tonight?

Lesson: A request for information has been cleverly reversed into a request for information from the other team.

Example 15.5 The best team negotiators keep their mouths shut
Opposing team member: What's with Dr. Dunlop? Why is she being so difficult?
Negotiation team member: I don't know. Why don't you go back and ask her?

Lesson: The team player has correctly refused to give out the requested information. Had he done so, he may have revealed critical information concerning the team's pressures, needs, and desires.

Goal Setting

The first and most crucial negotiation in team negotiations is the one amongst the team members when they set and agree upon their goals. The negotiation should include:

- selection of the lead negotiator for the team,
- deciding the team member's assignments,
- obtaining a consensus that the lead negotiator will do all of the speaking for the team, and
- setting up a signal or system for taking breaks when a team member feels it is crucial to caucus.

The team will be only as strong as its weakest link. If any team member is not fully invested in the team when this negotiation takes place, she should politely but firmly be asked to leave the team. The team leader should help ensure that the goals are practical, understood, and most importantly, agreed upon by *all* the team members. (See pages 112–14 on setting goals.) A unified front is needed to negotiate effectively.

Consensus building is crucial to the smooth running of a negotiation team. When a team member is unhappy about the negotiation's goals, she should be convinced or asked to leave the team. Nothing can be more damaging to a negotiating team than an unhappy physician who snipes at other team members and whose real goal is to prove them wrong. Team leaders need to get their team members to sign off on as many crucial decisions as possible *before* the negotiation process begins.

During the negotiation itself, the team will have to stay flexible (see pages 139 and 144 on flexibility). They may need to caucus frequently to redefine their goals. Team members should buy into this process before the negotiation begins, set their goals high, and leave themselves adequate room to negotiate. (See page 127 on adequate room to negotiate.)

Example 15.6 Get all the team members on the same page in advance
Doctor: (to colleagues) We have agreement for our bottom line on the length of the proposed contract, the geographic area covered, and the number of physicians required. The last item we need to agree on is cost. Nancy, I understand you feel strongly on this issue. Convince us....

Lesson: The team members either all need to agree or Nancy needs to be left off the team. Her presence on a team where she is negotiating something she does not believe in could be extremely detrimental.

__Signaling__

You need to anticipate the need to signal each other at key junctures during the negotiation. You should have prearranged signals for getting a team member to stop talking, notifying each other when an opponent is intentionally or unintentionally misstating the truth, and communicating that the team members need to caucus to discuss a change in strategy or make a key concession.

Be cautious not to inadvertently tip off your opponents that you need to talk or caucus. If you ask for a break/caucus as soon as an issue is brought up or comes to a head, this is a clear signal that you are concerned and are at least considering a compromise or concession. When you do ask for a break, you should have a prepared excuse for requesting it.

Example 15.7 Talking in code in front of the opposing team
Doctor: (to fellow team member, lightly) Fred, thank you for all of that information. Let's let Andy take the lead for a moment.

Lesson: What is being said here is, "Fred, shut your big mouth! Andy, please try to clean up this mess." This is much better than saying, "Fred, enough. I didn't want you to tell them that."

Example 15.8 More code to indicate team member misstatement
Doctor: (to fellow team member and opposition) We must be mistaken, then. I thought our research showed....

Lesson: This is a clever way to correct a wrong answer given by a team member. It should be used as a signal to say, "Be careful when discussing this area, we need to talk."

Example 15.9 A prepared excuse to break and caucus
Doctor: (to opponent and team members) I need to take a break. We old guys need to get up and stretch every few hours.

Lesson: A good excuse to have a break. A bad excuse would have been, "Let's take a break. Your offer is very tempting and I want to discuss it with my team members."

Example 15.10 Asking for a break can be a damaging signal to the opposition
Opponent: (to doctors during team negotiation) We need full coverage seven days a week at the emergency room. We know you offered four days, but what we need is seven days.
Doctor: We need to take a break right about now.

Lesson: This is a bad way to take a needed break. What you are signaling to your opponent is that since you want to discuss it immediately, seven days may in fact be acceptable.

Example 15.11 Disguising the motivation for taking a break by delaying the break until a few minutes after the problematic issue arises
Opponent: We need full coverage seven days a week.
Doctor: We need a lot of things also. How about more money, increased staff…?
Opponent: If you want to talk money, we can now.

Five minutes later…
Doctor: I need to take a break. We old guys need to get up and stretch every few hours. Let's take ten. Okay?

Lesson: The team will talk about the coverage issue during the break, but this point was well disguised by the doctor.

Taking Notes

You should assign one or more team members to take notes during the negotiation and to listen actively. This team member should be a good listener (see pages 58–68 on active listening skills) and should note not only what is being agreed to, but also the concerns expressed, important gestures, dissension in the ranks of the opponent, and other nonverbal cues. (See page 66 on nonverbal communication.) These notes can be very helpful during team caucuses.

All notes, deadlines, messages, etc. should be removed by the team members and not left lying on the negotiation table during breaks. You can assume that your opposition will most likely read notes left in plain view. Some negotiators specialize in reading upside down, so caution should be exercised even if your opponent is sitting on the opposite side of the negotiation table.

Example 15.12 What the listener/note taker should listen for
Doctor: (during caucus, reading from notes) Each time we talked about money, Jeff (opponent) would sit back in his chair and fold his arms. He would then whisper to Becky (opponent). It was Tom who seemed to be the most sympathetic. At one point he was starting to say we had a point but was cut off by Jeff. Leslie (opponent) agreed with almost everything Tom had to say. It seems to me that Tom is the key here. He is our best hope of getting a fair price.

Lesson: The note taker was able to make these detailed observations because his *only* role in the negotiations was active listening and note taking. The note taker is one of the most important members of the team. A good note taker is like a good offensive lineman in football. That person must be able to accept the fact that even though he is more important to success, the quarterback often gets 98% of the glory.

Caucusing

You should caucus as frequently and for as long as necessary to modify the team's goals and strategy. Caucusing may also be necessary to maintain consensus and goodwill amongst the team members. The comments of opposing team members should not deter you from caucusing as often as necessary. An added benefit of frequent caucuses is that such frequent meetings tend to disguise the fact that a caucus is being held because of some recently discussed issue.

During the break, it is essential to hear from all team members who have something constructive to say. The physician team leader will have to maintain tight control over the team during these short breaks in order to make the best use of the time available. You will need to maintain security and not permit your team meeting to become heated, loud, and overheard by the opposing team.

Example 15.13 Doctor firmly insists on taking break to caucus
Doctor: We will be taking a fifteen- to twenty-minute break to talk things over amongst ourselves.
Opponent: Another break? I think that is the fourth one already and we are not even finished with half of the issues. You guys need to get your act together.
Doctor: Why don't you use these few minutes to sharpen your proposal instead of complaining? Whining is not really consistent with your tough guy image.

Lesson: The doctor is not intimidated by his opponent's comments. He takes the break regardless and gains power by responding strongly to his opponent's negative comments.

Example 15.14 What to do during a team caucus
Physician team leader: (to team) Okay. We have twenty minutes. Let's spend ten minutes going around the room brainstorming and leave ourselves ten minutes to come up with our three best alternatives. Joanne, why don't you start? Fred, keep an eye on the time.

Lesson: The team leader keeps tight control on the meeting to assure that no time is wasted. The goal of defining the three best alternatives is set down before the negotiation recommences.

Example 15.15 The importance of keeping your voices down during a caucus
Doctor: (to team members) Do you hear the yelling and shouting coming out of their caucus room? I guess they are not all on the same page. We might be able to exploit this divisiveness.

Lesson: Make sure that the other side cannot hear what is being said in your caucus. If they can, you could be giving up highly damaging and highly confidential material.

Resolving Team Disagreements

You should anticipate that disagreements will arise amongst team members. You should set up an agreed-upon method for resolving these disputes *before* the negotiation begins. Getting the team members to buy into the method for resolving internal disputes will help reduce the chances that a team member on board at the onset of the negotiation will become unhappy, uncooperative, or destructive. If the team has to check with a higher authority, the team leader should make the call herself on a secure line. The team should disguise and not reveal to the opposition the specific issue(s) under discussion. Such revelations can undercut the apparent authority and power of the team and its leader.

Example 15.16 Setting in advance an internal dispute resolution mechanism
Team leader: (to team members) We agree, then, that if anyone has a problem with the way the negotiation is going, he or she will signal me. I will take a break. At the break, we will agree amongst ourselves on how to proceed. In the event that we cannot agree and we are deadlocked, I will cast the deciding vote. Are we all okay with this method?

Lesson: A strategy for resolving internal disputes is critical. A divided front during team negotiations can be fatal.

Team Negotiation Tactics

The two most commonly used team negotiation tactics should be discussed by your team in advance. These techniques are "divide and conquer" and the "weak link." Team members need to identify these tactics quickly and should respond appropriately.

Divide and Conquer

Divide and conquer involves your opponent trying to drive a wedge into the physician negotiation team. The hope is that this wedge will lead to squabbling, resulting in the team losing its focus and being substantially weakened. The person to whom the wedge remark was directed should respond to it. This will help display the most unified front possible.

Example 15.17 Wedge remark
Group practice leader: (to team of ten physicians being bought out) We have offered you $20 million. You have ten partners. That works out to $2 million each. (Looking at the youngest partner) How much more than $2 million each do you need? That is, of course, based on the assumption that each of you will be getting 10%. Since your income production was more or less equal, we just assumed that you would each get an equal share.

Lesson: The opponent's wedge is used to get the doctors' team fighting about money amongst themselves. This will naturally lead to disunity.

Example 15.18 Defeating the wedge by showing unity
Group practice leader: (to team of ten physicians) We have offered you $20 million. Each of you would get an equal share.
Young partner: Put your wedge back in your bag. This negotiation would be close to being completed if you offered us a reasonable amount.

Lesson: The target of the wedge attacked it head on. The team has stopped the wedge and gained power by showing its strength of unity.

WEAK LINK

In the "weak link" tactic, your opponent will quickly identify your team member who is most ill-suited to be a negotiator. This quick identification and exploitation of the weak link takes place in the animal kingdom as well. You probably recall watching scenes on television or in the movies of a herd of graceful antelope moving across an African plain. They are too quick for the natural foes and head toward a watering hole. Then the camera pans to one old, sick, and injured antelope who does not appear to be that quick or graceful. The dangerous music comes on and you know something bad will be happening. The camera pans to the lion in the fields who instinctively picks out the one injured antelope among hundreds. The lion singles him out and the rest is nature taking its course. Just like the injured antelope, the weak link in your negotiation team is easily identifiable and exploitable.

If a physician team member is unduly concerned about being liked, is inexperienced, or is unduly afraid of deadlock, then he is susceptible to becoming the weak link.

A sports analogy is helpful in explaining the weak link tactic. In basketball and football, the offense quickly identifies the weakest defender, isolates that person, and then takes advantage of the defender's shortcomings. The same tactics are used during team negotiations.

When you become aware of a weak link on your negotiating team, you should get that person off the team as quickly as possible. If this is not a practical solution, sit next to the weak link and do not let him or her out of your sight for even one minute. The weak link is particularly vulnerable in ongoing negotiations that are spread out over days or weeks. One well-placed phone call to the weak link by a savvy opponent can result in serious information leaks, major concessions, and fatal damage to the negotiation. Leave the weak link back in the office as far away as possible from the negotiation site.

Example 15.19 Going after the weak link
Team opponent: (to doctor during break) Joe, can you help me carry the box of printouts?

When Joe is isolated from the team…
Joe, I am telling you this as a friend. Nothing against your team and team leader, but they are ruining *your* career and *your* future in medicine. You have a reputation of twenty years of excellence, integrity, honesty, and now to throw it all away over these issues that have nothing to do with you. Other doctors have been talking. Don't let your team push you around. Remember, after all is said and done, it is *your* reputation.

Lesson: Joe should have been left back at the office. Failing this, he should not have been allowed to be alone with an opponent. The team leader should have "double-teamed" the opponent and sent another team member to escort the weak link.

Agendas

You need to deal effectively with any disparate agendas that physicians may have prior to, or which could develop during, the negotiation. Team members may try to impress the opposition, line up future consulting work or employment, and build up goodwill for future use. Each of these individual agendas can be damaging to the team as a whole. This problem is particularly troublesome if the team members are not co-employees or partners, but are instead independent contractors brought together with the express purpose of negotiating an agreement for their mutual benefit. The apparent and hidden agendas of the physician team members need to be addressed and reined in by the team leader and the team prior to and during the negotiation.

Example 15.20 Doctors on the same team as their opponents…
Doctor Washington: We are looking at developing a protocol. We would recommend a needs assessment, development of hard data, and interpreting the data. This consulting work should be done before we develop educational programs. We are looking at three to six months of consulting work. As you know, this is my area of specialty.
Doctor Lopez: While I agree with Joe that the data is important, I think we can proceed immediately to develop the distance learning programs and seminars. As you know, this is *my* area of specialty.

Lesson: Team members need to be team players. If they are not, they should not be on the team. If this situation occurs during an ongoing negotiation, the team leader should find an excuse to take a break and then take firm control of the situation.

Flexibility

Your team needs to remain flexible. The more rigid the team becomes, the less open it is to reason, compromise, and concessions. (See pages 139 and 144 on flexibility.) The team leader should remind the team periodically that just because they all agree on a point does not make it a fact and does not mean they cannot and should not remain flexible.

Example 15.21 Reminder that some flexibility may be needed
Physician team leader: (to team) We all agree to $3 million, not a cent less. Our practice is worth every penny. We all have worked too long and hard to sell ourselves short. We will hang tough, but we may need to rethink our goals if we can't get the $3 million.

Lesson: The team leader reinforces the unity of the team with the $3 million demand. He also, however, prepares them to be flexible if that goal appears to be unattainable.

Chapter 16 Negotiating for the Retention of an Attorney

Executive Summary

- Do not give the law firm a blank check.
- Make sure the lawyer you hire is actually the one who does your work.
- To get a read on how good your case is, ask the lawyer if he'll take it on a contingency.
- Contingency fee percentages are negotiable.
- Make sure the lawyer bills frequently so there are fewer surprises.
- Insist on tightly controlled expenses. Expenses can often be abusive.
- Push to settle a matter quickly.
- Do not wait until the last minute to hire the attorney.
- Hold out the possibility of future work with the attorney.
- Be a good client who the lawyer wants to keep happy.

Introduction

Retaining counsel or a law firm can be a traumatic and very costly experience. Unfortunately, it is likely that you will need to hire an attorney many times over the course of your career. The cost of legal services, however, are 100% negotiable. To successfully negotiate with attorneys regarding retention, you will need to understand law office economics, available legal fee arrangements, the best arrangements, the optimal time to hire an attorney, how to get better fee agreements by being a good client, and the criteria to use in selecting counsel.

Law Office Economics

You will reduce legal costs through a better understanding of law office economics. This understanding needs to be applied with the use of selected negotiating techniques. Most law offices are set up with the partners running the firm and obtaining new business. The routine, time-consuming work is then referred to less experienced associates. These associates are then "billed out" at a multiple of their salaries. The client pays a very high hourly rate for the partners, lower rates to train the associates, and as much of the expenses of running the law firm as the firm can get away with. ***You must also keep in mind that there is no limit***

to the amount of legal work that can be done on even a routine matter, if an attorney knows that she will be paid for it. The first rule in negotiating with an attorney is, therefore, to be very careful to not give the attorney a blank check. Consider the following examples.

Example 16.1 Giving the law firm a blank check
Law firm partner: Doctor, I understand the issue. The legal question is the validity of the covenant not to compete that you signed two years ago as a young, inexperienced physician. We will look at the corporate practice of medicine doctrine, anti-trust, and any other theory that we can come up with to invalidate your five-year covenant. We will need a $10,000 retainer and will apply that against our billing rate of $400 an hour plus expenses….
Doctor: Fine. I need to get out from under that covenant….It is stopping me from taking advantage of a wonderful opportunity.
Doctor leaves office
Partner: (to associate, who is being paid $100 an hour, as he tosses the file on her desk) Nancy, I need you to research this covenant not to compete. I want you to do a thorough job. I will need a detailed memorandum. The client will be coming in on Friday and I will need it before then. Take a look at the *Berlin v. Sarah Bush Lincoln Center* case at 664 N.E.2d 337 (1996) and *Holden v. Rockford Memorial Hospital* at 678 N.E.2d 342 (1997). They might help. Any questions?
Associate: Is there any limit on time or expenses here?
Partner: (laughing) We are dealing with a doctor who has agreed to pay the firm $400 an hour plus expenses.
Associate: Got it. You will have the memo on Thursday even if I have to work on it day and night until then.
Partner: I am glad we understand each other.

Lesson: The unsophisticated doctor has, in effect, given the law firm a blank check. He will be paying $400 an hour for work done almost exclusively by a new associate who is paid $100 an hour by the firm. The doctor has put no restrictions on the type of expenses, their cost, or their mark up. As difficult as it may be to believe, the majority of doctors who retain lawyers and law firms "negotiate" in the same way and achieve the same results as the doctor in this example.

Example 16.2 Keeping the law firm on a short leash

Law firm partner: Doctor, I understand the issue. The legal question is the validity of the covenant not to compete…$10,000 retainer…billing rate of $400 an hour plus expenses….

Doctor: Before we discuss fees, have you had much experience in these covenant-not-to-compete cases?

Partner: Yes. I have handled three or four cases like this in the past two years alone.

Doctor: I take it you will not be billing me for original research if you already have many of the issues briefed.

Partner: Well, each case is unique….They depend upon the facts….But, obviously, we will not bill you for work previously done.

Doctor: Will an associate be doing the research?

Partner: Yes, but I will be reviewing the work and giving you my opinion. That is what you are *really* paying for.

Doctor: Do you want to charge me a reduced rate for the associate's time or would a blended rate of $175 an hour work better for you?

Partner: (reluctantly) We can go with the blended rate of $175.

Doctor: As this is a routine research project, the only expenses should be the actual Westlaw charges and fax and copying costs, correct?

Partner: Yes. We will bill you those at our own cost.

Doctor: I would hope that this would not take more than ten hours of work. Would a $1,750 retainer be reasonable…?

Partner: (anticipating the next request) Yes…and I will call you before we exceed your retainer.

Doctor: Thank you.

Doctor leaves office

Partner: (to associate, throwing the file on her desk) Nancy, I need you to research this covenant not to compete and do a memo for Thursday. Pull out the memo in the *Jones* case and *Kahn* case. The issues are basically the same and look at the *Berlin* and *Holden* cases. Keep the bill under $1,750. No overnight delivery, overtime for staff, meals, or taxi rides. This doctor will not stand for that stuff….

Associate: One lean and mean memo…no fat, no frills, no extras.

Partner: I am glad we understand each other.

Lesson: The doctor did not give the attorney a blank check. He verified that the work would not be time consuming, that he would be billed a blended rate, that there would be no extravagant expenses, and that he would be notified immediately if his retainer was exceeded.

Bait and Switch

To win new clients, large law firms may use a highly regarded, well-known attorney to attract the business. Once the client is in the fold, however, the firm will transfer the actual grunt work to a new associate.

> Watch out for the "bait and switch routine": Once a client goes through the selection process discussed earlier to select a legal expert, make sure that expert is handling the case and not someone else or an amorphous and ever-changing "team." Many clients are attracted to a firm by the reputation of one partner, who makes a few guest appearances on the bill (usually to be briefed in preparation for the next performance for the client's benefit), while the guts of the matter have been delegated to others with less experience.
>
> Firms often excuse this bait and switch by suggesting they are doing clients a favor by pushing the work down to cheaper attorneys. Unfortunately, the client is often paying for on-the-job training for the junior attorneys, while the more senior attorneys then charge to correct or re-do their work. Junior attorneys two or three years out of law school billing at, for example, $125 per hour and more can bill well over $20,000 in a month—none of it worthwhile. The more senior attorney, with the great reputation, should not take as long nor suffer as many false starts.[1]

Reasonable Attorney Fees

Attorneys are ethically obligated to charge clients "reasonable attorney fees." Of course, what exactly *is* reasonable will vary on a case-by-case basis.

The Washington State Bar Association provides guidance on the factors that are to be considered when determining reasonable attorney fees. Many other states provide similar guidance.

---

[1] Toothman, "Managing Lawyers and Legal Fees: A Guide to Integrated Management of Legal Services," thedevilsadvocate.com/manage.html (2005).

Determining Reasonable Fees

Although exact fees cannot usually be determined in advance, the factors involved in computing charges are fairly standard. These factors include the following.

- Time spent on a particular problem. Time is a basic element in determining professional fees. For many matters, a straight-time hourly fee agreement will be arranged. Different lawyers value their time at different rates because of variations in experience, training, skills and law-office expenses. Most lawyers keep accurate records of time spent on each matter. Assistance from other lawyers, legal aids, and clerical staff also affect costs.
- The amount charged in a locality for similar legal services. Lawyers usually bill for consultation and meetings, telephone calls, document preparation, client representation in court, research of legal issues, and for other work that directly relates to a case. These charges should be itemized or explained to you. Legal services, unlike medical or dental services, are often performed when the client is not present. Documents and advice are frequently the products of many hours of analysis, research and preparation.
- Ability, experience and reputation. You should expect to pay more for a lawyer with proven abilities whose expertise in a specific area of law is in demand. Circumstances or unique problems sometimes require special services. A lawyer with a reputation as an "expert" or who concentrates his or her practice in a particular area of law may charge higher fees than someone less experienced. This lawyer may sometimes be able to handle matters in substantially less time, resulting in a lower total fee.
- Overhead and operating expenses. When hiring a lawyer, you hire the resources of a law office to work on your behalf. For a typical law office, overhead and operating costs (including such items as rent and utilities, professional and support staff, law libraries, equipment and supplies, taxes and insurance) may comprise 35 to 60 percent (or more) of legal fees.
- The results obtained. In some cases, the outcome and the amount involved may determine a fee. A "contingent fee" agreement, often used in personal injury or collection cases, is one example. [See Fee Arrangements section below.] No lawyer can guarantee results of a court proceeding. If a contingent fee has not been arranged, the lawyer will expect to be paid whether the client wins or loses the case.
- Time limitations imposed by the client or by the circumstance of the matter.
- The seriousness and complexity of the legal problem. If the problem involves established legal principles requiring routine skills and attention, a straight-time fee may be appropriate. However, if the problem raises difficult or novel questions of law, larger fees may apply.

- A client's ability to pay. Payment plans can sometimes be arranged, or legal aid might be available. Discuss these concerns before you hire an attorney.
- Other factors. The attorney-client relationship must also be considered. With a continuing relationship, the charge for a particular matter may be less than if employment is on a one-case basis.[2]

Legal Fee Arrangements

You need to understand the various legal fee arrangements that are available. You should strive to obtain the fee arrangement that reduces your exposure to legal costs while at the same time maintaining or increasing the attorney's incentive to successfully conclude the case. Box 16.1 describes the legal fee arrangements that are generally available and their uses. The best fee arrangement for you to negotiate will depend upon the type of case that you have and the type of lawyer you need.

Box 16.1

Types of Attorney's Fee Arrangements

1. *Contingent fee:* Your attorney will receive a percentage of your recovery (i.e., 33%–40% in personal injury matters), plus expenses. This method can also be used in contractual and some other types of disputes.
2. *Fixed fee:* Your attorney will receive a flat fee for representing you in a case (i.e., $2,500 for a minor criminal case).
3. *Hourly fee and expenses:* In complex matters your attorney will charge you his or her hourly billing rate plus expenses (i.e., $350 per hour and expenses).
4. *Blended fee and expenses:* The attorney will charge you a combination of the associates' and partners' billing rates plus expenses.
5. *Reverse contingency fee:* You and the attorney agree on a worst-case scenario and you agree to pay the attorney a percentage of anything she can save you from that amount.

---

[2] Washington State Bar Association, Legal fees pamphlet 11/18/2004 at http://www.wsba.org/media/publications/pamphlets/legalfees.htm.

CONTINGENCY FEE

When you are the plaintiff in a personal injury case or involved in a speculative case, you are normally better off seeking a contingency fee arrangement. There are three main advantages to this type of fee arrangement. First, you will typically not have to pay any up-front retainers, fees, or expenses to initiate the litigation.

Second, if you lose the case, you will not be obligated to pay any legal fee. (Note, however, that most contingent fee agreements do provide that you will be responsible for the attorney's expenses.)

Third, and most importantly, the attorney representing you has a substantial and significant financial incentive to win the case. If the attorney loses, she gets nothing. If the attorney wins, she gets 33% to 40% of the award or whatever the contingency fee is that you negotiated.

An example of a speculative case where you should attempt to get a contingency fee arrangement would be suing for lost profits in a medical practice. By requesting a contingency fee arrangement, you can quickly determine the viability of your claim. If one or more attorneys turn you down and insist on being paid by the hour, you should think long and hard before investing your time and money in hourly representation for the claim.

On contingency cases, you will frequently be presented with a standard form calling for between 33% and 40%. This fee is *always* negotiable. Because less than 5% of cases ever go to trial, one good tactic is to insist on a fee reduction if the case is settled before trial. You should also remember that, when hiring an attorney on a contingency fee, you should hire the best attorney that you can find.

Check to see if the attorney has actual trial experience and takes a case to trial when the settlement offer is unreasonably low. All too often, personal injury lawyers are reluctant to try cases due to their lack of experience or due to the large amount of work a trial requires. It is more cost-effective for some unscrupulous attorneys to settle quick and easy and move on to the next case. You will want to select an attorney with an excellent reputation who maximizes the recoveries obtained. Savvy physicians do due diligence and check the reputation of the attorney with other counsel before retaining an attorney in a contingency case.

Example 16.3 Asking the attorney to represent you on a contingency basis will give you a very good idea what he really thinks of your case
Doctor: (to attorney, showing him the documents) We would like to sue a former partner for breaching his contract, stealing patients, and for the profits our practice lost.
Attorney: (looking over documents) This looks like a solid case. We would be pleased to represent you. We will stand a good chance of winning.
Doctor: We would like you to represent us on a contingency basis....
Attorney: No can do. These cases are too speculative...there are too many variables.

Lesson: By insisting on a contingent fee agreement, the doctor has determined what the attorney really thinks about this case. If two or three other attorneys also refuse to accept such an arrangement, the doctor should strongly consider not pursuing the case.

Example 16.4 Negotiating the amount of the contingency
Attorney: Doctor, here is our standard preprinted contingency calling for a 33% legal fee. Please read it and sign it.
Doctor: I would like to make one change. I need the 33% reduced to 25% if this case is settled prior to trial.
Attorney: Well, Doctor, we do not normally reduce....
Doctor: (cutting him off) As you know, there are 7,500 certified trial specialists in this state. I am sure that when I call two or three....
Attorney: Give me a few minutes to make that change.

Lesson: The amount of the fee is *always* negotiable. This is especially true if you have a good case.

Example 16.5 Find the best lawyer you can when hiring based on a contingency fee
When Pennzoil sued Texaco, it hired nationally known trial attorney Joe Jamail on a contingency basis. He obtained one of the largest judgments of our time, $10.53 billion. His legal fee has been estimated at $350 to $500 million. They were happy to pay the fee because they knew that without Attorney Jamail, there would have been no $10.53 billion verdict.

Lesson: It is in your interest when prosecuting a contingency fee case to hire the best attorney that you can.

FIXED FEE

There are advantages and disadvantages to fixed fee arrangements. The chief benefit is that you know the cost of your representation and can budget accordingly. You need to understand the substantial drawbacks to this arrangement as well. First, the fee may be set too high to take into account things that might go wrong. Second, if the fee is too low, the attorney may lose interest in your case. Third, counsel may have a less experienced associate handle the case. Consider the following examples.

Example 16.6 Fixed fee gives incentive for lawyer not to spend time on your case

Doctor: You charged me $5,000 for this contract problem and you resolved it with one fifteen-minute phone call.

Attorney: It took me twenty years of experience to learn who to call and what to say.

Lesson: A fixed fee may result in overpaying for legal services.[3]

Example 16.7 Attorney loses interest in fixed fee case

Doctor: I have left twelve messages. You never return my calls.

Attorney: There is only so much time I can devote to this case due to our fee arrangement. I am doing the best I can.

Lesson: The attorney losing interest is a serious risk when the arrangement is for a fixed fee.

Example 16.8 Fixed fee case dumped on new, inexperienced attorney

Doctor: (to new associate in court) Who are you? Where is Attorney Relief?

Associate: He was tied up with another matter. Don't worry, I have been doing most of the work on your case anyway.

---

[3] In this case, $20,000 per hour.

Lesson: If the fee is fixed, you may end up with an inexperienced attorney doing the actual work.

HOURLY FEE

The successful physician negotiator understands that in most cases in which he retains counsel, a request will be made for payment of an hourly fee plus expenses. The hourly fee could range from $225 to $500 an hour or more. The expenses can range from photocopying charges to airfare, hotels, cabs, electronic research, meals, etc. A complex case in which the physician is paying by the hour can be a financially draining experience. The savvy physician negotiator knows ten ways to help reduce this exposure.

1. Ask for a reduced hourly rate

Example 16.9 Split the difference to reduce the usual fee

Doctor: I understand you normally charge $350 an hour. I normally pay $150 an hour. Can we split the difference (see pages 173–75 on splitting the difference) and agree on $250 an hour?

Attorney: Okay.

Lesson: The hourly rate is always negotiable. Note, however, that when attorneys reduce their rates, they can make up for it by billing more hours.

2. Ask for a reduced rate for associates' time and travel

Example 16.10 Reduced associates' time and travel

Doctor: (to attorney) I don't mind paying for associates' time and for travel, but can we agree to $150 an hour for associates' time and 50% for travel time if any is needed?

Lesson: If you don't ask for concessions, you will never get any.

3. Get an estimate of total cost

Example 16.11 Asking for a budget

Doctor: Can you give me an estimate/ballpark figure on what you anticipate the total cost of this case will be? (See pages 179–82 on estimates.)

Attorney: It will all depend on how cooperative the other side will be. A rough estimate is between….

Lesson: It will be difficult for the attorney to later exceed this estimate. The doctor has given herself some protection.

4. Request billing by the tenth of the hour

Example 16.12 Not suffering from "rounding up" errors
Doctor: (to attorney) In light of your hourly rate, I would prefer to get billed by the tenth of the hour and not by the quarter of an hour. This would be fairer to me and will more accurately reflect the time actually spent.

Lesson: This is a good argument and is difficult for the attorney to refute.

5. Set a maximum fee not to be exceeded

Example 16.13 Capping the legal fee
Doctor: Your fee is $350 an hour with a maximum of $15,000, correct?
Attorney: Yes, and we will do our best to resolve this case quickly.

Lesson: The savvy physician has capped his legal fee exposure.

6. Ask for reduced charges for standard forms and agreements

Example 16.14 Recognizing that attorney will just be changing a standard form
Doctor: This is boilerplate stuff, all you'll need to do is change your form. The time required will be minimal.
Attorney: It will require some modification.

Lesson: The doctor has lowered the fee expectations of the attorney.

7. Request weekly or monthly itemized billing

Example 16.15 Requesting monthly itemized billing
Doctor: I will need monthly itemized billing.

Lesson: This helps the client monitor the legal costs. Additionally, she knows exactly how the attorneys' time is being spent (e.g., 14 hours on inter-office conferences).

8. Request efficient handling of the case ("Ask or ye may not receive")

Example 16.16 Remind the attorney that you will be watching the expenses
Doctor: I am not the tobacco industry with unlimited resources. Do a good, thorough job, but no excesses.

Lesson: The attorney is put on notice that the legal bill will be scrutinized.

9. Request reduced billing for attorney conferences and for file reviews

Example 16.17 Recognizing a common abusive practice
Doctor: I don't want to be getting any bills for lengthy conferences or file reviews.

Lesson: The doctor has taken away some billing ammunition from the attorney.

10. Strive to resolve the case by settlement or alternative dispute resolution before incurring large legal bills

Example 16.18 Pushing the lawyer to resolve the case quickly
Doctor: I want you to make an offer to settle this now, before we go through all those costly motions and discovery.

Lesson: The doctor points out to the attorney he is interested in a quick, fair, inexpensive resolution.

Expenses

Many law firms substantially mark up their expenses and view them as an excellent additional source of revenue. You need to put strict limits on traditional law firm expenses such as photocopies, airline and other travel, copying, cell phone calls, overtime for paralegals and secretaries, hotel bills, legal research, meals, cabs, and limousines. You should demand itemized receipts for all expenses. You should also demand the apportionment of expenses if two or more cases/projects are being done at the same time at the same location.

Example 16.19 Putting attorney on notice as to abusive expense billing practices

Doctor: We have an agreement on your hourly rate. I am very concerned about the possibility of out of control expenses….

Attorney: I can assure you….

Doctor: That's what I am looking for…you to be personally responsible for keeping a sharp eye on expenses incurred and billed. What we both want to avoid is "utilization review" by a legal fee auditing company.

Attorney: What are you looking for specifically?

Doctor: No mark-up on faxes, photocopies, or phone calls, no travel or other expenses over $1,000 without my prior written approval. No eating at five-star restaurants on the road. No first-class airfares, taxi rides, or limo rides without my written approval. No overtime charges, hotel bills that contain extra charges for bar bills, x-rated movies, hair cuts, massages…We would prefer that large research projects be referred to legal research companies. You can outsource these overseas to save money as well. In other words, please treat my money as carefully as I do.

Attorney: We will do our best.

Doctor: Please prepare an addendum to my fee agreement reflecting our understanding and circulate it to the attorneys who will be working the case.

Lesson: Attorneys can and will bill you for any and all expenses they can get away with. You need to be proactive to prevent yourself from being abused by that practice.

When to Hire an Attorney

The best time to look for, interview, choose, and negotiate with counsel is when you are not desperately in need of services. As in all negotiations, the greater your need for counsel, the less negotiation power you will have. (See pages 75–91 on the best time to negotiate.) Keep in mind that there is a gross excess of attorneys in this country. You should, therefore, always have the power of alternative representation on your side.

Example 16.20 Procrastinating in hiring an attorney weakens the doctor's bargaining position

Doctor: (to attorney, handing him a large package of legal materials) We would like you to represent us in this lawsuit. As you can see, we have a hearing on a preliminary injunction in two days. The answer is due….How much will your fee be?

Attorney: $350 an hour plus expenses….We will need a retainer of…..

Lesson: If the doctor did not wait until the last minute, he could have shopped around. His delay has left him with few alternatives and very little power in the negotiation.

Example 16.21 A tough time to be negotiating

Doctor: You don't know me, but I am a cardiologist. I am calling from the Hingham police station. I was picked up a few hours ago for DUI. What I am looking for is for you to come down to the station house, arrange bail, and represent me in the case. This kind of case could destroy my reputation. My husband will be very upset.

Attorney: I will be down to the station house in thirty minutes. Don't say anything to anyone. Have your husband come down to the station with your checkbook. We will discuss my fee when I get there.

Doctor: Thank you.

Lesson: The doctor still has power, even in this situation. If the attorney wants to charge too high of a fee, she can fire her and retain new counsel after she is bailed out. The desperation in the doctor's situation, however, has given the attorney additional power in the negotiation.

How to Be a Good Client and Make It Pay Off

One of the most significant concessions you as a potential client can make is the promise to be a good client. Bar associations give this general advice to clients.

> **Reducing Legal Expenses**
> Lawyers are professionals with many qualifications and years of training. Time and advice are their stock in trade, so they must charge for them. By following a few suggestions, however, you can help reduce legal costs.
>
> - Gather pertinent information before meeting with your lawyer. Write down names, addresses and telephone numbers of all persons involved in the matter.
> - Be organized. Bring letters, documents and other relevant papers to the first meeting with your lawyer. Summarize essential facts. Write down questions you want the lawyer to answer.
> - Be concise in all interviews with your lawyer.
> - Answer questions fully and honestly. Be accurate and objective. Reveal all information, even if it may not be in your favor, and avoid letting emotions color the facts.
> - Avoid unnecessary telephone calls to your lawyer.
> - Be informed and keep your lawyer informed. Discuss ways you can help, such as by obtaining documents, lining up witnesses, or providing other assistance to reduce costs.
> - Consider "bottom line" or financial aspects of a legal matter and discuss them with your lawyer: be sure you understand advantages and disadvantages of a proposed action (for example, would court costs and legal fees be more than the amount of a bad debt you would likely recover?).
> - Try to prevent later problems by contacting a lawyer before committing yourself to a major obligation.[4]

This promise to be a good client can cost you little or nothing, but it will be very valuable to your attorney. The qualifications that make a client a good client are listed in Box 16.2. You need to also always keep in mind that the best client for an attorney to have is one that will be coming back to that attorney for significant work in the future. Remember that when an attorney has a difficult client, he may frequently (consciously or subconsciously) charge this client more than the good client.

---

[4] Oklahoma Bar Association Pamphlet (11/18/2004).

Box 16.2

The Ten Commandments of Being a Good Client

1. Promptly pay your bills. A physician client who brings in a check when he receives a bill is by *definition* a good client.
2. Have your story organized in a chronological fashion, typed neatly.
3. Have all supporting documents available and organized.
4. Make the names, addresses, phone and cell phone numbers, fax numbers, and e-mail addresses of all witnesses available to counsel.
5. Do not hide "bad" information or mislead counsel.
6. Do not wait until the last second to retain counsel so everything is done in a crisis atmosphere. If counsel has to drop everything to handle your case, it will cost you.
7. Do not continually call the attorney for progress reports. (Ask how often to check in.)
8. Be available. (Don't disappear without leaving contact numbers.)
9. Ask counsel how you can help and then follow this advice.
10. Mention additional work and refer clients. You will get VIP treatment and the best possible hourly rate once you become a significant source of additional legal work for your attorney.

Example 16.22 Holding out the possibility of additional work helps obtain a more favorable rate

Doctor: Before we talk about fees, I want to let you know that I will be an excellent client. Noncompliance by our patients is a big problem for us and this has made me extremely sensitive to the need to cooperate fully. I also hope to refer substantial amounts of new business to your firm. As you may know, I am president-elect of....

Attorney: We normally bill at $350 an hour. How about a $300 an hour excellent client rate?

Lesson: The promise of possible additional future work is a very powerful negotiating tool. With it, the doctor may turn a competitive negotiation into a cooperative negotiation.

Selection of Counsel

Cost is only one of the criteria for selection of counsel.

> The most critical tool for obtaining cost-effective legal services is first hiring the right lawyer. Hire the right lawyer[,] one who is attentive, with experience and efficient habits[,] and the representation should go smoothly. Hire the wrong lawyer[,] indifferent, inexperienced, or inefficient[,] and all the management effort in the world might get you where the right lawyer starts.[5]

You should also research and consider the attorney's experience in the specific legal area and whether she is too busy. Reputation is important and references should be checked. Finally, make sure that the attorney you retain will be your attorney. You do not want your case handled and managed by an inexperienced attorney in the firm. Always remember that there are a lot of attorneys out there. You can and should shop around.

Example 16.23 The right questions to ask when hiring a lawyer
Doctor: (to attorney) Your firm has come highly recommended. We are looking for a firm that has significant experience in this area. Will you send me a note with the names and docket numbers of your trials in this area for the past five years and their outcomes? We will need your assurance that you personally will take the key depositions and be lead counsel for any significant motions and the trial. I will need to see a draft sample fee agreement. Use your tightest language for the expenses, please, and give me the names of five references I can call. I know this is a lot of work, but we are trying to avoid the "beauty contest route."

Lesson: You need to be firm when dealing with attorneys. Do not be afraid to ask pointed questions. Attorneys ask such questions themselves all the time.

---

[5] Toothman, p. 9.

Chapter 17 Negotiating Employment, Managed Care, and Other Formal Written Contracts

Executive Summary

- Every word in a written contract counts.
- Never sign anything you do not read and understand. Be familiar with the meaning and effect of common boilerplate provisions in written contracts.
- You will be at an advantage if you have your attorney make the initial draft of the contract because the fine print will be drafted with your interests in mind.
- Plan ahead for future contingencies by inserting protective language into the contract.
- Make sure the contract clears up any ambiguities that could operate against your interests.
- If you want a change in a standard form contract, you'll need to ask for it.

Introduction

Many of your most important negotiations will involve formal written contracts, including employment, managed care, and purchase and sale agreements. An in-depth discussion of the issues and subtleties of negotiating each type of written contract is beyond the scope of this book. Indeed, to adequately cover those specific issues would require a series of books. This chapter is designed to assist you with general principles that apply to *all* negotiations involving formal written contracts.

Contract Law

You are probably not a lawyer. Reading this next section will not make you a lawyer. However, to be a successful physician, you must have a basic understanding of contract law in order to properly negotiate formal written contracts. In addition, you will need to be able to recognize when to retain a lawyer during negotiations that involve formal written contracts.

STATE-SPECIFIC

The law of contracts is state-specific; that is, it varies from state to state. Generally speaking, contract law is founded in the common law, which is precedent from previously decided cases. Although common law rules are considered judge-made law, the common law can also be modified by statutes passed by state legislatures.

INTERPRETATION

If a contract dispute regarding a formal written contract results in litigation, a key issue for the fact finder to decide is how to interpret the written terms of the contract. In both contract negotiations and disputes, the precise words and terms used in the written contract are closely scrutinized. A good lawyer plans for contingencies and drafts the tightest language possible to protect the client. Planning for contingencies and tightening language are major aspects of contract negotiation. It is also important to realize what a contract does *not* include and to add appropriate language where needed.

DAMAGES

The law of how to calculate contract damages is too complex to discuss in detail here. You should, however, appreciate three things about contract damages. First, contract damages may not, and generally do not, equal the price of the contract. For example, if you renege on a deal to purchase a new car for $35,000, the dealer's damages under the law will most likely be less than $35,000. However, damages in *certain circumstances* can be far greater than the contract price. For example, assume you reneged on a deal to sell 100 shares of stock to a friend for $5 per share. The stock then rises to $200 per share the day after the purchase and sale agreement was to be signed. In this case, you could be legally liable for far more than the $500 value of the contract for sale. Finally, and perhaps most importantly, professional and general liability insurance will not typically insure you for breach of contract. If you are sued for breach, you are likely to be personally liable.

Important Contractual Clauses

The language used in a contract is perhaps the most important part of the agreement. Most contracts are broken down into numbered paragraphs or clauses. Several boilerplate clauses appear in all types of formal written contracts and you should have a basic understanding of their significance. Boilerplate clauses are generally included by the parties in an effort to assert control over the outcome of disputes stemming from the contract. These clauses contain "legalese" and can have a significant impact upon the rights of the parties. Various commonly used clauses are discussed below.

CHOICE OF FORUM CLAUSE

A *choice of forum* clause sets forth in advance the forum or court in which the parties may bring a lawsuit involving the contract. Because more than one court may have jurisdiction (power to hear a case), a forum selection clause prevents what is known as "forum shopping" by the parties' lawyers. An example of a choice of forum clause follows.

Box 17.1

Choice of Forum Clause

The parties agree that all disputes arising out of this contract shall be tried in the courts of New York State, to the exclusion of all other courts that might otherwise have jurisdiction apart from this contract provision.

A forum selection clause has several advantages. First, it limits the parties' exposure to courts in other jurisdictions, thereby saving costs and fees associated with travel to other states. Second, parties can avoid litigation in states known for high jury awards.

Generally, courts uphold freely negotiated choice of forum clauses if the parties have not designed the clauses to discourage litigation. If a forum selection clause is rendered unenforceable, however, it does not mean that the contract itself is unenforceable. In such cases, the clause will simply be severed from the agreement, thereby allowing the plaintiff to bring a suit in any court that has jurisdiction.

What you should remember is that by signing a contract with a choice of forum clause, you may be assenting to being sued in a distant state should a dispute arise. This could be very costly and inconvenient for you, while giving your opponent a significant advantage.

Choice of Law Clause

Designating the location of the court to resolve a dispute does not necessarily mean that the court will apply the law of the state in which the court is located. For example, under certain circumstances, a Florida court may be required to apply New York law to decide a case. To prevent this from happening (or, in some cases, to ensure that this does happen), parties can insert a contractual clause that specifies a particular state's law to govern their dispute. Such a clause is referred to as a *choice of law* clause.

Like a forum selection clause, choice of law clauses are generally enforceable if they are freely negotiated (i.e., not the result of fraud, duress, or undue influence). For the chosen state's law to apply, however, that state's law must be reasonably related to the transaction. For example, a court would likely uphold a forum selection clause if one of the parties maintained an office in the chosen state. Box 17.2 contains an example of a choice of law clause found in a physician asset purchase agreement. Because the law of contracts varies from state to state, such clauses can have a significant impact should a dispute arise.

Box 17.2

Choice of Law Clause

Buyer and Seller agree that this contract together with the rights and obligations of the parties shall be construed under and governed by the law of the state of Illinois.

Arbitration Clause

Alternative forms of dispute resolution (ADR) are increasingly popular substitutes for formal civil litigation. *Arbitration,* the most common form of ADR, has the following advantages over litigation.

1. Efficiency. It often takes years before a case goes to trial. In addition, an appeal of the lower court's decision can add years before a final resolution of the dispute is reached. For an arbitrated dispute, the average time from filing date to decision is only 145 days.

2. *Lower Cost.* Lawyers charge by the hour, which becomes quite expensive if the litigation process drags on. Because arbitration is faster than going to trial, parties to an arbitrated dispute will pay significantly lower attorneys' fees. Arbitration also avoids court costs (although in an arbitrated dispute parties are still responsible for a private fee schedule).

3. *More Control.* Whereas in litigation the judge is assigned, in arbitrated disputes the parties create a list from which the arbitrator is chosen. Unlike a judge, the arbitrator is not constrained by precedent or rules of evidence. The arbitrator may therefore tailor the result according to the facts presented. Finally, the parties can agree on high-low or non-binding arbitration.

4. *Expert Arbitrators.* Arbitrators are not required to be judges. Arbitrators almost always have expertise in the field involving the dispute and may be more adept at resolving complicated or technical issues than a randomly assigned judge.

5. *Confidentiality.* The pleadings involved in a lawsuit are generally public record. Documents submitted with respect to an arbitrated dispute are not subject to public disclosure.

Parties can voluntarily submit to the arbitration process by including an arbitration clause in their contract. Arbitration decisions, also referred to as *awards,* are legally binding. Courts may review arbitration awards, but such review is limited to procedural aspects such as fairness of process and neutrality of the arbitrator. Courts generally will not undertake a review of the merits of the case. When signing a contract that contains an arbitration clause, you are giving up your right to have future contractual disputes litigated in a court of law or heard by a jury. Box 17.3 provides an example of an arbitration clause regarding medical treatment to a patient.

Box 17.3

Arbitration Clause

It is understood that any dispute as to medical malpractice, that is as to whether any medical services rendered under this contract were unnecessary or unauthorized or were improperly, negligently or incompetently rendered, will be determined by submission to arbitration as provided by California law, and not by a lawsuit or resort to court except as California law provides for judicial review of arbitration proceedings. Both parties to this contract, by entering into it, are giving up their constitutional right to have any such dispute decided in a court of law before a jury, and instead are accepting the use of arbitration.[1]

INDEMNITY CLAUSES

To *indemnify* means to reimburse or restore a loss already incurred. In a contractual sense, an *indemnity* clause requires one party to reimburse the other for past or future losses. Such clauses are designed to shift the entire loss from one party, who may be at fault, to another. These clauses are commonly referred to as "hold harmless" clauses because one party is held responsible for damages or losses sustained as a result of the other party's conduct. Depending upon the particular wording in the contract, an indemnity clause could subject a person to substantial and uncontrollable risk, regardless of fault. You need to be very careful before signing a contract that calls on you to indemnify the other party. You should always seek, where possible, to have the other party agree to indemnify you. An example of an indemnity clause follows.

Box 17.4

Indemnity Clause

Provider agrees to defend, indemnify and hold Managed Care Company harmless from and against any and all damages, liabilities, losses and expenses (including attorneys' fees) which in any way may arise from this agreement.

[1] Language recommended by California Civil Code, section 1295.

LIMITATION OF LIABILITY CLAUSE

A contract may contain a clause excusing one party's liability should that party breach the contract. This type of clause is called a *limitation of liability* or an *exculpatory* clause. An exculpatory clause is almost always unenforceable when it attempts to excuse a party from liability in the case of that party's intentional or reckless conduct. Even clauses that purport to excuse ordinary negligence are not always binding. The purpose behind the court's unwillingness to enforce such clauses is that the law of torts has been created to protect others from the unreasonable risk of harm. Therefore, if such limitation of liability clauses were always enforceable, parties would be able to circumvent the standards of conduct imposed to protect the safety of others. The inclusion of an exculpatory clause by your opponent can be used against him to prove a lack of good faith.

COVENANTS NOT TO COMPETE

Covenants not to compete are frequently included in physician employment agreements.

Such covenants function as a restraint of trade and will be closely scrutinized by the courts. To be enforceable, the clause must generally meet the following requirements.

1. Reasonably necessary to protect a legitimate interest.
2. Does not impose an undue hardship to the promisor.
3. Not likely to injure the public.

The term *reasonable* is hard to quantify because it depends upon the circumstances (such as size and nature of the business). Courts will examine the geographic scope and duration of restraint in determining whether to enforce the clause. Box 17.5 contains a typical physician's covenant not to compete.

Box 17.5

Covenant Not to Compete

Neither he/she, nor any professional association, partnership, or practitioner of medicine with whom the Physician is currently or may in the future associate, will open, own, operate or otherwise participate in any emergency center, emergency clinic, general or family or any similar practice with in five (5) miles of any such emergency clinic or emergency center operated by EPS or any of its affiliates.

The Physician hereby agrees not to contract to provide services (or otherwise accept employment) with any facility which has had a contract with EPS, or any affiliate of EPS for a period of one (1) year following termination of such contract at the facility.

Liquidated Damages Clause

As discussed above, the law of contract damages is extremely complicated. In some cases it may be difficult or even impossible to calculate the damages suffered by an injured party. Rather than leave this task to a jury, parties may insert a clause into their agreement fixing the damages at a certain amount. This clause is known as a *liquidated damages* provision because it specifies in advance the amount of damages to be awarded in the case of breach. To be enforceable, the liquidated damages must be reasonable in light of the anticipated or actual loss caused by the breach and the actual damages incurred must be difficult to prove.

A term fixing unreasonably large liquidated damages as a penalty is unenforceable on the grounds of public policy. Notice that the amount must be *reasonable*. This is because the damages must not be punitive (penalizing) in nature, but instead must be designed to compensate the injured party. Consequently, courts will not enforce excessive liquidated damages clauses. Box 17.6 contains a liquidated damages clause.

Box 17.6

Liquidated Damages Clause

In the event of a material breach of the agreement, the party breaching the agreement shall be liable for $50,000 liquidated damages. This clause is intended as full and final liquidated damages for the material breach and the parties mutually agree that this amount does not constitute a penalty.

If enforceable, a liquidated damages clause allows the injured party to recover nothing more than the amount stipulated in the clause. Upon a showing of breach, the injured party is entitled to the specified amount regardless of whether the actual damages were more or less than the liquidated sum.

Force Majeure

A *force majeure* clause expresses the parties' intention that certain specified events, such as labor strikes or acts of God, shall excuse performance of the contract. Inclusion of such a clause helps alleviate the problems associated with relying on the doctrines of impossibility and impracticability. A sample force majeure clause follows.

Box 17.7

Force Majeure

Neither party shall be deemed to be in violation of this agreement if either party is prevented from performing any of its obligations hereunder for any reason beyond its control, including, without limitation, strikes, inmate disturbances, acts of God, civil or military authority, acts of public enemy, or accidents, fires, explosions, earthquakes, floods, winds, failure of public transportation, terrorism, or any other similar serious cause beyond the reasonable control of either party.

SEVERABILITY

A *severability* clause operates to preserve the remainder of a contract where one or more provisions, such as a choice of law or choice of forum clause, has been stricken by a court. One major difficulty with severability clauses is that the enforcement of the contract without the stricken clause(s) may be problematic for the parties. A sample severability clause follows.

Box 17.8

Severability

If any provision contained in this agreement is held to be unenforceable by a court of law or equity, this agreement shall be construed as if such provision did not exist and the non-enforceability of such provision shall not be held to render any other provision or provisions of this agreement unenforceable.

NOTICE

Contracts are frequently used to convey information or requests from one party to another. The form of such communications may be governed by a *notices* clause. When negotiating a contract, make sure you are able to meet the notice provisions. Your failure to comply with the notices may result in breach. An example of such a clause is provided in Box 17.9.

Box 17.9

Notices

All notices or other communications required or permitted to be given under this agreement shall be in writing and shall be deemed to have been duly given if delivered personally in hand, by telephonic facsimile or mailed certified mail, return receipt requested, postage prepaid on the date posted and addressed to the appropriate party.

ASSIGNMENT

An *assignment* involves one party transferring its rights and/or obligations under a contract to another. Contracts frequently contain assignment clauses governing each party's right of assignment. An example of such a clause follows.

Box 17.10

Assignment

Neither party shall assign, transfer, nor delegate any rights, obligations, or duties under this contract without the prior written consent of the other party.

TERMINATION

Most contracts contain a clause specifying how and when the contract can be terminated. If you want to get out of a bad contractual relationship, this will be the crucial clause. Box 17.11 provides an example of such a clause.

Box 17.11

Termination by Provider

Provider may terminate this agreement at any time, with or without cause, upon sixty (60) days prior written notice to Managed Care Company.

Non-Form Contracts

Many important contracts will not be written as standard form contracts. Non-form agreements may include employment contracts, medical practice purchase and sale contracts, and business contracts. When negotiating and drafting such contracts, you should involve an attorney. It is important to note the tremendous advantage you gain if your attorney, rather than your opponent's attorney, prepares the first draft of the agreement. If she does, then the contract's fine print will be most favorable to you. Your opponent will then be anchored and will have to negotiate back from this draft. It could be very difficult for your opponent to subsequently negotiate away the fine print.

The disadvantage of having your attorney draft the contract is that you will typically incur greater legal costs. These costs stem from the increased time required to draft, as opposed to review, the contract and the time required to make any and all changes to future drafts.

When your attorney does not or cannot draft the original contract, you will often receive a one-sided document favorable to your opponent. There are ways to defend against this. First, you can threaten that, because the document is very one-sided, you will find other alternatives by using the other side's competitors. Secondly, you can exploit the promise of a long-term relationship to make the contract more fair. Third, you can simply state that you do not sign complicated contracts and demand that your opponent come back with a simpler document. Finally, remember that when negotiating any contractual term, you always need to have a credible rationale for why the term should be included or excluded. You should also look carefully for potential ambiguities and always ask yourself "what if." The time to resolve "what if" questions is when the contract is being negotiated, not when something goes wrong at a later date. Consider the following examples.

Example 17.1 The importance of understanding the "fine print"
Doctor: I thought you were acting in good faith until I saw the contract your lawyer sent over. You expect me to indemnify you for your *own* negligence and disclaim liability for any and all harm caused? And what's this about $50,000 in liquidated damages? I never agreed to any of that. I'm negotiating with three other doctors for shared use of my office space. None of them would ever come up with a document like this.
Opponent: I'm sorry, I didn't know. I'll have to talk with my lawyer. Why don't you have your lawyer make whatever changes you feel are necessary and send it directly to me?

Lesson: Through the controlled use of emotion (see pages 149–55 on emotion) and a good rationale ("I never agreed to that"), the doctor was able to negotiate changes to the terms of the contract. The implied threat of dealing with someone else was also helpful.

Example 17.2 Read the contract carefully and plan for future contingencies
Doctor: I'm looking for a long-term relationship here. Our practice is expanding and we'd love to stay in this property if we are treated fairly. We may even need to take over more floors in the very near future. This clause requiring written permission to make any and all alterations to the leased premises isn't going to work. And the $40,000 liquidated damages provision is patently unfair. What would happen if you rented the same space the next day for a higher rent? This lease is about the future and should be a basis for our future agreements. We need a fair document that protects both sides. This isn't it.

Opponent: I'm in it for the long term, too, and would love to have you. Let's make it work for both of us. Strike out those clauses and fax it back to me.

Lesson: The rationales of fairness and reasonableness can be effective for demanding changes to a written contract. Furthermore, it is *always* to your benefit to communicate to your opponent that you will be seeking to negotiate again in the future.

Example 17.3 The longer the contract drafted by your opponent's lawyers, the worse it will usually be for you

Doctor: I received your 17-page contract and, to be honest, I was a little taken aback. This isn't a complicated deal and it shouldn't take 17 pages to cover it. I'm not paying a lawyer thousands of dollars to review it. Send over something that's one or two pages long and then we'll talk.
Opponent: My lawyer says that we need this 17-pager to protect us.
Doctor: Are you saying you don't trust me? If you and your lawyer really think that you need a 17-page, two-sided document to protect yourself from me, then we probably shouldn't be doing business at all.
Opponent: I didn't mean to imply that. Let me draft something much simpler, have my lawyer review it, then send it over to you.

Lesson: If your opponent's lawyer is drafting the contract, it is usually in your best interest to have the contract be as short as possible. This is true because most, if not all, of the additional language in the contract will be for your opponent's benefit and your detriment.

Example 17.4 Clarify ambiguities that could prejudice you

Doctor: The contract you sent over states that I will be responsible to take calls "on a rotating basis." That is ambiguous. This could mean that I take calls every other night and weekend. Let's add a sentence that states, "In no event shall employee be required to be on call more than one night per week and one weekend per month."
Opponent: Fine. Mark up the document in red and I'll have my lawyer run the changes.

Lesson: The doctor had a good rationale for correcting the possible ambiguity. It would have been difficult for the opponent to refuse adding the requested language by providing a rationale for maintaining the ambiguous wording while still appearing to negotiate in good faith.

Example 17.5 Wise negotiators plan for contingencies and have escape clauses written into the agreement

Doctor: One final thing. Let's add a force majeure clause that says if I die or become disabled before the closing date, I, or my estate, will be excused from purchasing your practice.

Opponent: Well, let's hope that doesn't happen. Sure.

Lesson: The time to protect yourself from a possible bad turn of events is before the contract is signed. You have the power to plan for and protect yourself from certain contingencies. Think hard about your contracts and use that power.

Example 17.6 Doctor is much better off negotiating now rather than litigating later

Doctor: We need to talk about this covenant not to compete. I agree that you need to protect yourself. However, during my interview, you stated that over 90% of your patients are within a five-mile radius of your clinic. The covenant in this contract restricts me to areas outside of 20 miles from the practice. That's unfair, overbroad, and unnecessary to give you proper protection.

Opponent: Okay. We'll make it five miles.

Lesson: During the interview the doctor gained valuable information (through active listening), which she then used to negotiate the formal written contract. (See pages 35–74 on information.) The doctor was savvy enough to realize that the initial interview was part of the negotiation process. By conceding that the clinic needs protection, the doctor helped strengthen her rationale that the clause was overbroad and unnecessary. The doctor did not rely on a court to find the clause overbroad if a dispute arose at some later date. She successfully negotiated away potentially costly future problems.

Negotiating Standard Form Contracts

Many contracts today are standard form contracts. Standard form contracts include leases, managed care contracts, and consumer contracts such as those for the purchase and sale of an automobile. Applicable state law may give relief under some form contracts if something goes wrong. You *cannot* rely on obtaining such relief. You should try to negotiate more favorable terms even in standard form contracts. It can be done!

You will never get a change made to a standard form contract unless you ask for it. Due to the power of legitimacy (see pages 103–5 on legitimacy), many physicians do not even attempt to negotiate terms in these contracts. When you do ask for changes, you will need to have a rationale that is strong enough to justify them. Your opponents may indeed have the authority to amend their form contracts.

The same rules apply for all contracts. You will need to review the contracts carefully for ambiguities and carefully consider "what if" problems. You can also use the possibility of a long-term relationship and your ability to use your opponent's competitors to make changes to the standard form. Giving the impression that you are prepared to walk away may make your opponent significantly more flexible. Consider the following examples.

Example 17.7 Change of terms in form contract supported by powerful rationale

Doctor: Your company gets access under clause 6.2 to my patients' medical records. I will need you to add a clause stating that the plan will reimburse me for my expenses in copying those records.

Opponent: That's not part of the standard contract.

Doctor: That's not my concern. What's to stop you from frequently requesting voluminous medical records when you don't know exactly what you are looking for? Why should I have to pick up that cost? Under managed care I am supposed to accept incentives to become more efficient, so why shouldn't you?

Opponent: What language do you propose…?

Lesson: The doctor was not afraid to ask for a change in the standard contract after his "what if" analysis revealed a potential problem with medical record requests. He was prepared with a powerful rationale to justify the requested change.

Example 17.8 If you want a change in a form contract, you need to ask for it
Doctor: This provider agreement can only be terminated on 180 days advance notice. That's far too long. The other providers I am negotiating with all call for 60-day termination periods. That's the industry standard. You're looking for a long-term provider in this area and I want a long-term relationship with a provider who is in line with accepted practices.
Opponent: Okay. Cross out the 180 and insert 60.

Lesson: The doctor was not afraid to ask for a change. She used her alternatives (other managed care companies) and the possibility of a long-term relationship to gain power in the negotiation. The industry standard was a powerful rationale for her requested change. Note that her opponent did indeed have the authority to change the language in the standard form contract.

Example 17.9 Failure to respond builds negotiating power
Opponent: Doctor, we haven't heard from you in two weeks. I just wanted to follow up on the status of our negotiations.
Doctor: (sounding cold and noncommittal) Well, as you recall, I had some serious concerns about that standard agreement you sent over.
Opponent: (after a moment of silence) Ahh..., that's why I'm calling. I want to work with you so that we can get an agreement that's fair to both of us.
Doctor: Okay then. First, remove....

Lesson: Your opponent may be bluffing when giving you the impression that she cannot negotiate the terms of the contract. She may very well have flexibility. Furthermore, even when you think you need the deal more than your opponent, this may not be the case. A failure to get back to your opponent in a timely manner may communicate that you do not need the deal and may help you gain power in the negotiation.

Chapter 18 Closing the Deal

Executive Summary

- Using the assumptive close technique can help end negotiations.
- The final OK is a good opportunity to wrest an additional concession from your opponent.
- Pointing out your opponent's investment in a negotiation is a good way to close the deal.
- Don't leave any important items unsettled before reaching an agreement.
- Stressing your other options is a good way to help push the negotiation to a conclusion.

Introduction

Closing the deal is the final step in any negotiation and there is a series of techniques that can be used to help close a deal. These include the assumptive close, linkage, clear choice, and the power of investment. You need to understand when you have a deal and the importance of "face saving" to your opponent. Finally, you want to ensure that an ongoing or potential long-term relationship is not jeopardized, and is in fact strengthened, by the closing.

Assumptive Close

The successful physician negotiator recognizes when he has "won over" the opponent and has an agreement in hand. When an agreement is very close to being reached, the assumptive close is an appropriate technique to finalize the deal. The *assumptive close* involves your "assuming" that a deal has been reached and concluded. This psychological closing tactic forces your opponent to either say, "No, you are wrong. We don't have a deal" (which, at the very end of a negotiation, is difficult to do) or to accept that an agreement has been reached. Calling third parties, such as lawyers, accountants, or spouses, is another affirmation that the agreement has in fact been finalized. An assumptive close is very effective when all the major terms have been worked out but the opponent is having difficulty concluding the negotiation and saying the words, "We have a deal."

Example 18.1 Calling third parties to signal that the deal has closed
Doctor: (to opponent) Excellent! All of our hard work has paid off! I will call the venture capital people and tell them to start the paperwork. You can use my office, line three, to call your parties.

Lesson: The doctor has forced his opponent's hand. The opponent now needs to either assent to the deal or explain to the doctor why they have not reached an agreement.

Linkage

Linkage is one of the most effective methods of increasing the psychological pressure to achieve a deal. (See pages 131–32 on linkage.) In this context, linkage involves a quid pro quo in the form of a concession in exchange for finalizing the agreement.

Example 18.2 Using final agreement to leverage an additional concession
Hospital recruiter: (to prospective doctor employee) Doctor, as you know, we would welcome you to the faculty. The only remaining issue is the salary.
Doctor: It usually is.
Hospital recruiter: As I have mentioned repeatedly, our salary structure is such that we cannot exceed a starting salary of $140,000. Keep in mind that we have already agreed to your four weeks of vacation, health, disability and malpractice insurance, cell phone, pager, and relocation expenses.
Doctor: I appreciate all the perks, but I need $150,000.
Hospital recruiter: Our salary structure is such….
Doctor: If I agree to sign a letter of intent today, would you put in a $10,000 signing bonus? This would maintain your salary structure and give me and my family what we need.
Hospital recruiter: Let me make one quick call….We have a deal!

Lesson: The doctor listened carefully to the final objection (see pages 58–68 on active listening) and overcame the objection by linkage. His willingness to consent to finalize the deal was a concession that gained him $10,000.

<u>**Clear Choice**</u>

The clear choice closing tactic can also be useful in finalizing an agreement. The clear choice tactic involves focusing your opponent's choices in such a way that closing the deal is the best option available to her. When you know you may be losing time or money, the "clear choice" option can help cut your losses.

Example 18.3 Making opponent's best choice clear
Salesperson: The options are leasing the copying equipment for two years at $600 a month, or leasing it for three years at $500 a month and locking in the price for the additional year, or purchasing the equipment outright for $15,000.
Doctor: Why should I lease for two or three years when I could just purchase the equipment outright for the same price? At least this way I own the equipment.
Salesperson: Not many people have your grasp of finances, Doctor. Let me write up the sales agreement. For signing today, I will throw in one year of service and all the copy paper I have in my Prius. Just don't tell all the other doctors in this medical complex the deal you got!

Lesson: The salesperson effectively focused the doctor's choices and then made the decision easy and inevitable.

Example 18.4 Limiting options
Doctor: (to staff members) You have the option of taking off Christmas Eve, New Year's Day, Thanksgiving, or July 4th, which comes on a Saturday. Please pass around a sign-up sheet. As you know, we cannot close down on those days due to our patients' well being and the $5,000 a day we have in overhead.

Lesson: By limiting her opponent's choices, the doctor has made closing the deal more likely.

<u>**Power of Investment**</u>

The power of investment (see pages 101–3 on investment) can also be used as an effective closing technique. Pointing out your opponent's investment in a negotiation makes it much more difficult for him to walk away from the deal.

Example 18.5 Using your opponent's investment to close a deal
Physician head of nonprofit organization: (to prospective doctor author) Your idea for a book is viable…however, due to the fact that we are a nonprofit association and have our own publications, I am not sure we can proceed.
Prospective doctor author: (appearing overeager) Well, I know the book will be excellent. As you know, I am the leading authority on the subject.
Physician head of nonprofit organization: Doctor, your credentials are impeccable. No one here questions even for a moment your abilities. If we did, we would not have let you prepare the twenty-page outline, spend $847 in airfare, $500 in hotel expenses, and lose two days of work to come here to discuss the project.
Prospective doctor author: As you know, I have been working on this concept, outline, and even a few chapters….
Physician head of nonprofit organization: I don't want to see you come away empty handed after all the time, money, and effort you have spent. We can authorize "our" book. We will retain the copyright, set the price, be solely in charge of the marketing and the supplements, and will give you a 10% royalty payable twelve months after the end of our fiscal year, which is June 15th. We want the book as soon as possible.
Prospective doctor author: Thank you. I will get right on it.

Lesson: The doctor revealed her investment in the negotiation to her opponent. By doing so she disclosed damaging information. Her opponent used this investment against her to close an unfavorable deal.

Having a Deal

Making or having a deal occurs when the parties have agreed to all outstanding issues. The terms of the agreement should be written in an unambiguous memorandum and need to be such that they can and will be lived up to by all parties.

Outstanding Issues

After a lengthy and/or a complex negotiation session, parties commonly run into problems if some of the terms are not been spelled out in detail. Do not consider a deal closed until all the details have been worked out and curtail actions that could be detrimental if the deal falls through. Considering a deal closed prematurely can be very dangerous.

Example 18.6 Assuming deal is done before covering all the issues
Proposed employer: (to new doctor employee) We are all set. I will tell our attorneys to draw up the employment contract. You can have your attorney review it.
Doctor: Great! I look forward to starting on Monday.
Proposed employer: Actually, you start this Saturday. Under our call coverage plan, you work this weekend. You get every other weekend off and you cover at the emergency department every seventh day. Also, you have to cover the clinic at night.
Doctor: Wait just a minute. You never mentioned and I never agreed to this….
Proposed employer: Actually, if you remember, we agreed that you would have the same call coverage as the other physicians….This is what everyone is doing. You are a team player, aren't you, Doctor?
Doctor: Yes…but…I already told my spouse we had an agreement. I have to call her right away. She was going to give her two weeks' notice today at work.

Lesson: This doctor acted on the deal before all outstanding issues were finalized. He may now be trapped in a deal he would have otherwise walked away from.

Written Memoranda and Contracts

When it comes time to write up a memorandum of agreement, term sheet, contract, or letter of intent, the party who took detailed and clear notes during the negotiation holds the position of power. Also remember that the party whose attorney drafted the initial agreement will be in a position of power because the fine print in the initial draft will favor the drafting attorney's client. The opponent's counsel must then negotiate back from the initial document. The downside of having your attorney draft the contract is that you will generally incur greater legal fees than your opponent.

Example 18.7 The importance of accurate notes
Doctor: Just to summarize, you are looking for $1,000 a month retainer. For the $1,000 you will draft and copy both print and radio ads, place the copy, and determine the cost-efficiency of the ads.
Marketing group leader: That is correct.
Doctor: There are no additional or hidden charges to us.
Marketing group leader: That's right…one flat fee.
Doctor: Your group will not be paid anything over and above the $1,000 a month, right?
Marketing group leader: Well, it will not cost you anything else, but we do get the standard 20% ad agency commission.
Doctor: That should come back to us. We agreed to $1,000 a month….
Marketing group leader: It is standard practice for all agencies to retain the 20%.
Doctor: My notes of the negotiation session are clear. Your group gets $1,000 a month, no additional fees. If you refuse to live up to the agreement, we really can't do business with your group.
Marketing group leader: To be fair to us, this commission issue was not clearly spelled out by either party. We assumed we would retain it and you assumed, apparently, that any commission would revert back to you.
Doctor: We need to clear this up, as well as any other ambiguities, before we can sign the contract.

Lesson: Accurate notes helped the doctor gain power in the negotiation.

Living up to the Agreement

Any agreement or contract is only as good as the people who sign it. A party's intention and ability to live up to the agreement is critical. If you can demonstrate a track record of fulfilling your past agreements, you will be more likely to close the deal.

Example 18.8 Using a track record to close the deal
Medical education company representative: We would like you to help produce a video on informed consent, Doctor.
Doctor: As I mentioned, I am very interested in the project.

Medical education company representative: We have set up a timeline of three months to produce a final script and three months to shoot and edit the video. We are looking for twenty minutes.
Doctor: As you know, I have written thirty-six papers on informed consent and have lectured internationally on the subject. I would like to have a final script done in two weeks and have the whole project wrapped up in one month. The video should be sixty minutes long.
Medical education company representative: We want to have a realistic timeframe, Doctor. We have produced fourteen videos like this. Our experience has been that it takes two or three times as long as you might think. We have to line up a producer and director and reserve sets and equipment. We need to give you enough time to produce the work so that you do not fall behind schedule. Every hour we spend in pre-production saves us three hours in filming. We need only twenty high-quality minutes.
Doctor: I will trust your judgment. You have the experience. Let's go with the six-month timeline and twenty-minute video.

Lesson: The company was able to use its track record to gain a concession from the doctor and close the deal.

Saving Face

If there is any chance you may be dealing with your opponent again in the future, it is important for her to come out of the negotiating session looking good to her superior or employer. (See pages 134–35 on "the story.") You should use closing the deal as an opportunity to make your opponent look good. If you do, your future negotiations are more likely to be resolved favorably. As a corollary to this principle, you should never gloat or be demeaning at the end of a negotiation. Doing so serves no purpose and can be very detrimental to future negotiations and dealings.

Example 18.9 Making your opponent look good to her supervisor
Doctor: (on the phone to the negotiator's superior after a tough negotiation) I just want to congratulate you on your employee, Ms. Bonds. In the twenty-five years I have been a physician, she was the most effective negotiator I have ever faced. She listened, dealt with my concerns and issues, and was tough but fair. I don't think anyone else

could have gotten me to sign the contract on those terms. Even after beating my terms into the ground, she was so pleasant I couldn't be upset. I look forward to doing business with you and my worthy adversary, Ms. Bonds, in the future.

Lesson: Ms. Bonds will hear about the kind comments and will likely go out of her way to make future negotiations more favorable to you.

Example 18.10 Unwise gloating
Doctor: (to opponent by fax after negotiation) It was good doing business with you. Just as a point of information, I would have taken 30% less and still signed the contract.

Lesson: There is *no* efficacy to this fax. The doctor has made it much more difficult if he ever needs to negotiate in the future.

An Alternative Approach

One way to encourage your opponent to finalize a deal is to stress your alternatives should a deal not be reached. Hoping to gain further concessions from you, your opponent may try to delay or think over a deal for as long as possible. By stressing alternatives, you can motivate your opponent to close the deal. Objectively demonstrating the likelihood of you making a deal with another party will signal to your opponent that with further delay, your opponent could be left without any deal at all.

Example 18.11 Pressuring the opponent to close by stressing other options
Orthopedic surgeon: (to prospective physician employee) We have been negotiating for three weeks. I have listened very carefully to all your needs and have gone beyond my authority to try and meet almost each and every one of them. My partners have instructed me to reach an agreement today by 5:00 P.M. or else re-open our search efforts in order to recruit another orthopedic surgeon. If we can't reach a memorandum of understanding today, we will start the second interviews of other qualified and interested candidates.

Lesson: By stressing her alternatives, the doctor has gained power in the negotiation and made a timely closing of the deal more likely.

Example 18.12 Politely reminding your opponent of your other options to nudge them to close the deal

Doctor: We enjoyed the few days you have spent with us. The negotiation has been challenging but educational. We have put our best offer on the table. Sometimes when you are just starting out, it is hard to tell when someone is bending over backwards to be fair. Why don't you take all the time you need to think it over? In the meantime, we will invite several other doctors who are very interested in working in our office.

Prospective hire: May I call my wife? I do not need any additional time to think it over.

Lesson: By using a bit of reverse psychology and stressing the practice's alternatives, the doctor was able to push his opponent into making a decision.

Chapter 19 Negotiating an Employment Contract

Executive Summary

- Get an experienced lawyer involved as soon as possible.
- Make sure you understand the contract and that there are no ambiguities that can be used against you.
- Research your prospective employer before you start to negotiate.
- Negotiate your responsibilities first, then talk compensation.
- Negotiate fringe benefits before salary.
- Negotiate tight language so that you cannot be cheated out of bonuses, profit sharing, and the like.
- Protect your outside income (such as speaking and consulting fees).
- Think long and hard before agreeing to a covenant not to compete.
- Get as much medical malpractice protection, including a tail, as you can.

Introduction

Each year physicians lose substantial amounts of money due to poorly negotiated employment contracts. In addition to the significant monetary loss, physicians can lose freedom, restrict their professional choices, and impair their careers by signing unfair and unduly restrictive employment agreements. This loss adversely affects their families and family life as well. The key to the rights of both the employer and employee are the terms of the written employment contract. This means every word and every comma. Physicians need to be exceptionally careful as to what terms are contained in their employment contracts.

Consult with Counsel as Early as Possible in the Process

Many physicians negotiate the broad terms of their employment agreement, obtain a contract from their prospective employer, and then retain counsel to "look it over." The reasons they proceed this way are:

- they do not want to appear to be difficult,
- they do not want to jeopardize their careers, and
- "saving money" by getting the lawyer involved at the last minute.

By consulting counsel too late in the process, the physician has forfeited counsel's ability to provide the physician with guidance, checklists, demands, proposals, counterproposals, strategies, and tactics to achieve better terms, compensation, and working conditions. In addition, if counsel is involved early, counsel can negotiate the contract with the employer's lawyer for you. Having a professional negotiate the contract will likely result in better terms and will free the physician of the uncomfortable job of negotiating with a future employer.

> **Action Step:** Locate, consult, and retain an attorney experienced in negotiating employment contracts for physicians as early as possible in the process. Physicians who proceed in this fashion will do better financially, have more security, and enjoy better working conditions.

> **Tactical Tip:** When the broad terms of your tentative employment have been agreed upon, tell your opponent that your attorney will be handling the review and editing of the draft contract. Explain that your attorney reviews all your written contracts, which you've learned to do through a bad experience in the past.

Make Sure That the Negotiated Contract Terms Are Well-Defined and That You Understand Them

The employment contract you negotiate will contain defined terms. It is crucial that you understand what each and every defined term means prior to finalizing and signing an employment contract. Such terms are usually recognized on a contract by their being placed in quotes, bolded, underlined, placed in italics or made to stand out in another way. When a defined term is used in a contract, a court is likely to interpret the term according to its definition in the contract, not its commonly understood "Webster's" definition. In other words, what counts is what the contract says the term means, not what an average person thinks the word means in its ordinary sense.

For example, let's say the contract states that the physician "may be terminated immediately for *professional misconduct.*" Since *professional misconduct* is in italics, it is a defined term. What will govern precisely why a physician can be terminated is the definition of this term in the

"Definitions" section of the contract. Other defined terms may include the following.

- Employee
- Employee responsibilities
- Duties of a licensed physician
- Non-solicitation
- Confidentiality
- Termination

The definition of each and every defined term is open to negotiation. Physicians should not be intimidated into accepting standard definitions just because they are presented in a pre-printed standard contract.

Action Step: Understand each and every defined term in the proposed employment contract. If you do not understand what the term means even after reading the contract, have it defined with greater specificity before signing the contract. Look closely at the defined terms and think like a pessimist. If you can picture a situation under the definition that would adversely and unfairly affect you, it's time to negotiate a more favorable definition.

Tactical Tip: Use an absurd example or a point no reasonable person would disagree with to empower your request for clarified definitions. For example, if you can be terminated for *professional misconduct* and that term is very broadly defined, you can frame your argument against your opponent as follows: "You would agree that you will only be able to terminate me for good cause? This is important as I am putting my kids through school here, buying a house, and making a tremendous commitment to you. Unprofessional conduct, as you know, is sanctionable by the state licensing board. The way I read 'professional misconduct,' it could be construed to mean that you can fire me for anything you deem (fairly or unfairly) to be 'unprofessional,' such as showing up late for work one day. Let me suggest adding the following clause that will clarify…."

Duration of Employment

The duration of the contract (term) needs to be negotiated and clearly spelled out. How long the physician will want the contract to run will depend on many factors, including:

- the physician's responsibilities,
- base compensation,
- bonuses/profit sharing,
- partnership potential,
- fringe benefits,
- malpractice insurance,
- non-compete provisions, and
- termination provisions.

The physician may want to maintain some flexibility on the term of the contract to increase her bargaining power.

Once the term is agreed to, it should be read in conjunction with other provisions in the contract, for example, in conjunction with the *termination* provision. A two- or three-year employment contract may provide that it can be terminated with only 30 or 60 days notice upon the happening of specified occurrences. It is the interlocking provisions of the contract (one dependent on another) that make these contracts challenging to negotiate.

Action Step: The length of the contract is a crucial provision and one that affords the physician substantial leverage. The employer will generally want to "lock-up" the physician for a lengthy period of time. The physician can use this desire by the employer to link certain provisions to the term.

Tactical Tip: Use the duration of the commitment to leverage additional concessions from your employer. Focus on your commitment. For example, "You are asking for a long-term commitment. As you know, the demand for my specialty is forecast to increase dramatically. In all fairness, the commitment you are looking for deserves greater flexibility in terms of call, profit sharing, and hours…."

Perform Due Diligence on Your Prospective Employer Before Negotiating

Physicians often start negotiating over salary with a prospective employer before they are prepared to do so. Why negotiate with a potential employer before doing some basic research on the practice/group?

Physicians concentrate so much on the salary and other proposed provisions of the employment contract that they often neglect to do their due diligence on the employer. While the promises (written and oral) of the prospective employer are important, of equal importance are the past actions of the employer. Physicians should research:

- the reputation of the practice/group in the community,
- physician turnover and *why* this occurs,
- the percentage of physicians who make partner,
- past profits,
- payouts in past years,
- adequacy of support staff,
- malpractice claims pending,
- contracts with providers, and
- pending litigation.

Action Step: Physicians should perform a comprehensive due diligence check on the practice, group, and physicians before negotiating specific terms of employment. What the physicians and practice have done in the past may be more significant than what they promise to do in the future.

Tactical Tip: Ask lots of questions to research the above points and listen very carefully when dealing with your opponent. It is a good idea to have a checklist of due diligence questions to ask and to get your opponent's responses in writing. Notice everything in their office. Does the staff seem to get along? Does the place look well organized or is it a medical malpractice claim waiting to happen? Ask questions of your colleagues to "get the scoop" on the practice. Why have doctors left the practice? Ask if you can talk to former employees to see why they left. Conduct a computer or news search to see any mention of them. When negotiating and committing years of your life and your reputation to a new employer, you can never have too much information at your disposal.

Determine Specifically What Your Duties and Responsibilities Will Be

Physicians should negotiate a carefully delineated list of their duties and responsibilities in their employment contracts. This complete and comprehensive job description will avoid any surprise duties you may find yourself responsible for once you arrive on the job.

Physicians often overlook whether the employment contract specifically deals with the actual conditions of employment. What physicians will be called upon to do and where and how they will be expected to perform are crucial aspects of any physician employment agreement. This should be negotiated prior to the compensation issues.

A detailed list of the specific proposed duties for the physician should be negotiated and clearly spelled out in the employment contract. These include the following.

- Call
- Patient appointment hours
- Hospital rounds
- Responsibilities and schedule
- Office duties
- Location of work to be performed
- Whom you report to
- Who will report to you
- Input you will have in hiring decisions
- Types or numbers of procedures expected to be performed
- Review of blood work/lab results
- Phone calls
- Medical record documentation
- Pre-operative consultations
- Availability to nurses and support staff

Action Step: Physicians, with the assistance of experienced counsel, should draw up a checklist of proposed duties and responsibilities to use during employment negotiations. When, and only when, the duties are agreed to, should physicians negotiate compensation issues. The responsibilities of the employer should be specified as well.

Tactical Tip: If faced with vague or no terms regarding working conditions in the written contract, get specific, concrete terms that protect you added to the contract. For example, let's say the draft contract says that you are to take call on a "rotating basis in accordance with Group's established practices and procedures." Ask what this means. When the oral answer comes back "one night a week and one weekend a month," insist that the contract be amended to specifically clarify this (which is only reasonable). You don't want to be surprised to find out that the group's rotating basis practices and procedures requires the new physician to take call much more often than the partners! If you are working with a written contract and the terms are not in the contract, you may be out of luck, regardless of what oral promises or assurances you received when you were being hired.

Negotiate Fringe Benefits Before Salary

The physician who can negotiate the term of the contract, duties and responsibilities, and fringe benefits will be best positioned to then negotiate salary and other compensation. The salary the physician is paid is of primary importance. However, many prospective physician employees overlook the breadth of potential negotiable fringe benefits. A few of the more common benefits include the following.

- Tuition and CME reimbursement
- Health insurance
- Malpractice coverage
- Car allowance
- Vacation
- Sick leave
- Maternity leave
- Life insurance
- Professional dues
- Paid holidays
- Journal subscriptions

- Relocation expenses
- Dental insurance
- Profit sharing
- Disability insurance (short-term and long-term disability)
- 401(k) and other retirement plans
- Parking
- Flex time
- Loans
- Retirement benefits

Action Step: Physicians, with the help of counsel, should create a checklist of negotiable fringe benefits. These potential benefits should be prioritized and a "must-have" section created. The salary and compensation offered should be analyzed in light of the total package offered.

Tactical Tip: Prepare a compelling reason why you either deserve or require fringe benefits that you have not been offered. The most compelling and powerful reason would be a competing job offer. Also, like other key terms, make sure your fringe benefits are specifically included in writing in the final contract. You don't want to get into a situation where fringe benefits were merely paid out of tradition and future fringe benefits are subject to the whims of management.

Obtain as Much Specificity as Possible Regarding Your Proposed Compensation

Prior to negotiating salary, the physician will want to research industry standards that vary with specialty, years of experience, and location. These industry norms should be a starting point for your negotiation. It is important that you do not fixate or permit yourself to get anchored to these average salaries. Ask yourself, are you an average physician?

The three general methods for compensating physicians are:

- base salary (guaranteed amount),
- base salary plus production (the more you work and produce the more you get paid), and
- production less overhead.

Factors that physicians will want to consider when negotiating compensation follow.

- What are the sources of revenue of the practice/group (private insurance, Medicare, out-of-pocket, Medicaid)?
- What is the time between services provided and monies collected?
- If compensation is based on "production" or a "production schedule," obtain a definition of the formula to be used.
- What are the collection percentages of the practice/group?
- To what extent will your compensation be based on factors outside of your control? (Such as office overhead, the production of other physicians, etc.)
- To what extent are your bonus and other income protected by the proposed contract? (See below.)

Action Step: Physicians will first want to obtain a guaranteed base salary upon which to build a total compensation package. These physicians will then want to lock in "bonus" and "additional income" with objective, realistic triggers.

Tactical Tip: If the employer tries to paint an unrealistically rosy picture of the bonus potential, do not be afraid to ask instead for 75% of the "pie-in the sky" bonus as a guaranteed salary. The same is true with equity grants. Ask what they anticipate the equity will be worth, then ask for 75% of that as cash. As always, the best way to achieve a higher than average compensation package is by developing competing bids for your services and playing one employer against the other. (Of course, this must be done with the utmost amount of tact since it may adversely affect your job responsibility or taint the relationship.) Remember that most employers do not offer the most of what they are willing to pay initially. Assume that they have flexibility and understand that the only way you will get more compensation is if you ask for it.

Tie Your Bonus to Objective, Realistic, Obtainable Triggers

Many physicians sign employment contracts without adequate information regarding the additional compensation (bonus) they can expect to receive under the contract.

Incentive plans (bonuses) in many physician employment contracts are written to protect the employers and not the physician employees. Some clauses physician employees should be particularly careful about include the following.

- The ability of the compensation committee to *cancel* or *prospectively revise* the incentive plan.
- The need for a site to break even before the plan takes effect.
- The precise calculation of the physician incentive.
- The definition of key terms (for example, positive net income, negative variance, percentage, gross revenues, etc).
- When the bonus is payable (at the end of the contract year, quarterly, or semi-annually).

The physician will want to tie her bonus as much as possible to things under her control (for example, the amount billed). Physicians will want to exercise great caution in tying their bonuses to factors completely outside their control (such as profits after payment of salaries and collections, which may be hampered by office inefficiency and outside contingencies).

Action Step: With the assistance of counsel, a physician should negotiate the proposed incentive plan until the physician completely understands the plan. The plan should preferably have objective triggers that cannot be manipulated against the interest of the physician by an unscrupulous employer.

Tactical Tip: Negotiate incentive terms based on gross income, which is objective and is somewhat under your control, not net income, which includes expenses not under your control and which can be manipulated. When offered a net deal, always remember what 25% of zero works out to be.

Physicians Should Negotiate Diligently to Protect Additional Income

Physicians generally will be expected to sign a contract provision that calls for them not to provide medical services that will detract from, or adversely affect, the quality of services provided to the patients of the group or practice.

Negotiate for the right to generate additional income from outside activities that is readily available to many physicians. This outside income, depending on the circumstances, the work ethic of the physician, and the physician's specialty, can be substantial. They may include the following.

- Directorships
- Honoraria for lecturing
- Royalties for writing treatises and articles
- Consulting work
- Testifying as an expert witness
- Inventions
- Patents
- Copyrightable works
- Discoveries
- Other intellectual property
- Medical-legal consulting

Action Step: Physicians should be cautious about signing away their rights to outside income, especially when this income is generated on their own time (nights, weekends, or vacations). Employment contracts should contain specific language that states that the physician retains all outside or additional income. Not addressing this issue in the contract can lead to misunderstandings and bad feelings at best, and litigation and termination at worst.

Tactical Tip: The physician negotiating this contractual provision should point to the fact that this can be a win-win situation. A physician who writes a well-received medical textbook will help grow the practice. Thus, the practice/group would be wise to encourage the physician to pursue this additional income and favorable publicity for the practice. In fairness, do the partners share their outside income with the practice? Finally, what you do on your time is your business. If you do extra work to generate additional income, you should be able to keep the proceeds.

Negotiate Fair and Balanced Termination Provisions

Physicians who are negotiating and signing employment contracts should be acutely aware of the full implications of the termination provisions of the proposed contract. Physicians can have an otherwise excellent employment contract that is eviscerated by onerous one-sided termination provisions. If the contract provides that the physician can be terminated *without cause* with just 30 or 60 days written notice, the physician does not really have the protection afforded by his "two-year contract."

Physicians should pay particular attention to the events listed that can trigger a termination, including:

- failure to provide duties in a "manner satisfactory" to the employer,
- *any event* deemed by the employer to be detrimental to the employer,
- suspension of privileges,
- "material" breach of contract,
- illness,
- disability,
- license suspension,
- expulsion or discipline by a professional organization,
- conviction of a felony or crime involving moral turpitude or unethical conduct, and
- inability to obtain malpractice insurance.

Action Step: Physicians and their counsel should take a long, hard look at the termination provisions of the proposed contract to see if they are fair and reasonable. Provisions that are too one-sided may portend difficulties with the employer. Vague provisions should be clarified.

Tactical Tip: If the employer insists on a termination without cause provision with 60 days notice, the physician should be given the right to similarly quit the practice with the same 60 days notice. If termination is only for "good cause," ask that the reasons constituting good cause be clearly and objectively spelled out in the contract.

Negotiate a Fair and Not Unduly Restrictive Covenant Not to Compete

Employers may request/demand that the physician joining their practice sign a covenant not to compete. In some states, the courts have construed these provisions to be enforceable if they are no broader than necessary to protect a legitimate interest of the employer and are not unduly burdensome to the physician and are not harmful to the public interest. Physicians frequently go into a negotiation with little or no concern about the covenant not to compete clause in the proposed employment contract. This is due to the fact that the physician is operating in good faith and has the hope and expectation of long-term employment.

Physicians may be asked to sign a provision stating that they will not compete with the employer in a specific geographic area, 5–50 miles, or for a specific period of time, say, one to three years.

Action Step: Physicians should concern themselves with the non-competition sections:

- length of term (years/months),
- geographic limitations (miles, states, etc.), and
- provisions for exception (for example, teaching, work for an insurance company, work as medical director of a non-competing company).

Physicians negotiating this provision should consider how the other provisions in the contract affect the covenant not to compete. For example, if the employer can terminate the physician without cause with just 60 days notice and the physician cannot practice within 50 miles of the group, the physician may be forced to uproot her family and relocate to continue to practice medicine or she may need to commute a long distance.

Tactical Tip: The physician can suggest a non-solicitation provision as an alternative to a covenant not to compete. The patient ultimately dictates if he wants the physician to continue to treat him.

Negotiate for Medical Malpractice Protection

Physicians will want to negotiate for full and complete malpractice coverage. Employers can be requested to provide coverage of $1,000,000 per incident/$3,000,000 aggregate up to $2,000,000–$4,000,000. The key is the type of coverage.

- *Occurrence:* coverage is in force no matter when the claim is made
- *Claims made:* is in force only when the policy is in place

The physician will want to obtain an endorsement or *tail* to cover her once she is no longer employed at the practice and the claims made policy is no longer in effect. The physician's goal is to avoid gaps in coverage.

Action Step: Physicians want to obtain complete and continuous malpractice coverage. The tail coverage provisions should be spelled out permitting the physician to obtain tail coverage without paying for the premium or a substantial deductible.

Tactical Tip: As an employee, you are not in on the upside, so you cannot afford downside risk. Use this argument to insist on complete malpractice coverage, including a tail. If they want you to pay your own premiums and thus share in the risk, ask to be made a partner who will share in the potential benefits of the practice.

Conclusion

There are many additional provisions to consider and negotiate for in your employment contract. Some of the more common are:

- partnership potential,
- performance evaluations,
- assign ability,
- dispute resolution,
- patient notification,
- employer's responsibilities,

- access to records, and
- recruitment incentives.

Physicians who understand the contractual issues, obtain counsel early, negotiate aggressively, and are able to assess the contract as a whole will be best positioned to achieve a fair, reasonable, and secure employment contract.

Additional Resources

- "Employment Contracts Can Be Crucial to Your Future," American College of Foot and Ankle Surgeons (2005)
- "Prescription for Avoiding Conflict," William Fleming, The Doctors Advocate, http://www.thedoctors.com/publications/docadv/2005q3matters.asp
- "Restrictive Covenants in Physician Contracts," *AMA Legal Issues* (2005)
- "Negotiating Employment Contracts: Do's and Don'ts, Bruce D. Armon, Esq. (May 2005)
- "A Physician's Guide to Employment Contracts," Minnesota Medical Association (2004)
- "Medical Group Management Association Physician Compensation and Production Survey" (2004)
- "Contracts: What You Need to Know" and the "Annotated Model Physician Employment Agreement," American Medical Association, www.ama-assn.org (2003)
- *Physician Employment Contracts: Understanding Your Employment Contract: A Model for Physicians,* Payne, Rosenbaum, American Medical Association, November 15, 2000
- *The Successful Physician Negotiator: How to Get What You Deserve,* Babitsky, Mangraviti, SEAK, Inc. (1998)
- *How to Negotiate a Physician's Employment Contract,* Hirsh & Wilcox, American Medical Association (1995)

Chapter 20 Negotiation of a Managed Care Agreement

By Dennis Hursh

Introduction and Executive Summary

Even the largest managed care company is usually willing to negotiate its participating provider agreements to some extent. Amazingly, however, many physician practices sign the first draft that is presented to them. By doing so, they not only "leave money on the table," but they also permit administrative hassles for their staff to develop that could have been avoided with aggressive negotiation of all managed care agreements. The bigger the managed care company's share of the market, the more important it is to assure a reasonable agreement is reached. Physicians must aggressively protect their rights through negotiation or risk continuing reductions in their income and increases in workload.

Have an Experienced Health-Care Attorney Review the Agreement

Managed care companies utilize experienced legal counsel to draft their agreements. It is unrealistic to assume that a physician, a practice administrator, or an attorney who does not focus on this area will understand both the legal ramifications and the practical issues presented by a managed care agreement.

> **Action Step:** Locate, consult with, and retain an attorney experienced in reviewing and negotiating managed care agreements. The fees of such attorneys are likely to be recouped many times over through decreased staff time in dealing with administrative problems and through potentially increased compensation.

> **Tactical Tip:** The state or local county medical society may have recommendations. If not, talk to physician or office managers at practices who have utilized an experienced attorney for their input.

Require a Verifiable Fee Schedule

Few physicians would sign an employment agreement in which they agreed to be paid "the salary schedule in effect from time to time." However, many practices sign managed care agreements where they agree to be paid "the fee schedule in effect from time to time." The fee schedule should be either a specified dollar amount for specific CPT codes or should utilize an objective methodology such as a percentage of Medicare payments for a specified year. The fee schedule should have an automatic inflation adjustment and should not be subject to unilateral amendment by the managed care company.

> **Action Step:** Make sure you understand exactly what you will be paid under the agreement. Your office manager should be able to audit payments from the managed care company easily to determine if you are being paid appropriately.

> **Tactical Tip:** Do not fall for the oldest trick in the book: increasing the proposed compensation from "100% of the then-current fee schedule" to "115% of the then-current fee schedule." Consider proposing a reasonable fee schedule to the managed care company to begin negotiations. If specific CPT codes appear to provide lower compensation than the ones provided by the company's competitors, make sure the company is aware of that discrepancy. Pay particular attention to the CPT codes most often used in your practice.

Make Sure You Will Be Paid for Your Work

Many managed care agreements provide that only services that are "medically necessary" will be covered. The definition of medical necessity can often be paraphrased as "whatever we (the health plan) determine it is."

Action Step: Attempt to negotiate a definition that is based upon a "prudent physician" standard.

Tactical Tip: At a minimum, require that the determination of medical necessity be made in a "good faith" or "reasonable" manner.

Make Sure You Know with Whom You Are Contracting

Preferred Provider Organizations ("PPOs") are frequently among the best payors. However, the definition of "Payor" in PPO agreements is critical. Many plans define a "Payor" as "an individual, organization, firm or governmental entity, or self-insured account that has executed an agreement with the plan." This definition would allow the plan to "rent" its network in a manner that could be deemed a "silent PPO."

Specifically, if a patient with insurance through a small regional company located far away from your practice becomes ill and presents at your office, you would expect to receive your usual, customary, and reasonable fees for this office visit. However, if the patient's health plan or third party administrator is able to obtain access to your practice's negotiated rates with a local PPO, you will receive a greatly reduced discounted fee for seeing the patient. In short, a "silent PPO" has the effect of changing UCR payments to discounted fees.

Action Step: To address this issue, the definition of "Payor" should very clearly state that the term relates solely to the plan, affiliated entities in the insurance company holding group, and self-funded employee benefit plans that use the plan only as a third party administrator. Make sure that the definition of "Payor" specifically provides that the discounts being negotiated will not be accessible to any party other than those described above.

Tactical Tip: Some health plans are willing to provide a list of self-funded employers that have access to these discounts. It would be prudent to assure that such a list is given and to check the list against explanations of benefits received to assure that the discounts negotiated with the plan are not being "rented" to other parties.

Protect Yourself Against the "Bad Apple"

Most PPO agreements bring all "Payors" under the umbrella protection of the agreement. Therefore, even though you may be very pleased in general with payment and other terms of the plan contract, your practice might suddenly realize that it is not being paid with respect to enrollees of one employer. Frequently, your only option in this case is to claim a breach of the agreement by the plan and either terminate the entire agreement or "grin and bear it." A better alternative would be to negotiate a provision in the agreement to the effect that both parties acknowledge that agreements are being made between the plan and employers, and that your practice is a third party beneficiary of these agreements. This clause should give you the right to sue directly any employer who is not paying for services, without terminating the rest of your PPO agreement.

> **Action Step:** You should obtain specific provisions to the effect that, if a given employer is in default of its obligations, then the PPO will provide your practice with a copy of its agreement with the employer and make a demand for payment to the employer on your behalf. In any event, it should be made clear that your obligation to treat enrollees of that particular employer will be released upon your notification to the plan that the employer is a deadbeat.

> **Tactical Tip:** Initially, propose a provision requiring the PPO to make a demand and to provide that if payment is still not forthcoming within a reasonable period of time, then the PPO has two options: either pay the claim itself, or assign all its rights under the PPO/employer agreement to you. This approach tends to force the PPO to objectively evaluate the risk of a "bad apple."

Learn from Past Problems

Many practices have a relatively small number of CPT codes that account for the majority of the practice's income. Often, at contract renewal, the biggest complaint by the practice will be that the plan treats a given CPT code unevenly. Typically, the relevant scientific literature supports a given treatment modality under specified conditions. However, plan patients presenting with these conditions are frequently denied payment for this modality based upon an alleged lack of medical necessity. It is not uncommon for some significant portion of patients presenting with these conditions to be denied payment by the plan. Sometimes, every plan enrollee is initially denied payment, but, upon appeal, coverage is granted. Many health plans utilize proprietary software in their decision-making process. The licensing agreements with the software companies often prohibit wide-scale distribution outside of the plan. Accordingly, provider relations representatives will earnestly assure you that they cannot provide you with the decision-making criteria.

Action Step: The best outcome in situations such as this is to utilize the relevant scientific literature as an attachment to the agreement, specifically stating that a given modality is appropriate under the circumstances described in this exhibit. Another approach, somewhat more common, would be a simple statement attached to the agreement that a given modality will be approved under certain defined circumstances.

Tactical Tip: The licensing agreements of most decision-making software companies do allow sharing of specific criteria for a given CPT code to a physician disputing payment. Thus, although the plan is most likely prohibited from providing you the decision-making criteria for all CPT codes in your specialty, it is most likely not prohibited from sharing the decision-making criteria with respect to a given CPT code, particularly if you are currently disputing a decision made based upon that criterion. This is an extraordinarily difficult provision to negotiate, since the plan quite rightly will be concerned about treating enrollees with identical conditions differently, depending upon which practice treats them. However, to the extent that the plan's medical director can be involved, that individual is likely to want to assure uniform correct treatment (and treatment payment decisions) for all patients. Therefore, if the criteria are appropriate and generally recognized, the plan's medical director may become an ally in contract negotiations on this point.

Limiting the MCO's Ability to Retroactively Reduce Previously Paid Claims

Most managed care companies strictly limit the amount of time in which a practice may amend a claim—frequently to just 90 days after the service was rendered. However, few agreements place any limitation upon the period of time in which the plan can review a paid claim. Accordingly, practices have faced retroactive adjustments with respect to claims paid six years earlier. Although *medical* records may be maintained for the distant future, detailed *financial* records with respect to individual claims are not commonly retained for long periods. Accordingly, the practice is likely to be unable to efficiently contest any retroactive adjustment based upon services performed more than a year or two before the adjustment is claimed by the plan.

> **Action Step:** Most managed care companies are willing to place some outer limit (e.g., two to three years) on the period of time in which they may retroactively reduce previously paid claims.

> **Tactical Tip:** First, propose a "good for the goose, good for the gander" reciprocal provision that allows retroactive claim reduction for the same period of time that the practice is given to submit claims. By tying these two concepts, you can often increase the time given to submit claims, while limiting the time the plan can retroactively reduce claims.

Aggressively Limit the Plan's Right to Offset Money Owed to the Practice

Most managed care agreements provide that, should the plan determine that it has overpaid any money to the practice, then the plan may simply offset this money against money owed for services rendered. The problem with this approach is that if a major payor determines that it has overpaid a large dollar value of claims, cash flow to the practice can be seriously jeopardized. Even worse, the practice manager will not be aware of this impending cash crisis until it hits, as the first inkling will be receipt of an explanation of benefits that shows an amount owed for services and reflects an offset. A major adjustment by a large payor could be financially ruinous to a practice.

Action Step: To avoid this result, negotiate contract language that requires the plan to give your practice reasonable advance notice of a proposed adjustment, together with an opportunity to contest the adjustment.

Tactical Tip: A minimum of 60 days advance notice should be provided. This will allow your practice administrator sufficient time to determine the scope of the problem and the accuracy of the plan's calculations.

Maintain Your Leverage at Termination

Many managed care agreements provide that the plan, alone, is responsible and authorized to notify enrollees that your practice no longer participates in the network. This provision has the effect of tying your hands if you get into a dispute with the plan and want to terminate your agreement. Most plans provide for a 90-day "without cause" termination. In the event of a serious dispute, you might wish to invoke this provision and provide a notice of termination. The patients of the practice can be the most effective advocates of the practice if this occurs. Moreover, your practice administrator will be placed in an extremely difficult position if your patients in a given plan are attempting to schedule appointments or procedures after the effective date of termination, and he or she is prohibited from informing the patient that the practice will no longer be participating in the patient's insurance plan after a given date.

Action Step: Make sure that your practice has the ability to notify patients in the event of a termination (or the giving of notice of a future termination) of the agreement.

Tactical Tip: Termination of the agreement is the "atomic bomb" in your arsenal. Although this should be used only when absolutely necessary, sometimes it is the only way to get the attention of upper-level decision-makers of the plan.

Do Not Allow the Agreement to Continue while a Dispute Is Pending

Many managed care agreements require the practice to continue in the network while a dispute is pending. This can have the effect of preventing you from escaping from a contract, even if the plan has breached the agreement. Working through the plan's internal grievance mechanisms, then proceeding to mandatory arbitration can take months or even years. This could be devastating to the practice if the plan is breaching its agreement.

> **Action Step:** Make sure that there is some reasonable limit (i.e., 120 days after the initial notice of a dispute) on the amount of time that you will be forced to continue to honor the agreement if you get into a dispute with the plan.

> **Tactical Tip:** Termination of the agreement because of a breach by the managed care company is a vital right you must maintain. This right becomes meaningless if you are forced to remain in the agreement long after the plan has breached its obligations to you.

Do Not Violate Anti-Trust Laws by Discussing Compensation with Colleagues

It is natural for physicians to discuss managed care compensation with their colleagues in other practices. Do not do it! Antitrust law prohibits "actions in restraint of trade" among competitors. Two practices in the same specialty are considered to be competing for the business of managed care companies and their enrollees. Even though both practices are extremely busy and may have no desire (or even ability) to see new patients, the law still views them as competitors. Accordingly, a discussion of fees or other material terms of managed care agreements with colleagues in your area risks legal prosecution.

> **Action Step:** Avoid the temptation to join forces with other practices in your area to obtain better fees.

> **Tactical Tip:** Your best chance of obtaining a reasonable agreement comes from utilizing experienced legal counsel to scrutinize carefully all the provisions of the agreement. Focusing solely on fees or relying on other practices to

determine what is reasonable would likely not lead to the best result, even if it were legal.

Conclusion

In today's challenging environment, physician practices have to be tough to survive. Effective negotiations with managed care companies can no longer focus solely on basics such as fee schedules. Every detail of each contract must be scrutinized, evaluated, and negotiated.

Additional Resources

- "Managed Care Contracting 401," Dennis G. Hursh, *Physicians News Digest* (2004)
- "A Silent PPO Primer," Dennis G. Hursh, *Physicians News Digest* (2006)
- *The Successful Physician Negotiator: How to Get What You Deserve,* Babitsky and Mangraviti, SEAK, Inc. (1998)
- *Health Care & Antitrust Law: Principles and Practice,* John J. Miles, West Group, Inc. (2000)
- *Influencing Third-Party Payers: A How-to-Guide for Physicians, Medical Societies and Group Practices,* American Society of Internal Medicine (1993)
- "Model Managed Care Contract," American Medical Association (2003)

About the Author

Dennis Hursh is a principal in Hursh & Hursh, P.C., a Middletown, Pennsylvania, law firm concentrating on representation of physicians and physician group practices. Dennis' practice is concentrated on healthcare contract drafting, negotiation, and interpretation. He represents physicians in all areas of contracting and practice management, and is involved in the design, organization, and representation of employer welfare benefit plans, physician organizations, preferred provider organizations, hospital-physician joint ventures, coordinated care organizations, insurers and third party administrators. He may be reached by telephone at (866) DOC-LAW1 or by e-mail at Dennis@PaHealthLaw.com.

Chapter 21 Negotiating a Real Estate Lease for a Medical Practice

By Lisa D. Taylor, Esq.[1]

Introduction and Executive Summary

With the exception of the acquisition of certain types of equipment such as MRI machines and investments in facilities such as ambulatory surgical facilities, a physician's office space will be the biggest financial investment made in connection with the operation of his or her practice. Aside from the fact that a physician's office space will project an image for the physician, the office space can be a major factor in the success of the medical practice. This is not just because location and amenities can affect accessibility and convenience for patients, but also because a real estate lease can facilitate or impede the operation of a practice and can provide certain competitive advantages and disadvantages. Therefore, it is crucial that physicians critically evaluate the business terms and legal requirements contained in a real estate lease and be prepared to undertake extensive negotiations to obtain the best deal possible.

Be Prepared to Negotiate and Assemble Your Team

Physicians *must* be prepared to negotiate the terms of the real estate lease for their medical practice's office space. Commercial real estate leases are almost always negotiable and virtually always require some revision before execution. This is because the form of document initially presented to a prospective tenant by the landlord is usually overwhelmingly favorable to the landlord and often unreasonably burdensome to the tenant.

Physicians sometimes are reticent about undertaking a negotiation, especially one that is often necessary. The reasons for this reticence include the following.

- They may believe that real estate leases are not negotiable.
- The fear that the landlord will not be willing to negotiate.
- The fear that they will lose the space to a more accommodating tenant.

- They are busy focusing on other business aspects of the medical practice such as staffing, professional liability insurance, and the acquisition of equipment, and/or they want to be able to consummate the deal as quickly as possible.
- They do not want to incur the cost of legal counsel and other professionals.
- The real estate broker discourages them from negotiating.

Physicians must not allow any of these factors to prevent them from undertaking negotiations. As stated above, commercial landlords *anticipate* that the real estate lease will be revised and it is for this reason that the initial version of the lease is so one-sided; landlords often build negotiating room into the initial version of the lease expecting that it will be a draft. Given the cost not only of the monthly lease payment, but also the other costs associated with lease of space for a medical practice which often include utilities, real estate taxes, and insurance on the building, along with a portion of operating expenses of the building, physicians cannot afford not to invest the time, effort, and money in getting the best terms possible.

Moreover, it is important that physicians not rely on the real estate broker as if the broker is a trusted adviser. Real estate brokers can be very helpful in identifying real estate that is available for lease and providing some idea of prices in a given geographical area. However, commercial real estate brokers' commissions are generally paid in full by the landlord and they may unconsciously have some loyalty to the landlord, rather than the physician-tenant. Furthermore, a real estate broker's primary goal, regardless of who pays the commission, is to close a deal. A real estate broker cannot be relied upon to advise a client when to walk away from a situation that is problematic, although there are some who will do so.

Action Step: Locate, consult with, and retain professionals to assist in negotiating a real estate lease. An attorney will certainly be required and must be retained. Physicians should retain an attorney experienced with leases for medical office space. Commercial leases, especially those for medical office space, are specialized. Even a general real estate attorney may not be qualified to provide advice if, for example, the bulk of the work the attorney handles is residential real estate or the sale of commercial real estate. Also, an attorney should be sensitive to the factors that will be important to a medical practice tenant. An attorney who predominately represents landlords may have a pro-landlord mindset. If use of the space will require construction or renovation, known as "fit-out," "fit-up," or "build-out," assistance of an architect, space planner, and/or interior designer may also be necessary.

Tactical Tip: Do not commit to any particular business or financial term or orally to the space until consulting with your professionals. This will reduce your ability to negotiate. Tell the broker that you will want your professionals to review all documentation and advise you. Be certain to tell your professionals about all of your plans for the space and your understanding of the terms so they can advise you appropriately and try to protect your interests. Be aware that unless understandings made orally are included in the lease or an exhibit, they will not be binding and have no force or effect.

Obtain Confirmation that the Space Is Suitable for Medical Use

It is imperative that physicians confirm that the office space they are considering leasing is suitable for medical office use. Physicians and the brokers who show space should not assume that any commercial office space is actually useable by a medical practice for its office. The reasons commercial office space may not be appropriate for use as a medical office include the following.

- Zoning restrictions in some localities
- Inadequate parking
- Insufficient access/accommodation for mobility or sight-impaired visitors
- Insufficient electrical current or plumbing/sewage capacity

With respect to zoning, be aware that some localities treat medical use differently than other commercial uses and will not allow a medical practice to locate in space unless it is specifically zoned or approved for medical use. Sometimes the ability to use the space for medical use is dependent upon available parking. This is because medical use typically requires more parking than other commercial uses. Patients usually spend more time at a physician's office than they do shopping, for example, so the spaces do not turn over as quickly or as frequently as they would if the patient were shopping. Also, patients are more likely to travel to a medical office alone or with only one other person. By contrast, patrons of a restaurant, for example, are more likely to come to the restaurant in groups of at least two persons but often in greater numbers. This allows a restaurant to serve a greater number of customers who have traveled in a smaller number of cars.

Even if parking does not affect zoning, sufficient parking (or convenience to public transportation) is essential. Patients may miss appointments or be late for appointments if transportation or parking is inconvenient.

Impediments for patients who are visually or mobility impaired also need to be considered. Although federal law, specifically the Americans with Disabilities Act, and state laws which mandate accessibility, have forced landlords and "places of public accommodation" to provide accessibility, physicians need to assure that accessibility is not ephemeral.

Sufficient electrical current and plumbing/sewage capacity also need to be confirmed. Medical practices virtually always have greater plumbing/sewage needs than other commercial enterprises because of the need for sinks for hand washing. Some practices need extra restrooms for patients to provide urine samples. Similarly, medical equipment often requires much greater electrical current than typical office equipment requires. Dedicated circuits or special 220 volt circuits may be necessary to run some types of medical equipment.

> **Action Step:** Physicians should request their real estate broker to obtain written confirmation that the space is zoned for medical use and ask their lawyer to ensure that the landlord provides such a representation in the lease. So that other tenants in a multi-tenant building do not over-utilize parking space, physicians should seek to have a certain minimum number of reserved spaces that can only be used by practice visitors. This should be in addition to unreserved spaces.
>
> Assure that if ramps or elevators will be required for patients to gain access to the medical office that the obligation to maintain them is guaranteed in the lease so that they will be available when needed. If Braille on elevators or stairways is not present, a written commitment

for installation by a specific date should be made along with a commitment that the Braille will not be obscured during the term of the lease.

Physicians should consult with an architect, and, if necessary, an electrician or a plumber to determine whether the electrical and plumbing capacity in the space contemplated to be leased is sufficient for medical practice needs. Electrical and plumbing requirements need to be specified in the lease as well.

Tactical Tip: If space has previously been used by a medical tenant or is located in a building that is primarily or entirely leased to medical tenants, it may be more suitable for medical practice use than other space. However, a physician must not assume that prior use by another medical tenant or the proximity of other medical tenants will prevent problems. Physicians' practices are not identical and specific needs will vary greatly by specialty. For example, a radiologist's office will have substantial electric needs for the imaging equipment utilized, while urology office space typically requires extra restrooms.

Make Certain that Your Lease and the Leases of Other Tenants in a Multi-Tenant Building Protect Your Specialty

Physicians need to assure that the operation of their particular type of medical specialty is allowed pursuant to their lease. They also need to ensure that another tenant's lease does not preclude them from practicing their specialty or providing certain types of services. Prudent physicians also will want to try to avoid competitors, if possible, from being in close proximity and should enlist the assistance of their attorney in accomplishing these goals. This is because leases for commercial space, and medical office space in particular, often include provisions for:

- permitted uses and
- exclusive uses.

A permitted use is the purpose for which leased space may be utilized. An exclusive use is a service or function which only the designated tenant may perform.

Action Step: Physicians must ensure that their attorneys review, negotiate, and possibly re-draft the provisions which provide for permitted uses and exclusive uses. The provisions for permitted use need to include all uses which the medical practice-tenant contemplates. A permitted use provision might state, for example, that "the premises shall be utilized for the operation of a medical office, specifically the provision of professional medical services to patient-invitees, and associated business and administrative functions including billing, collection, and preparation and storage of medical records."

So that a physician does not have a competing practice in close proximity, a provision for exclusive use should also be sought. Being the only practice of a particular type in a multi-tenant building will enhance the chance that referrals from other physicians in the building will be received and that patients will select the practice if they require services of the specialty offered. This will also reduce the chance that patients will be encouraged to seek the services of a competitor. An exclusive use provision for a radiology practice would state, for example, that "tenant shall have the exclusive right to provide radiological and imaging services in the building, including, but not limited to, x-ray, ultrasound, CT scan, magnetic resonance imaging (MRI), mammography and such other technologies that may be developed, during the term of the lease and any renewals thereof." The lease should also provide that "the landlord shall have the obligation to enforce this covenant." This means that the landlord cannot lease to anyone else to perform such services and must take steps to prevent other tenants from performing such services by including a prohibition against performing such services in the leases of other tenants and taking steps to stop violations by other tenants.

Tactical Tip: To preserve flexibility, a physician should enlist their attorney to seek to negotiate permitted and exclusive uses that are as broad as possible. Be aware though, that the landlord will seek to have the clauses as limited as possible so that the landlord will have flexibility when leasing space to other tenants.

Review the Rules and Regulations

It is not unusual for landlords to adopt rules and regulations that govern use of the commercial space. This is in addition to what is contained in the lease and may address such items as:

- the hours during which heating, ventilation, and air conditioning (HVAC) are provided,
- deliveries to the building,
- use of approved vendors for construction, cleaning, and other services within the physician's office space, and
- noise.

Action Step: It is important that a copy of any rules and regulations are obtained from the prospective landlord and reviewed and evaluated early in the process. They are often non-negotiable and can substantially impede a tenant's ability to use its space. For example, access to the building may be limited during certain hours for security reasons. Deliveries of equipment and supplies may only be allowed at certain times which can make it inconvenient for such deliveries to be made. In other instances, additional, and sometimes substantial costs may be incurred in order to utilize the space as needed. For example, overtime costs for HVAC may be imposed during evenings, weekends, and holidays which can be prime times for some medical practices to operate since sickness and illness do not abide a clock.

Tactical Tip: Assure that the lease requires that the landlord enforce the rules and do so uniformly with respect to all tenants. No one should be burdened by rules that they do not benefit from and steps must be taken to assure that cannot readily happen.

Triple Net Can Mean More than Triple the Cost

Physicians need to be aware that commercial office space, such as a medical office, is often leased on a "triple net" basis. This means that in addition to paying rent, the tenant medical practice will also be required to pay a portion of the:

- real estate or property taxes assessed on the building,
- insurance on the building, including property and casualty and premises liability insurance, and

- utilities for the common areas of the building, such as outside or hallway lighting.

These amounts can very significantly increase the actual cost to the medical practice of leasing the space. It is also important for physicians to understand that these amounts are in addition to any costs incurred by the medical practice to insure itself, for example.

Action Step: Before leasing space, physicians should ascertain the estimated cost of real estate taxes, insurance, and utilities attributed to the space. Since these are amounts incurred by the landlord that are passed on in full to the tenants, often the landlord has no incentive to control such costs. Space that is not leased on a triple net basis will usually have a higher square foot charge than space that is leased on a triple net basis, but may be less expensive overall.

Tactical Tip: Assure that the lease allows for a right to audit such costs to confirm that the costs are not "marked up" and assure that the lease does not permit the landlord to mark up such amounts.

Additional Rent Can Really Add Up

In addition to real estate taxes, insurance, and utilities, leases can also provide for payment of "additional rent." This means that the tenant-medical practice would have to pay a pro-rata share (known as "proportionate share") of such items as, but not limited to:

- landscaping and snow removal,
- maintenance and repairs,
- janitorial services,
- replacement of equipment such as the common HVAC (heat, ventilating, and air conditioning) system, and
- a management fee.

Sometimes these costs are referred to as common area maintenance or "CAM" charges rather than additional rent.

Action Step: As with the costs of real estate taxes, insurance, and utilities, these amounts can really add up. The lease should specifically state the medical practice's proportionate share since this will affect the percentage of the total costs the tenant will have to pay. It is important to assure that the proportionate share is not greater than the percentage of the actual space in the building leased since that will mean that the medical practice is subsidizing the costs incurred by another tenant and paying more than the actual share of such costs.

Tactical Tip: As with real estate taxes, insurance, and utilities, the lease should allow for a right to audit such costs to confirm that the costs are not "marked up." The lease also should not permit the landlord to mark up such amounts.

Reserve a Realistic Right to Audit

Given the costs in excess of monthly rent that lease of medical office space entails, physicians are well advised to assure that the lease affords them the ability to have their accountant or other financial professional audit the additional costs, including triple net items and additional rent, to ensure that the amounts charged to the tenant medical practice are both legitimate and permitted under the lease.

Action Step: Physicians should request that their accountants review the audit language prior to lease execution to ensure that the rights afforded are sufficient to allow a thorough and complete review. Physicians should facilitate communication between the attorney and accountant for the medical practice.

Tactical Tip: Audit timing can be critical. Sometimes leases do provide a right to audit, but the timeframe to do so is so limited that an effective audit cannot realistically be performed. Doing so would require virtually constant review throughout the calendar year or performing the audit at the beginning of the calendar year for the prior year and this is a time most accountants are already burdened with tax preparation responsibilities.

Take Steps to Protect Your Security Deposit

As a condition of entering into a lease, landlords typically require a security deposit. This is some form of collateral to protect the landlord in the event of such occurrences as:

- damages to the premises,
- nonpayment of rent or other monetary obligations, and
- costs arising out of the tenant-medical practice's failure to comply with a term of the lease or breach of some other obligation such as violation of a local ordinance that results in a fine.

Often, the security deposit is in the form of a cash deposit and can be the equivalent of a month's rent or more. If the dollar value of the security deposit is very high or the tenant medical practice wants to preserve liquidity, security in the form of a bank letter of credit that the landlord may draw on and convert to cash in the event of stated occurrences as set forth in the lease may be provided. In either event, physicians should take steps to protect the security they post.

Action Step: Leases should specifically set forth the circumstances pursuant to which the landlord will have a right to all or a portion of the security deposit. Leases should also include detailed timeframes for returning the security deposit upon lease termination.

Tactical Tip: Physicians should take steps to ensure that the lease requires that a cash security deposit be held in a segregated account and not be co-mingled with the assets of the landlord. Ideally, the landlord should be required to pay all or at least a portion of the interest on the security deposit to the tenant-medical practice. To assure that a letter of credit is returned promptly, since the bank will continue to charge a fee (usually some percent of the letter of credit amount) until the original letter is returned to the bank and cancelled, consider providing in the lease that the letter of credit will be held in escrow by a third party, such as a lawyer, and that the third party will have an obligation to return the letter of credit to the tenant medical practice upon termination of the lease.

Consider Subleasing and Renewal Options

At the time a physician leases medical office space, the physician should consider and negotiate subleasing and renewal options. The longer an initial lease, the longer the initial commitment will be. Moreover, terminating a lease early and even subleasing space to another tenant can be a difficult, expensive, and sometimes impossible task. Certainly, physicians should have their attorneys negotiate the most flexibility possible and try to assure that the lease allows the physician to sublease the space without too much difficulty. Nevertheless, physicians should be cautious about entering into leases that are too lengthy. However, physicians also do not want to have to relocate their medical practice when patients and referring providers have gotten used to the location unless it is their choice to do so. Moreover, moving is expensive both in real dollars and in the time that is taken away from medical practice functions in order to relocate. Therefore, it is important for physicians to negotiate renewal terms and include parameters for renewal in the initial lease so that they are not forced to relocate at the end of the term or acquiesce to a landlord's unreasonable demands in order to remain in the space. Renewal terms should include:

- timing for exercise of the option,
- duration of renewal terms, and
- formula or other basis for calculating rent during the renewal terms.

Action Step: Physicians should ensure that their medical practice leases contain reasonable parameters for subleasing and renewal. Ideally, the lease should provide that the physician may sublease the medical office upon notice to the landlord. If consent must be obtained from the landlord, it should not be unreasonably withheld. The lease should also contain specific terms for notice by the physician in order to exercise the option to renew, the length of the renewal term or terms, and a basis for calculation in the rent. References to "market value" or "fair market" rent should be avoided if at all possible since what constitutes such an amount is readily subject to dispute.

Tactical Tip: Ideally, the lease should provide for a cap on the increase in the amount of rent during renewal term or terms. A fixed percentage or an increase based upon the increase in the consumer price index (CPI) are two options to consider.

Be Sure the Lease Includes a Requirement that the Landlord Obtain a Non-Disturbance Agreement from All Existing and Future Lenders

A non-disturbance agreement is an agreement whereby the landlord's lender(s) is required to honor the terms of the lease in the event of a default under the lender's loan documents which results in a subsequent foreclosure action. Without a non-disturbance agreement, upon the foreclosure of the property, the bank or subsequent owner can terminate the lease after the foreclosure, which could be during the lease term. The practice may have a significant investment in the build-out and fixtures and a replacement office may not then be easily available or available at comparable cost. Moreover, moving will result in disruption and cost for the practice. Thus, the provision is of paramount importance.

Action Step: The physician should ensure that there is a clause in the lease which requires the landlord to obtain non-disturbance agreements from all current and future lenders and provide them to the medical practice-tenant.

Tactical Tip: A landlord may not be willing to commit to obtaining such a clause from its lender. In such case, the landlord should at least be obligated to use its best efforts to obtain the non-disturbance agreement. Also, physicians should consider obtaining and reviewing information (such as a Dun & Bradstreet report) regarding the landlord before entering into a lease to ascertain whether the landlord is having financial difficulties which might ultimately lead to a foreclosure action.

Do Not Overlook Signage

Physicians must also not overlook signage both inside and outside the building. Signage noting the existence and location of the medical practice is important to assure that patients and other visitors can readily locate the office. Signage can also be valuable as a means of advertising.

Action Step: Rights to signage must be reserved in the lease. Ideally, signage should be obtained both inside and outside the building, even if the cost of the sign itself has to be assumed by the physician.

Tactical Tip: Regulations governing medical practice in many states mandate particular signage. Consult the rules and assure that compliance can be facilitated without violation of the lease or the rules and regulations of the building.

Conclusion

Physicians must be prepared to extensively negotiate the lease for medical office space and engage the assistance of experienced professionals to assist them. Since a lease for a medical office is a costly and long-term commitment, it is imperative to consider legal, business, and operational terms and be prepared to invest time and effort to obtain the most favorable terms possible. Physicians should also try not to become too committed to leasing particular space until the deal is finalized so that they will be in a position not to proceed with a deal that is too limiting, too onerous, and/or too expensive.

About the Author

Lisa D. Taylor, Esq., is a partner with Stern & Kilcullen, L.L.C. in Roseland, New Jersey. She is serving her fifth term as Vice Chair of the American Health Lawyers Physician Organizations Practice Group and is a member of the Board of Directors of the New Jersey State Bar Association Health and Hospital Section for which she previously served as Chair. Ms. Taylor received her B.A. from Barnard College of Columbia University, her M.A. and J.D. from Duke University and is licensed to practice law in New Jersey, New York, Pennsylvania, Florida, Tennessee, and the District of Columbia. She can be contacted at ltaylor@sgklaw.com or 973-535-2634.

Peer reviewed by Michael F. Schaff, Esq., Wilentz, Goldman & Spitzer, P.A., Woodbridge, New Jersey, mschaff@wilentz.com or 732-855-6047.

Chapter 22 Negotiating the Sale of a Medical Practice

By Michael F. Schaff, Esq., and Peter Greenbaum, Esq.

Introduction and Executive Summary

It is commonplace for a physician or group of physicians to sell their medical practice to a third party. Regrettably, physicians often fail to take the necessary steps to protect their interests and to maximize the benefits of the transaction. Medical practices are developed over many years, however, a slight miscalculation could have a substantial negative impact on the value of the practice. Fortunately, physicians can take certain basic steps during the process of the sale of their practice to maximize the value of the practice. This article identifies some of these steps with regard to the sale of a practice to a third party. This article focuses on the sale of a practice to an unaffiliated third party and, although certain action items are applicable, is not intended to address the issue of taking on a "partner" with the eventual sale to that "partner."

Retain Experienced Advisors Early in the Sale Process

Many physicians feel they are capable of identifying all significant terms of a sale, and are thereafter capable of negotiating such terms, without the assistance of trained professionals. Just as it is imprudent for a lay person to practice medicine on himself, it is unwise for a physician to attempt to sell her practice without consulting with, and obtaining the advice of, professionals who are experienced in the sale of a medical practice.

Often, physicians do not realize that it is important to consult with professionals. Other times they will not retain advisors to save money. It is important to retain experienced advisors early in the sale process. Failure to do so may result in a physician's failure to realize the maximum net value of her practice.

> **Action Step:** A physician should seek to have her "team" in place at the beginning of the transaction, preferably as early as the time she begins to think about selling her practice. Retaining an attorney who is experienced in the sale of medical practices will assist to guide and strategize with the selling physician, as well as highlight the customary legal and business concerns associated with the sale of a practice.

Additionally, engaging the services of an accountant who practices in the health care arena can help maximize the "take home" financial terms of the transaction.

Tactical Tip: As a practical matter, sellers and purchasers will sometimes negotiate certain terms directly with each other. A seller should prepare prior to such a direct negotiation by discussing the issues with her advisors. If the discussions become too heated or not completely understood, you should table that point by stating you need to consult with your advisors.

Understand the Goals of Each Selling Physician

The initial question which must be analyzed by each selling physician is the following: "What are my goals and the goals of the other selling physicians?" Before a practice can be sold, the physicians must understand what they desire to achieve from the sale. If there are two or more selling physicians, it is highly possible that their primary and secondary goals may be different. For example, the selling group may contain a mix of older and younger physicians. Some may want to retire after the sale, while others may want to continue employment with the purchasing group. Some may be risk adverse and desire to structure the transaction as an all cash deal (without installment payments) so there is no risk of a default in the payment of the purchase price by the purchasing group, while others may not be as risk adverse and willing to finance all or a portion of the purchase price by accepting installment payments. In any event, understanding each seller's desires and goals early in the process will assist with the transaction.

Action Step: The sellers should discuss the various issues related to the sale of the practice, with the assistance of their advisors, to identify their common goals and objectives as well as to identify any differences. Doing this early in the process will assist in the identification of a viable purchaser and the negotiation will be more efficient.

Tactical Tip: The guidance of experienced representatives can assist to identify necessary topics of discussion and provide alternative solutions and common grounds.

Use of a Confidentiality Agreement

A soft drink manufacturer has information that it desires to keep confidential, such as the formula to its cola. Similarly, a medical practice has information that the sellers wish to keep confidential. Specifically, this includes its patient list (including the names, addresses, phone numbers, and relevant personal information of such patients), as well as the identity of referring physicians. Additionally, a medical practice may desire to keep certain employment related information confidential, such as the names of its key employees and their salaries and benefits. Such information often is gathered and developed by a practice over a long period of time.

An early step in every sale of a medical practice is to have fundamental discussions with prospective purchasers. By disclosing confidential information to a prospective purchaser without entering into a confidentiality agreement, the selling physicians may inadvertently allow the purchasers to acquire beneficial information about the practice without paying for same.

Action Step: Prior to disclosing any patient information, referring doctor information, employment information, or any other confidential information, the sellers should insist that the purchasers enter into a confidentiality agreement—this agreement will prohibit the purchasers from using such information, disclosing such information to third parties, or allowing third parties to use such information, other than for the evaluation of the purchase of the practice. The confidentiality agreement should also require that all written confidential information be returned to the sellers upon their demand. Further, the confidentiality agreement should prohibit the purchasers from hiring or attempting to hire key employees of the sellers if the sale does not go through. By negotiating a confidentiality agreement prior to the disclosure of such sensitive information, the sellers will not inadvertently jeopardize the value of the practice.

Tactical Tip: The presentation of a confidentiality agreement to prospective purchasers will demonstrate to the prospective purchasers that the sellers are prepared and ready to sell the practice.

Use of a Letter of Intent

During the early stages of negotiations, the sellers and purchasers will exchange information and conduct rudimentary discussions regarding the potential terms of the transaction. The parties may believe that they have agreed upon the basic terms of the transaction, such as the purchase price and payment terms. It is important at this stage to memorialize, in writing, their agreements to make sure that they are "on the same page."

A letter of intent is a non-binding document that sets forth the basic terms of a transaction. It is a useful tool, although it is not required. The letter of intent summarizes, early in the transaction, the significant business points of the transaction. The document is not the final, definitive agreement. Rather, it is intended to merely summarize the deal points.

Action Step: Consider whether a letter of intent is appropriate for your transaction since it is a useful tool to assist in focusing on the most important issues and to keep the process moving.

Tactical Tip: The definitive agreement which memorializes the terms of the purchase and sale is called a purchase agreement. If the parties agree to the content of the letter of intent, it will often lead to a more efficient negotiation of the definitive purchase agreement. Conversely, if the parties are unable to agree on the basic terms of the letter of intent, it is better to learn that a deal will not work early in the transaction (before significant financial and other resources are dedicated to the proposed transaction).

Understand Due Diligence

Due diligence in the context of a sale and acquisition of a medical practice is the process by which potential purchasers review the books and records of the sellers to learn what they are purchasing. Potential purchasers will conduct a due diligence investigation of the practice to learn of its financial strengths and weaknesses and operating structure, to ascertain the true value of the practice. The sellers may also conduct a due diligence investigation of the purchasers to determine their "makeup" to ascertain, for example, the purchasers' financial wherewithal or whether the sellers desire to continue employment after the closing with the purchasers or desire to "hold paper."

Action Step: Due diligence activities, and the ease and time to complete them, depend not only on the size of the practice, but the preparation of the physicians. The sellers should ensure that their books and records are in order, including tax returns and balance sheets, contracts with employees and vendors, patient and referral source lists, and other items. The more organized the practice is, the quicker and less disruptive the due diligence process will be. Additionally, if the sellers desire to conduct a due diligence investigation on the purchasers, they should ask their counsel for a due diligence investigation list which outlines the information which may be relevant to them.

Tactical Tip: Often, the requested information can be voluminous and detailed. In this regard, you should identify a "point person" who will coordinate the process. Again, it is strongly recommended that the sellers request the purchasers to enter into a confidentiality agreement before disclosing any confidential information.

Structure the Transaction to Take Advantage of the Tax Laws

Most transactions are significantly affected by their resulting tax consequences. In this regard, there may be a significant distinction in the end value (after consideration of the tax effect) that the sellers receive. Thus, an issue is whether the individual sellers will sell their ownership interest in the medical practice (that is, for example, the shares of stock in the professional corporation that is the medical practice) or whether the medical practice will sell its assets (such as the patient lists, equipment, telephone number, goodwill, etc.).

Generally, if the medical practice sells its assets, the portion of the purchase price which exceeds the entity's basis may be taxable income to the entity and then again taxable when distributed to the individual sellers. The exact tax consequence varies depending on many factors, including whether the entity is an S corporation, C corporation, or limited liability company. On the other hand, if the transaction is structured as the acquisition of the ownership interest, the sellers will be afforded capital gains treatment which results in less taxes paid by the sellers.

In sum, it is best from the sellers' perspective to negotiate for and structure the transaction as an ownership (stock) sale, which will result in capital gains treatment. Keep in mind that the tax laws are such that generally what is most favorable for the sellers from a tax perspective may not be as favorable for the purchasers from a tax perspective.

> **Action Step:** It is imperative that the sellers consult with their tax advisor when analyzing the tax consequence of the transaction before agreeing upon the purchase price and terms. If the sellers wait until after the purchase price and terms have been agreed upon, they may find that they will have less money "in their pocket" after the deal is consummated than they intended due to the tax effect on the proceeds.

> **Tactical Tip:** If structured as an ownership (stock) sale, often certain third party consents will not be needed. For example, it is common for real estate leases to require that before the lease is assigned, the landlord's consent must be obtained. However, if the transaction is structured as an ownership sale, the medical practice will still be the tenant after the closing, thus often eliminating the need to obtain the landlord's consent.

Payment of Purchase Price

Many sellers believe that once the purchase price has been agreed upon, the rest of the terms will fall into place. However, many sellers do not focus on how the purchase price will be paid. The purchase price can be paid in full at closing, in installments, or a portion at closing and the rest in installments. Sellers typically want to be paid all or most of the purchase price at closing and want to finance as little as possible. By doing so, the sellers reduce (or eliminate) their risk that the purchasers will default on the installment obligations. On the other hand, purchasers typically desire to pay the purchase price over the longest period of time. By doing so, the purchasers need not have a large reserve of available cash and need not borrow funds from a bank. Paying in installments allows the purchasers to free up cash that can be used instead for working capital.

Action Step: If the sellers are willing to finance all or a portion of the purchase price by allowing the purchasers to pay in installments, the sellers must conduct a due diligence investigation on the purchasers to determine that they have adequate resources to make such payments. Further, among other things, the number of installments, frequency of installments (monthly, quarterly, etc.), interest rate, and collateral must be discussed.

Tactical Tip: Often, sellers will agree to finance the transaction with an increased purchase price and/or higher interest rate to compensate the sellers for the additional risk that they are assuming.

Obtain Adequate Collateral

In the event that all or a portion of the purchase price is paid in installments, the sellers should insist on some form of collateral to secure the payment obligations. Specifically, if the purchaser is a newly formed medical entity, the purchaser will have no real assets which the sellers could pursue should the purchaser default in its payment obligations.

There are numerous forms of collateral and the appropriateness of each depends upon the amount of the purchase price which the sellers are financing as well as the creditworthiness of the purchasers, among other things. At a minimum, the personal guarantees of the purchasers (and their spouses) should be requested. Further, the sellers can request a security interest in the assets of the purchasers' practice and/or a security interest in the ownership interest owned by the purchasers in the practice. Such security interest will give the sellers the right to reacquire the assets and/or the purchasers' ownership interest upon a default of the payment obligations. Additionally, should any purchaser own a house, a mortgage in the name of the sellers can be placed thereon. Appropriate insurance (that is, life, disability, business interruption) on key persons or the practice can also be obtained naming the sellers as beneficiaries.

The foregoing are the more common approaches to secure the purchasers' payment obligations, however, there are numerous other methods.

Action Step: First, the sellers should identify the forms of collateral they feel are necessary. Then, the collateral should be negotiated with the purchasers simultaneously with the discussion of the payment of the purchase price.

Tactical Tip: The amount and value of the collateral which is supplied by the purchasers can be used by the sellers to negotiate other financial terms. For example, if the purchasers are unwilling to provide what the sellers believe is adequate collateral, the sellers can request a higher purchase price and/or interest rate to compensate them for this increased risk.

Addressing Other Post-Transaction Obligations

It is important to remember that once the financial terms of the transaction have been agreed upon, there are other obligations and topics which are customarily discussed.

Some or all of the sellers may be employed by the purchasers after the closing. Often, the sellers want to continue to work. Other times, this may be done to help the purchasers transition the practice. Regardless of the reason, the basic employment terms must be discussed, such as compensation, benefits, malpractice insurance payments, and the time of the commitment.

Purchasers often request a formal patient introduction. Sometimes, a patient letter is sent to the patients. Other times, one or more of the sellers will remain with the practice after the closing to make the introductions. The exact method is dependent upon what is most appropriate for the transition and to what the parties are willing to agree to.

Another topic which must be addressed is the handling of the sellers' accounts receivable which exists on the closing date. The sellers must determine the best way to collect the receivables after the closing. If the sellers are collecting, the sellers may need access to the premises after closing to access the records and to use the billing system and/or the billing staff. Alternatively, it may be appropriate for the purchasers to perform the collection services.

Action Step: With respect to the continued employment after the closing, it is important to remember that the sellers must identify each of their desires early on in the process. Some may want to retire and not perform any services after closing, while others must continue to work after the closing to support their families. Identifying the extent any selling physicians must continue employment will assist with the negotiations.

The sellers should be leery of sending patient letters and advising patients that the practice has been or will be sold, prior to the actual closing. If the purchasers back out of the transaction prior to the closing, the damage may be irreversible. In any event, the cost of the patient introduction services (and who pays such costs) must be considered.

Finally, the sellers must determine whether they want to collect their accounts receivable or request that the purchasers collect same, and in either case, access to the purchasers' resources and the cost relating to such collections are negotiation points.

Tactical Tip: The foregoing transition obligations are often left to the end of discussions as they are not deemed as important as the other terms. However, these items frequently become major discussion points.

Understand the Restrictive Covenant

A significant discussion point is the post-closing restrictive covenants to which the sellers will be bound. It is customary that purchasers will request that after the closing, the sellers be bound by restrictive covenants pursuant to which they agree that they will not engage in the practice of medicine, nor solicit the patients, referral sources and/or employees for a specified period of time in a geographic area. The purchasers do not want to pay for a practice only to have the sellers open a new practice in the locale and solicit patients, employees, and referral sources which they just acquired.

Many physicians believe that restrictive covenants are not enforceable. States vary on the extent to which they will enforce a restrictive covenant (if at all), so it is important that the state laws in which the practice is located be analyzed.

Action Step: It is important that the sellers be aware of their respective goals. A seller who is retiring is less likely to care about the extent of the restrictive covenant. Conversely, a seller who intends to continue practicing will pay significant attention to the restriction during negotiations.

Once the sellers determine the importance of the restriction, it is left to determine the time period during which the restriction applies and the geographic area in which they will be prohibited from practicing. Additionally, sellers can request "carve-outs" (exceptions) to the restrictions.

Tactical Tip: In the event that the purchasers are paying all or a portion of a purchase price in installments or have other significant post-closing obligations, the sellers should insist that in the event the purchasers have breached any of such obligations, the restrictive covenant automatically terminates.

Limit Representations and Warranties

The representations and warranties of the sellers regarding the medical practice are typically the most extensive provisions in the purchase agreement. The representations and warranties are statements made by the sellers regarding the practice. Should a representation or warranty be learned to be inaccurate or false, and should the purchasers be damaged relating thereto, the purchasers may seek redress against the sellers.

Action Step: The sellers must carefully review the proposed representations and warranties. Too often, sellers gloss over the requested representations and warranties and do not confirm their accuracy. A careful review of the proposed representations and warranties before the closing can minimize the risk that the purchasers will make claims against the sellers after the closing.

Tactical Tip: All sellers, as well as key employees (such as the office manager), should carefully review the representations and warranties. One physician may not know whether a representation or warranty is accurate, however, someone else in the group may be more familiar with the subject matter thereof. Thus, all parties with knowledge should be asked to review the proposed representations.

Further, the more organized a practice is, the easier the review of the representations and warranties will be. For example, a customary representation requests that all contracts to which the practice is a party be identified. A practice with orderly books will be able to more efficiently tackle this task.

Additionally, try to qualify representations and warranties so as not to be open-ended and make them "to the sellers' knowledge."

Limit Indemnification of the Sellers and Obtain Adequate Indemnification from the Purchasers

Sellers should seek to be indemnified by the purchasers for a breach of a term, condition, representation, or warranty, and from claims that the purchasers failed to honor their post-closing obligations (such as payment of installments).

Similarly, purchasers typically seek to be indemnified by the sellers for a breach of a term, condition, representation, or warranty from pre-closing claims that are asserted against the purchasers after the closing, and from claims by the sellers' vendors that the sellers failed to pay for all supplied goods and services.

Action Step: The sellers should insist that no individual seller will be held liable for actions of another individual seller. Further, they should insist that there be a "cap" on the indemnification, pursuant to which the maximum liability to which the sellers are exposed does not exceed a certain dollar threshold, and should request a "basket," pursuant to which the sellers' indemnification obligations do not kick-in until the total indemnification obligations exceed a certain dollar threshold. Finally, the sellers should insist that the indemnification obligations terminate on some specified date (so that the obligations do not linger in perpetuity).

Tactical Tip: A thorough review by the sellers of the requested representations and warranties will reduce the risk that these are inaccurate and correspondingly reduce the risk of a claim of indemnification by the purchasers.

Determine Whether "Tail" Malpractice Insurance Is Necessary

Malpractice insurance is generally characterized as claims-made insurance or occurrence insurance. A claims-made policy is a policy that provides coverage for a malpractice claim in the event the claim is made during the covered period. An occurrence policy is a policy that covers a malpractice claim regardless of the date that the claim is asserted as long as the event occurred during the covered period. A claims-made policy can effectively be converted into an occurrence policy by the acquisition of a "tail/prior acts" policy.

> **Action Step:** The sellers should review their policies to determine coverage requirements and whether tail insurance is appropriate. In the event one or more sellers will be employed by the purchasers after the closing, the parties must discuss who will maintain (pay for) the malpractice insurance on behalf of such sellers and, if applicable, it should be determined who is responsible for the tail premiums.

> **Tactical Tip:** The sellers should consult with their insurance carrier regarding malpractice insurance coverage prior to negotiations. Often, if a physician is retiring or of a certain age, an insurer will not charge for tail insurance.

Consider Including Dispute Resolution Procedures

Unfortunately, it is not uncommon for a dispute to arise between the sellers and the purchasers after the closing. Disputes arise from, among other things, inaccuracies of representations and breaches of obligations. Thus, it may be useful to set forth the dispute resolution procedures in the definitive agreement.

Dispute resolution provisions customarily fall within one of two categories: the resolution of disputes through court procedures or resolution through mediation and arbitration procedures. Often, if arbitration is the selected forum of a dispute, the procedures set forth by the American Health Lawyers Association are the guiding policies.

Action Step: Each method of dispute resolution has pros and cons. Thus, the sellers should discuss the methods with their representatives to determine which is more appropriate for their specific circumstances. Also, should the sellers and purchasers be located in different geographic areas (such as different counties or a great distance apart), the sellers may wish to identify the venue of the action to be the court or arbitration office closest to their office or home as the location in which the dispute will be heard.

Tactical Tip: Generally, the court process has more stringent rules and takes a longer period of time to be resolved. Conversely, an arbitration proceeding tends to have less stringent rules and is often heard by an arbitrator in a shorter period of time. The foregoing varies from locale to locale and the sellers should determine which they feel is important.

Consider Estate Planning

Hopefully, the sellers will reap a purchase price which they feel adequately reflects the value of their practice. Without careful estate planning, however, the sellers may not fully realize the financial benefits of the sale and/or wind up giving Uncle Sam much of the proceeds.

Action Step: Each seller should consult with his or her accountant and/or estate attorney with respect to the financial terms of the sale. It is only with wise planning that a seller will truly realize the full potential of the proceeds of the sale.

Tactical Tip: As noted earlier, sellers may have different goals. The nature of estate planning as it relates to the sale is dependent upon the ultimate goals of each seller.

About the Authors

Peter Greenbaum, Esq., is a shareholder with Wilentz, Goldman, & Spitzer, P.A., and practices on the Business Law Team and the Healthcare Team. His business law focus is on general corporate law and corporate counseling. He has extensive transactional experience in stock and acquisitions representing both buyers and sellers. He has expertise in contract drafting and negotiation and providing legal consultation and document review to business entities of all sizes, both publicly and privately held. Mr. Greenbaum structures professional practices for healthcare professionals and provides healthcare-related advice. He frequently lectures on behalf of the New Jersey Institute of Continuing Legal Education as well as to professionals and business owners at association meetings and organizations. Mr. Greenbaum has had articles published in many periodicals, including the *New Jersey Law Journal* and *New Jersey Biz Magazine,* as well as chapters included in books such as *Representing Physicians Handbook.* He can be contacted by telephone at (732) 855-6426 or by e-mail at pgreenbaum@wilentz.com.

Michael Schaff, Esq., is a shareholder and head of the Corporate and Health Care Departments of Wilentz, Goldman, & Spitzer, P.A., which maintains offices in New Jersey, New York, and Pennsylvania. Mr. Schaff has lectured extensively on health care matters across the country. He is the immediate past chair of the American Health Lawyers Association Physician Organization Practice Group, and a former chair on the New Jersey State Bar Association Health and Hospital Law Section. Mr. Schaff, who has published extensively on various health care topics, including physician representation, has a BA, joint JD/MBA (specialization in finance), and an LLM (in taxation). He is listed in *Best Lawyers of America* and is admitted to practice in New Jersey, New York, and Maryland. Mr. Schaff can be contacted by telephone at (732) 855-6047 or by e-mail at mschaff@wilentz.com.

Peer reviewed by Lisa D. Taylor, Esq., Stern & Kilcullen, L.L.C., Roseland, New Jersey, ltaylor@sgklaw.com or 973-535-2624.

Chapter 23 Negotiating the Purchase of an Established Medical Practice

By Bruce D. Armon, Esq.

Introduction and Executive Summary

The opportunity has arrived. Whether you have been in practice for many years or are a freshly graduated resident or fellow, the opportunity to acquire the practice of a retiring physician can be very appealing—and nerve wracking. This is likely one of the most important negotiations and acquisitions you will make in your lifetime. For many physicians it is more expensive than the purchase of their primary residence. The negotiation and purchase of an established medical practice may be also one of the best long-term investments you ever make because it can sustain you and your family's livelihood for your entire professional career and then be sold for a significant sum when you decide to retire.

Below are 10 tips that you should follow when you decide to negotiate and, hopefully, purchase an established medical practice. While this article is focused on buying out the interests of an established medical practice, many of the same tips are applicable to a physician who is becoming a "partner" in an existing practice and would like to make sure the investment—financially, professionally, and emotionally—is warranted.

What Are You Negotiating to Buy?

As a prospective purchaser, once you have identified a potential practice, you should identify what you are buying. There are two types of acquisitions: an asset purchase or a stock purchase.

Absent unusual circumstances, the purchaser should insist upon an asset purchase arrangement.

The seller of a medical practice would likely prefer a stock purchase agreement because all of the gain becomes taxable to the seller at capital gains rates. By contrast, as the buyer of stock only, you will not get any tax deduction for any portion of the purchase price.

The other main drawback with regard to a stock purchase agreement, from a buyer's perspective, is that in addition to acquiring the assets of the practice (see below), you are also acquiring all of the liabilities now and in the future of the medical practice.

The potential liabilities of any medical practice you may inherit as part of a stock purchase agreement include accounts payable and professional liability claims and any other litigation. In addition, the potential liability also includes settlements resulting from any fraud investigations from the federal and/or state governments and other third party payers for circumstances that occurred prior to your acquiring the practice and for which you might not even be aware until notice of the investigation is sent to your attention as the new owner of the medical practice.

It is imperative that you understand what you are negotiating and why.

An asset purchase agreement should be drafted so that it clearly delineates the respective liabilities and responsibilities of the purchaser and seller of the medical practice. Using this technique, both parties will know, as of the closing date of the acquisition, where each party stands with regard to matters pre-closing and post-closing. As a practical matter, it might be worth paying a slight premium to ensure an asset purchase agreement is acceptable to the seller. You should negotiate from a position of strength and understand where the prospective seller might have concerns.

What Entity Will You Establish to Buy the Medical Practice?

Assuming that you enter into an asset purchase agreement rather than a stock purchase agreement, you should have established an "entity" to make the actual purchase of the medical practice.

Depending upon the state(s) where your medical practice is located, there are different entity choices that will be available to you. Your choice of entity should be selected for legal and tax reasons. This does not involve negotiations with the seller—it is strictly a decision for you to make.

As a practical matter, you should probably not choose to practice as a sole proprietor. Under this model, you would not "incorporate" your practice. The biggest detriment to practicing as a sole proprietor is your potential litigation liability since you do not have the "protection" of any corporate entity.

Many states permit physicians and other licensed professionals to establish a professional corporation or professional association. Be aware that each state has its own rules regarding with whom a physician may "partner" as part of the professional association.

Many states permit an individual physician to establish a limited liability corporation (LLC). An LLC generally offers liability protection that is similar to that provided to corporations but is treated as a partnership for tax purposes. Note that a partnership is not going to be a viable option for an individual purchaser of a medical practice because, by its very nature, a partnership requires two or more owners.

What Items Do You Want to Negotiate to Buy?

This is perhaps the most obvious, and most often misunderstood, aspect of the negotiation and purchase of any established medical practice. Negotiating to buy a medical practice is, in some respects, like buying a car. At the end of the day, the purchaser will have the medical practice (or car) but there are lots of different options which you can purchase. There are no right or wrong answers. Depending upon what you purchase, however, the cost may be very different.

Understanding what should be included (and already be a given) in your negotiations will help make the process smoother for you and for the seller. Very few items are a part of every medical practice acquisition but there are some items generally included in every medical practice acquisition.

Medical Charts

The most important item that must be included is the practice's medical charts. This is the lifeline of every medical practice. You can be the best clinician in your specialty in your community but if you do not have a substantial patient base, you will not be a successful businessperson. Be aware that a patient always has the option to move his or her charts to another provider. As the purchaser of the medical practice the patient has to contact you, preferably in writing, if they want a copy of their chart to go elsewhere. States may have rules governing the transfer of charts from one provider to another and the charges (copying and administrative fees) that may be levied as part of this process.

Medical Supplies

Depending upon the type of practice you are acquiring, there may be a good deal of or very few medical supplies. Ensuring that there is an adequate inventory of needed medical supplies without any surge in purchases just prior to the closing date is essential to determining the fair valuation of the medical supplies and ensuring there is adequate supply for the demand the practice is likely going to encounter.

FURNITURE, FIXTURES, AND EQUIPMENT

In most cases, you will acquire the furniture, fixtures and equipment that are a part of the medical practice. It is very important that these be itemized and you know the condition and expected useful remaining life of each of these items. You also need to confirm who owns each of these items. Does the practice itself own the items? Does the departing physician individually own any of these items? Is any of the equipment leased or rented? If it is leased, what are the terms of the lease and can the lease be assigned to you without any penalty? If the item is being rented, what are the terms of the rental arrangement? If an item is leased or rented, rather than owned, you should not be paying for this item as part of the medical practice because the item has no "value" to you since the item will be returned at the completion of the lease or rental arrangement.

As part of your due diligence process, you should ensure that each of the furniture, fixtures, and equipment owned by the medical practice is free and clear of all liens and encumbrances so it will be transferred to you upon acquisition of the practice without any other party having an ability to claim any interest in any of the items.

How Do You Negotiate What the Medical Practice Is Worth?

There is no right answer to this question. It really depends upon the expectations of the buyer and seller. For the seller, this may be the last large pay day that he or she is going to receive for professional achievements. Accordingly, the seller is going to want as much as he or she can possibly get—preferably in cash at closing.

As the purchaser you don't want to pay more than you think you should, and you want terms you believe are fair. In your negotiations with the seller, you must understand what is the maximum amount you can afford. Through negotiations, you should learn what is the minimum that the seller will accept.

How do you bridge the professional differences? An independent valuation may be in order. There are many dimensions to a practice valuation. The seller will need to provide substantive information to the evaluator. Items that will likely be necessary to perform a valuation include: income statements and practice income tax returns for the previous three (3) years; balance sheets for the practice for the previous three (3) years; inventory and projected value of equipment owned by the practice; inventory and projected value of medical and office supplies; the physician's monthly productions and collections for the past several years; accounts receivable balances; patient inventories and demographics; lists of referring physicians and related information; and details regarding the compensation and expenses for the practice's staff.

The more that you and the evaluator can learn about the past and current state of the medical practice, the better prepared you will be to understand the potential future of the medical practice and determine what you believe is a fair price for the same. Like any negotiation, give and take will need to be a part of the process.

How Will I Pay the Bills When the Practice Is Mine?

If you do not acquire the accounts receivable of the medical practice as part of your acquisition, you will not have any cash flow upon the first day you own the practice. Even if you have a full book of patients ready to see on day 1, you will likely not see any revenues from these patients (outside of modest co-pays) for forty-five to sixty days (assuming that you have billing operations in place as of day 1).

Even if you will receive accounts receivable as part of your acquisition, you need to ensure that you have enough money to pay all of your upfront expenses (in addition to the purchase price for the practice). If you do not have sufficient personal savings, a bank or other lender may be your best option.

Banks are generally amenable to providing loans or a line of credit to a physician who acquires a practice. However, the bank will want access to many of the due diligence documents you and/or your independent evaluator have acquired so that they can make a reasoned judgment about the viability of the practice. In some circumstances, the bank or other lender will insist upon a personal guarantee from you of any loan or line of credit provided.

Keep in mind that negotiating the deal with a lender can be just as difficult as your practice negotiations. If you require funds to pay the seller at closing (in addition to your initial expenses for running the medical practice), you need to start negotiating with lenders as soon as you identify a potential practice opportunity.

You will have some opportunity to negotiate with the bank(s) as they are looking for your business. In a competitive lending environment, you should not hesitate to tell a bank that you have a better offer from another institution and see if they can match the offer.

Instead of securing a loan from a lender, the selling physician may also act as a lender and finance your acquisition of the practice. This may make your negotiations with the physician a bit trickier since he or she will be selling you their practice but they will not be reaping the full economic benefit from the transaction until the length of the financing is complete.

What Do I Need in Place or to Negotiate for My Practice to Run from Day One?

Whether you start a brand new medical practice or acquire the assets of an existing practice from a retiring physician, there are a number of items that need to be completed so you can effectively run the practice on the first day that it is yours.

Some items will take longer than others to accomplish. If you are new to the community, you will need to consider and, if you decide to move ahead, complete the necessary paperwork to become a participating provider in Medicare and the state's Medicaid program. The same process holds true for the various private third party payers in your community. There are no negotiations in your interactions with a third party payer—all you can ask is that they process your completed application in a timely way.

In some jurisdictions, you may be required to have a business license to operate a medical practice and may need to secure state and/or local approval. You will also need to get credentialed by the hospital(s) to which your patients likely will be admitted. Third party payer and hospital credentialing can take many months. To help ensure timely turn-around of these credentialing applications, be sure that your applications are accurate and thorough.

If you are staying in the current office where the practice is located, you need to ensure the lease is assigned to your practice (assuming the office location is not also going to be acquired by you or an entity you create for that specific purpose). You will need also to secure appropriate property insurance.

If you are keeping phone and fax numbers from the current physician-owner, you need to ensure a smooth transition is in place with the telephone company.

In addition to having your state license and DEA (and state counterpart, if appropriate) current, you will need to ensure that you have secured appropriate and sufficient professional liability coverage.

Computers and other necessary electronic equipment will be imperative, particularly if you intend to use electronic medical records. You will need to be sure this equipment is secure and that you are compliant with the HIPAA obligations.

You will need to make sure that you have sufficient staff in place to handle patient arrivals and records and third party payer billings or that you have negotiated and executed a billing agreement with a private vendor.

Creating a time-line and checklist can help you get up and running as efficiently as possible.

Remember, this is only a partial list of the items you will need to ensure are in place so your office can operate smoothly (not effortlessly) as of your first day as the owner.

How Do I Negotiate to Ensure the Selling Physician Stays Retired?

This is an important consideration. While many physicians might think they have had enough when they sell their practice, the lure of staying in the game or making a few extra dollars can be a compelling motivator. As the purchaser of a medical practice, the last thing you want is the selling physician to later become a direct competitor of yours—even if it is on a part-time basis.

Non-Competition Provision

There are at least two ways to prevent this from occurring. First, you should be sure to negotiate and include within the asset purchase agreement a non-competition provision. The negotiations should specify the geographic radius and length of time in which the selling physician shall not provide medical services. The scope of included medical services should be carefully negotiated. Significant financial penalties should be delineated if the selling physician violates the restrictive covenant. One way to ensure adherence to a non-compete provision is to negotiate to hold back a portion of the purchase price pending the adherence of the selling physician for the duration of the noncompete period.

NON-SOLICITATION CLAUSE

The negotiations relating to the covenant may also include a non-solicitation clause to prevent the selling physician from encouraging referring physicians and others in the community to change their referral patterns, and to prevent the selling physician from contacting your office staff and your patients and their family members. As part of this process, you should be sure to include in your negotiations that a carefully crafted letter will be signed by you (and ideally the retiring physician) and sent to the "community" on or before the closing date of the acquisition. This may help to prevent any encroachments upon your purchase and the price you paid.

EMPLOYING THE RETIRING PHYSICIAN

A third negotiating option is for you to employ the selling physician in some capacity—part time or full time—and also include restrictive covenant provisions in that employment agreement. If you employ or hire the departing physician as an independent contractor, there may be some tax benefits depending upon how the purchase price of the practice is structured. This may also help ensure the loyalty of existing patients as you start the practice.

Am I Even Negotiating about the Right Practice Opportunity for Me?

The timeline to buy a medical practice can be long or short—but it will always be fraught with anxiety for the purchasing physician. There is probably no perfect practice acquisition opportunity. Even starting a brand new practice from scratch has risks.

Your due diligence needs to be thorough and you need to be kept apprised of new developments affecting the practice throughout the negotiation process. You should negotiate and get the selling physician to agree to allow you to spend a few days in the office with the selling physician. This will help give you a sense of the dynamics of the practice and its staff and give you ideas for items you would like to change and keep the same.

As part of your negotiations, you should try to learn why the physician is willing to sell the practice. Did a prior partner leave the practice and is the practice now on the verge of financial collapse? Has he or she lost significant numbers of patients and/or revenue in the past several years? Are third party payers squeezing reimbursements for your specialty?

Or, do you find through the course of your negotiations that the retiring physician's reasons are all plausible? Has he or she had a long and successful career and is truly more interested in spending time with a spouse and/or grandchildren? Is there a significant health issue affecting the physician or a close family member? Is the physician simply tired of working and would like to enjoy retirement?

Depending upon the answer to these and other questions, your negotiating strategy to purchase the practice may be different. You need to work to find common ground early so the negotiations can proceed. If there are too many differences to overcome in the early stage of your negotiations, you will either have to change your strategies or end the negotiations. Gain as many facts as you can, and then act accordingly.

What Should You Negotiate to Be in Writing?

Everything. This is a short and the only logical answer.

Misunderstandings and miscommunications can be limited dramatically if the deal parameters are negotiated and placed in writing from the start. A carefully crafted letter of intent, precise deal documents and schedules and exhibits help ensure that both parties understand exactly what is expected of them and what they will receive in return.

It is very important that everything be in writing if the transaction is one between family members or there is a close personal relationship. Business deals can be difficult enough without adding the familial or close social interaction dynamic. You do not want to ruin a personal and/or family relationship because one side took something or someone for granted and there is no writing to memorialize exactly what each party agreed to.

Do I Need Help in My Negotiations to Purchase a Practice?

Physicians, by nature, are very bright individuals. However, clinical excellence does not always translate to business acumen. As described earlier, negotiating and buying a practice is one of the most expensive purchases you will likely ever make.

Having an experienced attorney assist you is invaluable. The attorney, if you prefer, can negotiate with the selling physician's attorney on your behalf. Alternatively, you can use the attorney as a behind-the-scenes resource. You will need to negotiate with your attorney on how you would like to use his skills.

The attorney can help you delineate what exactly you are purchasing, the appropriate type of entity to select to use to purchase the practice, help ensure that you are ready to practice as of day one, and value or consult with a valuation expert to appraise your purchase and help predict future economic viability. These are each essential elements of your successful practice negotiation and acquisition. You will likely have to sign a number of documents to purchase the medical practice. You will then have to prepare a series of documents to make sure your practice is operating smoothly—e.g., employment agreements, third party payer agreements, vendor agreements, compliance plan documentation, and personnel policies.

The selling physician is very likely going to have someone specifically representing his or her interests, as will each of the other parties with whom you interact from a business perspective (lenders, third party payers, vendors). You should do the same. The earlier in the process you retain and utilize your attorney, the better. You do not want to be in the position of having made numerous tactical, financial, and legal mistakes and then turn to counsel for assistance. By then it might be too late to salvage the opportunity.

The old Latin phrase, *caveat emptor,* is appropriate for physicians looking to negotiate and acquire an established medical practice. While the buyer should certainly beware when initially considering and then throughout the negotiations and acquisition process of an established medical practice, these tips will help the buyer become *more* aware of the great opportunity that may be presenting itself and how to negotiate to ensure that the purchasing physician is adequately protected.

About the Author

Bruce D. Armon is a partner at Saul Ewing, LLP. He can be reached at barmon@saul.com or 1-800-355-7777, x7985. Bruce has assisted physicians and physician practices in various health care corporate matters including: the establishment and merging of physician practices; drafting and reviewing employment and other practice agreements; HIPAA compliance; review and analysis of regulatory issues including Anti-Kickback Statute safe harbors, Stark II, Medicare, Medicaid, and private third party payment issues; and drafting physician and billing company compliance plans.

Mr. Armon regularly lectures to a variety of medical audiences on health care-related legal issues. A complete list of Bruce's articles can be found at //www.saul.com/publications/publications.aspx?attID=385.

Chapter 24 The Biggest Mistakes Medical Organizations/Journals Make in Negotiating with Medical Publishers

Executive Summary

- Develop power by playing publishers off one another.
- Do not sign away ownership of the publication.
- Insist on compensation based on gross revenues and not on profits that can be manipulated.
- Get a guaranteed minimum royalty by asking the publisher to stand up to his rosy financial projections.
- Ask for a signing bonus.
- Do not be afraid to retain professional assistance to help negotiate the deal.

Introduction

This chapter is an introduction to the negotiation of a medical journal publishing agreement. As medical organization and journal editors become better informed, they will improve the quality of the publication and assure its financial viability.

Not Retaining Ownership

Medical publishers will attempt to retain ownership of the journal to enhance their control of the publication and the negotiation process. The publishers will attempt to own the:

- copyright,
- trademark,
- inventory,
- electronic files,
- subscriber lists, and
- content (including back issues), etc.

A publisher with greater ownership will have stronger negotiating posture. Medical societies/journals will have to attempt to gradually regain ownership. The publisher can be expected to wrest significant concessions from the society in exchange for ceding ownership.

Lesson: Medical societies/organizations should not permit publishers to seize or maintain ownership of the publication. When the publisher has complete or partial ownership, the medical society may have to regain ownership gradually over a period of time.

Ill-Defined and Inadequate Royalties

Medical publishers may seek to pay the society an inadequate or ill-defined royalty or share of the profits generated by the publication. Publishers may offer one of several formulas.

Share of Profits

The publisher may offer the society a percentage of the *annual profit* generated by the publication. The percentage offered may vary widely (for example, 20%–50% or more). The share of the profits formula has an inherent and dangerous weakness. It permits the publisher to "write off" a whole series of expenses before splitting up the profits. These expenses can include the costs of:

- paper,
- printing,
- binding,
- postage,
- editorial,
- administration and management,
- production,
- order fulfillment,
- selling and marketing, and
- general administrative (legal, accounting, management, and corporate overhead).

The above formula encourages and rewards the publisher who runs up substantial expenses and writes off as much overhead as possible.

Auditing publishers who are permitted to use this formula can be a daunting, difficult, and expensive process.

Thus, the percentage of profits formula should generally be avoided by medical societies and organizations.

Royalty Based on Total Journal Revenue

Here the publisher tacitly acknowledges the inherent difficulties with the percentage of profits formula. The publisher will, when pressed, offer a royalty based on the total journal revenue. The percentage offered may vary greatly depending on the profitability of the publication and the negotiating strength of the parties.

The total journal revenue can and should include:

- all subscriptions,
- sponsored subscriptions,
- electronic searches and databases (for example, OVID),
- reprints (commercial and author),
- back issues,
- color charges,
- pay-per-view,
- rights permissions, and
- collections of past articles converted to books/monographs.

The royalty based on total revenue encourages all parties to spend efficiently and avoids the inherent conflicts of a share of the profits model. In addition, as changing technology permits new profit centers, the society will be positioned to share in these additional revenues.

Lesson: Medical organizations/societies generally are better served by negotiating for a royalty based on total revenue. They may be able to ask that both models be applied and that the society be paid based on the one with the largest revenue for the society.

Not Obtaining Guaranteed Royalties

Many publishers will not offer guaranteed minimum annual royalty payments unless pressed by the medical societies and organizations. When pressed, publishers will offer up to 50% or more of the projected revenues as annual guaranteed payments. The larger the projection offered by the publisher (to help win the publishing rights), the larger the resulting guaranteed payments. In essence, the publisher is forced to put its money where its mouth is.

Lesson: Medical societies/organizations should negotiate aggressively for guaranteed minimum royalties. Not only does the guaranteed revenue assure financial security, it will incentivize the publisher to follow through on the promises made during the negotiation process.

PERMITTING DELAYED ROYALTIES

Publishers are notoriously slow in paying royalties to medical societies/organizations. Most medical publishers will propose quarterly or annual payments. With a guaranteed royalty, there is no rationale (other than keeping the money to make interest on it) for the publisher to delay payment.

Lesson: Medical organizations/societies should negotiate for prompt payments of their guaranteed royalties.

SIGNING BONUS NOT ASSURED

Medical societies and organizations who own profitable journals can expect substantial interest from publishers desiring to take over the publishing of the journal. Many medical journals generate millions of dollars of profits annually. In addition, publishers recognize that once they "take over" a new journal they may continue to publish it for an extended period of time. The amount at stake in negotiating to take over a journal can be very significant.

Example: The ABC medical journal generates $10 million in annual revenue with a profit of $5 million annually. If the publisher can win over the journal, it is likely to continue to publish it for 20 years. The amount at stake in the negotiation is thus between $100 million (profit) and $200 million (revenue).

It is for this reason that publishers can be requested to pay a significant signing bonus to "land" a new medical journal. The amount paid will depend on the profitability of the journal and the bargaining strengths of the parties.

Lesson: Request and obtain a significant signing bonus for granting the publisher the right to publish the medical journal.

Editorial Support Lacking

The quality and reputation of a medical journal depends in large part on the continuing strength of its editor and staff. All parties have an interest in maintaining a strong, highly dedicated editorial staff. Publishers will have to market the journal based on its reputation and impact factor (the measure of the frequency with which the average article in the journal has been cited in a particular year).

It is for these reasons that medical publishers are willing to negotiate and pay annual editorial support stipends. In fact, publishers will pay stipends which exceed the society's actual out-of-pocket editorial costs to win over the publishing rights.

Lesson: Medical societies/organizations should be vigilant in protecting the quality of the journal and its editorial staff. Obtaining a significant annual editorial stipend is the first step in this process.

Advertising Revenue Not Maximized

A significant part of the revenue generated by many medical journals is from advertising. The level of commitment, effort, and success by the publisher for generating advertising revenue will depend on the terms negotiated in the contract. The opportunities for generating advertising revenue from the publication can include the use of:

- article reprints,
- belly bands,
- classified advertising,
- journal supplements,
- patient education tablets,
- premium positions,
- special positions, and
- special sales.

The challenge for those negotiating the contract is how to get past the sales language to assure peak advertising sales performance. The solution will often be:

- performance metrics and
- advertising guarantees.

Lesson: Those negotiating with medical publishers should require guarantees, performance metrics, and guaranteed marketing budgets to be used solely to attract additional advertising revenue for the journal. Frank discussions about potential conflicts of interest with other journals owned by the publisher should take place and the solutions should be committed to writing.

Term of the Contract Not Considered

Medical publishers acquiring a new journal or attempting to retain publication rights of a journal they currently publish are interested in stability. These publishers generally seek long-term contracts of five, seven, or ten years or more. The long-term contract will permit the publisher to invest in its brand, development, and future. Unfortunately, a long term contract can lead to neglect and lack of commitment. In addition, the publisher recognizes that it will be costly (time and additional concessions) to negotiate new contracts.

The medical society/organization/journal uses the publisher's need for a long-term contract to guarantee quality control, responsiveness, and financial security. Leaving oneself an "out" after a set period of time will put additional pressure on the publisher to perform.

Lesson: Journals, organizations, and societies should use the publisher's need for security and long-term contracts to assure performance. Contracts with options to renew (at the discretion of the society/journal) as well as substantial financial guarantees are most likely to result in optimum performance by the publisher.

No Negotiating Alternatives

One of the most significant mistakes societies/journals make in their negotiating process is not generating competing proposals with other publishers. These organizations/journals conduct detailed and often lengthy negotiations with their current publisher but have no leverage due to the lack of a viable alternative. It is an indispensable negotiating strategy to have a series of alternatives in hand when negotiating with a publisher.

Lesson: Organizations/journals should generate a detailed request for proposal (RFP) and send it out to a minimum of six medical publishers. The organizations can expect detailed proposals that will help them make informed decisions and generate the most favorable terms.

Not Obtaining Professional Assistance

Organizations/journals usually assemble a negotiating team of physicians to deal with the "contract" issue. Frequently, these are accomplished doctors who are extremely busy with their clinical practices and other demands. The publisher will use the fact that the negotiating team may be too busy to research alternatives, send out RFPs, interview publishers, accumulate financial data, spend hours with editorial staff, and make the time commitment necessary to assure the most favorable outcome. Negotiation teams may not start the negotiation process early enough and may be left with no alternative other than to go with the current publisher. Inertia and lack of time can be the negotiation team's worst enemies. In addition, negotiation teams may lack the experience that the medical publisher has in these types of negotiations.

Lesson: Negotiating teams have a fiduciary obligation to maintain the quality of their publication and its economic stability and viability. Engaging a professional to help with the negotiation process will eliminate many of the publisher's advantages and force it to negotiate on a level playing field. The negotiation teams should retain a professional early in the process to give her time to perform the many tasks needed to assure the best result.

Additional Negotiation Issues

A contract for the publication of a medical journal is a complex agreement with numerous matters to be negotiated. The areas of concern mentioned above do not even scratch the surface of the issues to be considered and negotiated. Additional issues to be negotiated include the following.

- Ability to conduct searches in native language
- Abstracting and indexing coverage
- Color pages
- Control of subscription price
- Digitization of back files
- Editorial board meeting support
- Electronic delivery of content
- Foreign language issues/translations
- Library (sales, consortia, and content collections)
- Living textbooks
- Non-compete agreements
- Online access
- Online platform
- Performance metrics
- Points of contact
- Production workflow and schedule
- Quality control steps
- Retention of points and online materials
- Subscription price
- Timeliness
- Transparency
- Video (articles, streaming video, podcasting, etc.)
- Web-based peer review

INDEX